THE ACCIDENTAL TOUR-IST

(FINAL) DISPATCHES FROM THE ROAD

NED BOULTING

BLOOMSBURY SPORT

LONDON · OXFORD · NEW YORK · NEW DELHI · SYDNEY

To Kath

BLOOMSBURY SPORT
Bloomsbury Publishing Plc
50 Bedford Square, London, WC1B 3DP, UK
Bloomsbury Publishing Ireland Limited,
29 Earlsfort Terrace, Dublin 2, D02 AY28, Ireland

BLOOMSBURY, BLOOMSBURY SPORT and the Diana logo are trademarks of Bloomsbury
Publishing Plc

First published in Great Britain 2025
This paperback edition published 2026

A catalogue record for this book is available from the British Library

Library of Congress Cataloguing-in-Publication data has been applied for

ISBN: PB: 978-1-3994-1981-9; eBook: 978-1-3994-1980-2

2 4 6 8 10 9 7 5 3 1

Typeset in Minion Pro by Deanta Global Publishing Services, Chennai, India
Printed and bound in Great Britain by Clays Ltd, Elcograf S.p.A.

To find out more about our authors and books visit www.bloomsbury.com and sign up
for our newsletters
For product safety related questions contact productsafety@bloomsbury.com

CONTENTS

1

THE ACCIDENT

I was already in mid-air when I understood what was happening.

Instead of gliding along the darkened road, savouring the crisp metal tang of an early autumn evening in Kent, a few hundred miles away from Paris where the 21-year-old Tadej Pogačar had raised an arm aloft in triumph, I was suddenly propelled into the night, airborne, still attached to a bicycle and very surprised by this new and unexpected turn of events. The ground had abruptly and simply disappeared without fanfare from beneath me, followed almost instantaneously by my bike, decoupling pedal from foot and bars from hands with the grace of an Apollo mission separation.

After that, all that remained was to wait for the contact that was rushing towards me, as only things which are inevitable do, with unforgiving violence. The world can be a right bastard.

It was clear that I had broken my arm very close to the shoulder joint from the instant that I landed in the shallow stream of water among the scattering of stones at the bottom of the ditch. I knew because I heard a distinct crack, processing as best I could the unusual sound of a human bone snapping, one that belonged to me no less, with one ear submerged under the trickle of water and my cheek resting on a rock covered in pond weed. I do not know where my legs were, nor what angles they described as they'd followed my pirouetting torso and flailing arms into the ditch, but I wasn't sure they had landed alongside the rest of me. For all I knew they were sticking comedically up into the air, as if I had planted myself headfirst into the abyss. None of my 51-year-old collection of limbs, muscles, fingers and feet made much sense any longer; nothing was correctly aligned. All that had changed in the instant that I mistook thin air for a bridge.

So I lay in this irrigation ditch in a state of furious confusion probably for no longer than a couple of seconds, a tiny slither of time really, but one that I remember as almost endless, outside the ordinary rules of time. I was dimly aware of the world around me, the canopy of ancient oak trees, the presence in the night sky of Venus, very bright I remember during those late summer weeks of 2020. Chris Boardman and I had often pointed it out to one another as we'd strolled back from another pub dinner at The George, wondering which planet it was until Chris had decided to settle the issue and downloaded one of those star-gazing apps.

And not far removed from my ditch-bound hide there was the impassive, ancient bulk of a 12th century castle, surrounded by a moat on which swans would be seeking cover in the reeds which fringed the waters. The old stronghold would by now be lit from the inside by yellow lights visible to those outside in the September gloom through the castle's leaded windowpanes. This, would you believe, was my intended destination. And I had fallen 50 metres short of its front entrance.

I sprang to my feet. Perhaps some deep, unconscious muscle memory had been activated, but my body instinctively leapt into action, mimicking the response I had witnessed in riders countless times at bike races. Unless they are actually knocked unconscious by a crash, riders are programmed by hours of conditioning and the actual insanity of their profession to get instantly to their feet. Never mind how much blood might be pouring from any number of wounds, nor how little of their Lycra shorts might remain to preserve their dignities in front of a gawping worldwide television viewership. Once righted, they reach blindly and unquestioningly for their bikes in an attempt to remount. The race must go on! At all costs!

Battling the steep sides of the ditch, I reached something approaching upright only in jerky stages, a faintly ridiculous sequence of silhouettes marking 'The Ascent of Man From A Ditch', squelching myself into a kind of hunched-over Marty Feldman-type standing position. Squinting through one muddy eye and another madly swivelling one, and through the drops of moat water which fell across my vision from the wet side of my head, I could make out the chrome and orange gleam of my bike, whose descent down the slippery side of the ditch had been arrested halfway by a sapling that had taken root in the bank. The whole incident would later remind me, albeit in a slightly less dramatic way, of Team Barloworld's John-Lee Augustyn in 2008 tipping over the side of the mighty Col de la Bonette and dropping down a vertiginous Alpine scree slope. They never found his bike it had fallen so far.

I found mine though, reached down with my right arm, forgetting that it was only attached to the shoulder by a snapped humerus bone, and grabbed hold of the frame. Then I tried to pull.

The swans will have heard the cry from across the still waters of the moat, perhaps raising in unison their slender necks to better sense which animal was in trouble. Likewise the rooks and owls, the hares and foxes of the woods around the castle, will have paused for a moment their nocturnal business and cocked an ear in the direction of the scream. They will have had no understanding that the voice they heard in torment was mine; that it belonged to a middle-aged cycling commentator who had just completed his 18th Tour de France, and, without bike lights, had ridden back to his hotel in the dark and had completely missed the bridge that would have led him safely to the gateway of Leeds Castle, where a delightful, warm, soft four-poster bed awaited him.

Several minutes later, some evening diners were just passing through an old portcullis and gate on their way home after a Sunday night dinner, as a limping silhouetted figure, dripping wet and groaning like some Dickensian spirit, passed by them in the opposite direction, one arm hanging uselessly at its side and mud covering one half of its crumpling form.

But that's the Tour de France for you. You never know what's around the corner.

2

THINGS CAN GO WRONG

I finished writing the last lines of *How I Won The Yellow Jumper* in a hotel room in Eindhoven in 2010, 15 years ago. I have always hated the title of my first book. I want it put on the record that I didn't come up with it, it was the work of my publishers. I thought I'd written *War and Peace*, not a frankly disposable account of being out of my depth on the telly, but there you go. It was a tale of my first few years covering the Tour de France for ITV; years that began with bewilderment and ended in confused enchantment. The title came about as a result of my first day broadcasting from the Tour, back in 2003. Amazingly, I managed to refer to the 'yellow jersey' as a 'yellow jumper'. If ever knitwear should have sunk a career, it was then.

I was in Eindhoven in 2010 to report on a football match, a thing I did in one of my previous lives. It was very early one September morning on the day of the game, I seem to recall. I had ironed my work shirt for later and was gazing out over the railway tracks at the back of the hotel, watching commuters on trains glide past my window on their way to work. My fingers were poised over the keyboard as I readied myself to type the closing lines of *Yellow Jumper*. Then two things happened at around the same time.

On the other side of the world, in Australia, David Millar had just claimed a silver medal in the World Championship Time Trial. He had finished just over a minute down on the all-conquering Fabian Cancellara, who was at the peak of his powers. In David's remarkable, if troubled, career, this had been a tremendously meaningful ride. It was a clean medal after the doping mess that he'd embroiled himself in back in 2004. Many years later, I would fully understand how much that moment meant to him.

But at pretty much the exact same time, back in Europe, news had just broken of Alberto Contador's positive test result for clenbuterol at the 2010 Tour de France. This would in turn signal the start of a tedious procedure that ended with him being sanctioned anyway, despite protesting his innocence with a defence that involved a contaminated steak that he had specially requested to be fetched from Spain, while the race was in the Pyrenees. Contador would be stripped of his 2010 Tour title.

Somehow, in my mind, these two events wound themselves around one another, speaking to me about the chaos of professional road racing; its corrupting effect on human behaviours and the path to validation it offers to others. These riders, I was beginning to understand, were just human beings doing a human thing. It's just that, for the most part, what they experienced sat outside our understanding.

It was time to write the final words of *How I Won The Yellow Jumper*. My publishing deadline beckoned. But I remember at the time thinking how unsatisfactory it was to break off there, with the story continuing to unfold in jerks and jolts. That's the funny thing about time. It doesn't seem to want to come to a satisfactory end. At least, not until the final star in the universe has collapsed and extinguished. But, according to Brian Cox off the telly, there are, 'More years until that happens than there are atoms in the universe.' So Tadej Pogačar's still got plenty of time to win every single Monument.

I was, of course, in no position to know back then that 15 years later I would pick up the now-yellowed pages of the book I had just completed and re-read the final line of the last chapter. It comes in response to a text message I receive from Australia. David, who I barely knew back then, was replying to the congratulations I had sent him:

'Thanks Ned. What a joy it was to rip that first lap. D'

What a joy, indeed. I did not yet know how that joy, that passion for this great sport, would deepen over the many years to come and that I would share it with the man who'd composed the message that lit up just beneath the black glass of the phone, sent from the other side of the world.

* * *

But things don't always go to plan. For years I had assumed I would be commentating on television with David Millar at the Tour de France for the remainder of my working life. This was naïve of me, of course; it was complacent to assume that nothing ever changes. But I hadn't wanted to imagine my summers any other way. So, when I embarked on writing this book, I wasn't expecting to have to write about how it will now come to an end. When the news broke in the autumn of 2024 that ITV had decided to relinquish the rights to the Tour, David messaged me: 'I thought that it was a forever job.'

We were both wrong. This summer of 2025 we will commentate on our last Tour de France for ITV. What began for me, in notoriously haphazard fashion in 2003, will come to an unexpectedly early close on the Champs-Élysées, 22 years and 23 Tours later. I am not looking forward to that moment. It will be a hill of beans, in the grand scheme of things: a small, bad thing happening in someone's life and not of any global consequence. But, when it comes, it will also be quietly devastating.

I've got all my accreditations, dating back to 2003, at the back of a drawer in my desk. It's the same one I am sitting at now, writing these words. I don't get them out to look at them. That would be weird and would take me to a depth of self-indulgence which I hope I have not yet plumbed. But I like to know that all those lanyards are there. I feel strangely delighted by the knowledge that these calling cards from history are tucked away in the dark recesses of a desk drawer in London.

Of course, as you will read on the pages that follow, my work in cycling commentary has extended far beyond the considerable confines of 'just' the Tour de France. There are many other great, and less great, races across the world, many of which I have been lucky enough to witness at first hand.

I hope, for example, that I will continue to commentate at the Giro d'Italia for many years to come. For those readers who don't know, the Giro is like a really stylish, occasionally freezing cold version of the Tour de France. There are a number of clear differences between the two grand tours. For example, the sheer number of middle-aged men at the Giro who stand around the race with hair held in place by oil, wearing skinny jeans and elaborate puffer jackets. That's the main point of difference, now I come to think of it; one which needs to be examined in the pages that follow.

The similarity between the two rival grand tours is that Tadej Pogačar can seemingly win them simply by turning up and without even trying. There will be time, too, in this book to reflect on the tufted genius from Slovenia, just as there will be the opportunity to recall the unexpected twists and turns that cycling has taken me on since I was first introduced to it in 2003. My journey in this sport still has a long way to run, I hope, even if a quarter of a century of working for ITV at the Tour has come to this unwanted end.

In the meantime, I want to lay down all those memories so that with time, as they gather dust on the shelf, they will mature into a personal, but also communal, record of a quarter of a century in which cycling has changed beyond recognition, as we all changed with it. Thus are races raced and lives lived: never truly in isolation. It's all connected.

So, for one final time this summer, David and I prepare to embark on another long French journey; one that will, as it always does, surprise, delight, sometimes bore, amuse and enrich us. I do not know who will win the race. But I know already that the moment is getting very close now when, as the sun sets behind the eventual *maillot jaune* of 2025, casting its golden light through the Arc de Triomphe, catching on the seams and the cuffs of the yellow jersey, and glancing off the smoothed tops of the cobblestones on the Champs-Élysées, we will sign off for the last time.

Before that moment comes, here's an extended list of all that bike racing has given me, from a moderate to severe case of haemorrhoids during the entire 2024 calendar (alleviated eventually by repeated and confusing visits to pharmacies in Florence and in Zürich in which my Italian and Swiss German language skills were put to the test), to occasional and sublime memories of bike races past, such as the sadly defunct Tour de Yorkshire, a race which almost saw a sudden wave sweep Gary Imlach into the North Sea at Scarborough in 2015.

I'm not kidding. It very nearly did.

3

THE ROAD TO SCARBOROUGH

The day when the briny deep nearly claimed one of television's most treasured and underused anchormen was also the first day I ever tried to commentate on a bike race. It was in the spring of 2015, just under 12 years since I had been introduced to the world of cycling. Had Gary actually slipped in his tasselled loafers and been carried away in his Fred Perry blouson towards the North Sea's oilfields and, beyond them, Norway, then I am sure I would have remembered the day differently. But that only happened in the multiverse.

In the actual Scarborough that we both inhabited, he kept his footing as he mounted the steps from the beach to the embankment, staying upright under extreme duress. When an unexpectedly brisk and playful wave decided to crash into the stairway, forcing the great man to scamper up the last three steps, microphone in hand, it was as close as I have ever seen Gary come, in a quarter of a century as his colleague, to losing his dignity. But instead he managed to deliver an immaculate opening line to the first ever Tour de Yorkshire. It was to be my debut in commentary. So, in a way, one of us was indeed swept away in an infernal angry tide and drowned, but not Gary.

* * *

I didn't have a clue how to prepare to be a cycling commentator. There is no school that you can attend; not even a strange private one housed in a detached Edwardian house with a cheap looking logo above the front door somewhere that aspires to being posh, like Wimbledon. The only people offering advice on how to commentate on YouTube are certifiably insane. And besides, when I set out on the journey, there were probably fewer than 10 people who did my job in the English language in the whole world. It's not a broad church. It's barely even a cult.

So, given that there was no template for the new career that ITV had somewhat foisted on me and that I was offered the sum total of no help or advice of any note, I found myself once again in the regrettable and by now tediously predictable position of having to make it up as I went along. But on this occasion, unlike when I made my 2003 debut at the Tour as a reporter, I did at least acknowledge that I would need to work very, very hard at it. After all, it appeared from the outside like an impossibly difficult job; something my first impressions only seemed to confirm when I started to think more closely about how to set about it. How do you talk about pretty much the same thing for five hours? How do you tell the riders apart, when eight of them are identically dressed and they're all basically skinny, young, white European men? How do you know what's really happening in a bunch sprint when the chaos kicks in? The whole proposition seemed absurdly difficult; a test of quick-wittedness and mental acuity that had me shrinking inside before I'd even tried it.

But the suggestion from ITV's producers that I at least try it ushered in a surprisingly sustained period of diligence as I prepared to assume the role of commentator. This approach was markedly different from my preferred method of (not) preparing to be a Tour de France reporter that I outlined in *How I Won The Yellow Jumper*.

In 2003, faced with the immensity of my knowledge deficit, I simply threw my arms up in instant and abject surrender. Back then, before being sent out to cover my first race, I didn't realise, for example, that there were teams at the Tour de France. I thought it was just a lot of people riding a bike (which, in a way, I still maintain it is). And even if I had known about the team thing, I really wouldn't have been able to explain why there were teams, what they were for or what it was that the various teammates did. Let alone what a negative split in a time trial was, how a train of climbing domestiques might be best marshalled, how it's possible to compete for the green jersey by targeting breakaways on mountain stages, or how headwinds can actually, counterintuitively, play into the hands of determined late attackers: all the stuff that matters, that makes road racing the beautiful mystery that I now understand it to be. Remembering the aftermath of a pretty chastening first meeting in a Soho coffee house with the immensely well-informed Gary Imlach (actually, I think he's genuinely allergic to inaccuracy) I wrote the following:

> Deciding that the depth of my ignorance wasn't going to subside overnight, I had embarked on a course of doing not a lot. I could have buried myself in research. But I had so much to learn that I decided any late lunge for expertise this late in the day would have been quixotic, so I learnt nothing. It was a technique that had got me through school and university and I wasn't going to abandon it now.

Back in 2003, realising quite how much ground I needed to make up to become even vaguely conversant in the language of cycling, I simply turned smartly on my heels and walked rapidly away without so much as a pang of conscience. After all, it was only cycling. I probably wouldn't even be back the following year.

Except that's not how it turned out. I returned to the Tour and never left. Ten years went by in a flash, travelling at the breakneck speed of the Tour de France.

I came back again as a reporter in 2004, despite having effectively resigned from the production the previous autumn due in part to the shame I felt at the job I'd done in 2003. When the dust had settled from July, I wrote an email to our producers, which should have ended my Tour de France career there and then. It detailed very precisely how terrible an experience it had been, what a dysfunctional production team it was and how I had produced, as a result, some of the worst work I had ever been responsible for. I didn't expect them to require my services again, but such was the paucity of the talent pool, like a bad penny I turned up again. It was the best thing that ever happened to my haphazard career.

* * *

In 2004 I spent another three weeks listening to Lance Armstrong lie to me at very close quarters and watching Jan Ullrich from afar as he avoided even having to lie to me. I said goodbye to Armstrong (or so I believed) after his final 'win' in 2005, then spent the next three or four years flipping around like a pinball in a game called 'Doper', bouncing off the various catapults and alarms with names like Landis, Schumacher, Rasmussen, Vinokourov and Riccò, before Armstrong reappeared once more in 2009 and finally exited the stage for good in 2010, en route to losing money and his reputation, both of which, astonishingly, he has since partly or completely regained.

Team Sky launched in 2010, and with their limitless budget and scant regard for what went before almost instantly made implacable enemies across the traditional cycling world. Most of that antipathy towards the new kids on the block was only partially, if at all, understood by British cycling fans. From this distinctly non-cycling island just off France that I call home and others call Britain, a lot of people rallied to the predominantly black flag of Team Sky. Bradley Wiggins, long before he'd ever heard the word 'podcast' or started to hang out with people like James Cracknell, won the Tour ahead of their ambitious schedule in 2012. In doing so he saw off the not insignificant internal threat of Chris Froome and also managed to overcome the spectacle of his wife Cath and Froome's girlfriend Michelle tearing chunks out of each other on Twitter, only to be put in their place by Peta Cavendish, in what became known as cycling's 'Wag-gate'. Wiggins was basically a track rider, or so I had always thought. I wasn't really interested in the track back in 2007 when we first met, so perhaps I never really took him seriously, not least because I found his name amusing. Bradley Wiggins sounded more like he should be a viola player in a provincial orchestra or a solicitor in Rochdale. He didn't *sound* as if he would one day win the Tour de France, not with a name like that. And he didn't look right either.

At least that's what I thought when I was first introduced to him, waiting patiently for me to finish interviewing David Millar outside a posh function room in a Kensington club on the eve of the 2007 Tour de France. I remember him being distant, shy, distracted, uncomfortable; characteristics which endured throughout his mostly unhappy relationship with his public persona and with the media landscape in general. The genuinely razor-sharp, viciously funny and evidently intelligent Bradley Wiggins would appear from time to time, as would the philosophical version of this highly complex human, but you were never sure when you entered into a conversation with him how it might turn out.

Even in 2012, when I spent half an hour in his company, locked into a tiny Campanile hotel room outside Chartres watching his masseur working on the legs that had just won the Tour de France, I was still not quite certain of my relationship with him – or lack of it. And the manner in which his post-racing career has navigated choppy waters of his own stirring, and of the knotted tale of TUEs, Russian hacks and jiffy bags, has meant that his prodigious achievement, his place in history, has perhaps been knocked a little further into the sidelines than any of us might have imagined when he sat on the golden throne after winning a final Olympic gold medal at the London games.

Only Britain could have produced Bradley Wiggins, for clear sporting reasons as well as for cultural ones. After he'd brought the curtain down on the Champs-Élysées with the best-conceived quip in Tour history ('Right – we're just going to draw the raffle numbers'), Wiggins went on to take the time trial gold at the London Olympics. For most of the British viewing public that gave him far greater credit than the fact that he'd just won the actual Tour de France; a race still widely believed by much of the UK population to be a bit of an amateur lark. Even in 2012, there was ingrained ignorance in the UK about the Tour de France.

Fundamental misconceptions about the true, unfathomable nature of the *grande épreuve* were evidenced in 2014. I remember a friend from Welcome To Yorkshire, the local organisers of the *Grand Départ* that year, showing me emails they had received in the immediate run-up to the race. Many of them were enquiries about how to get a place in the starting line-up: 'Dear Sir, please could you tell me how my grandson can apply to ride the Tour de France. He's been a keen cyclist for years and this would make a lovely birthday present for him.' That's what British Cycling has forever been up against and why the successes of Cavendish, Wiggins, Thomas et al have been so unexpected and counter-cultural.

By the time Yorkshire hosted the race, I'd spent getting on for a year of my life at the Tour. Perhaps for the first time I now felt qualified to offer the occasional opinion about the race. I'd seen at first hand the profoundly special Mark Cavendish rack up a crazy number of stages, and embark on a new and agonising series of high-profile exits from the race, quite a lot of his own making and others entirely outside his control. Then I would watch on in shared agony as his slow-motion assault on the Merckx record dwindled to a painful trickle and then seemingly stopped altogether, stymied for years by undiagnosed illness. That story wasn't even close to an end back in 2014. I'd been there since before his debut and during his long reign of dominance, but wasn't to know that his story wasn't even halfway through.

I'd watched Chris Froome's slender figure emerge from the equally skeletal shadow of Bradley Wiggins to dominate the Tour de France with Team Sky's crushingly effective and almost entirely charisma-free approach to getting the job done. And though I had found the years following the summer of 2012 to be parched and deficient in the otherwise happy texture of eccentricity and vainglory that I so admired in this particularly pyrrhic sport, I had noted how they had cemented my fate. The Tour de France had quite taken me over.

For almost a decade, through Cavendish to Froome, the unfortunate UK viewership had grown accustomed to my occasionally shonky interactions with the riders at the Tour. I suppose my voice had become familiar to those many viewers who tuned in to the highlights show with obsessive regularity: I had experienced the sometime glares of Cavendish, the inscrutability of Nibali, the excessive pre-answer nodding from Froome and the sheer oddness of Peter Sagan, though it would take me years to be able to replicate that particular nasal laugh that was his trademark when the absolute loon was at the height of his powers.

Whether I liked it or not, those short interactions with exhausted, overly-skinny men became the thing that I was known for, which is not something I had planned when I was first went to the careers adviser back at school. Air traffic controller had been their slightly more mundane suggestion. But, and I have no idea why, these fleeting moments of 'Rider talks to journalist on the top of a mountain' contained a curious power. A well-known football manager, who may be Alan Pardew and with whom I had feuded for years, even absolved me of the profound grievances he held against me, because of my work at the Tour de France. 'It's all right, mate,' Pardew had said to me in the tunnel at Brighton and Hove Albion's ground. 'You done the best interview ever this summer.' I had grabbed Bradley Wiggins at the end of the Tour in 2012 as he appeared at Mark Cavendish's side and had been forced to bat away the attentions of Wiggins's press minders who were trying to extract him.

Through some weirdness of association, a bit of me had now seemingly been spliced into July and the succession of hot, wet, slow, blistering race days that marked out our shared summers, shaping the days and weeks at the centre of our year with numbers, names, mountain profiles and polka dots. I guess I now felt at home in people's homes.

* * *

It wasn't my idea to uproot my career once more by switching roles. The ITV producers had been nagging away at me for some time to consider moving from reporting to commentating. Perhaps they too were simply tired of hearing the same old questions tumble forth from my mouth every summer. But for well over a year of their gentle insistence, I flatly refused to entertain the notion of trying my hand at commentary. I could not imagine the size of the leap in responsibility from asking three or four pertinent questions of riders, having watched the race and having had time to consider what had happened, to having to explain in real time what had just happened, what was happening right now and what might be about to happen in the race. Such vision and understanding seemed to me to be pure sorcery and way beyond the reach of my capacity. And that was before I even considered the verbal bedlam of navigating a bunch sprint commentary without simply resorting to shouting, 'Blllrrrrghhhaaarg!' But eventually, and under sustained pressure, I succumbed to their persistence. There was a limit, it seemed, to the number of times I could tell them that I had absolutely no intention of attempting to commentate the Tour de France and that I'd be more likely to enrol in a zookeeper's course in Belarus.

One day, during the 2014 Vuelta, I was invited by ITV to take a seat in a commentary box in London and try my hand (wrong part of the body, but 'try my larynx' sounds overly exact) at calling a stage of the race. The commentary would obviously not be used on the telly and would be incinerated and destroyed so as to prevent any future embarrassment. The test run was merely a way of finding out whether or not I would fall emphatically at the first hurdle. With a comical degree of cloak and dagger, ITV even paid for an experienced former pro co-commentator (thank you Matt Stephens) to sit alongside me, on the understanding that he was to say nothing to anyone in public about what was about to happen. Somewhere in the same building, Phil Liggett was in a different studio, doing the actual commentary, quite oblivious to what was happening down the corridor. The subterfuge heightened still further the sense that the entire operation was potentially career-ending. As I cycled across London to the studios that afternoon, attempting to commentate on my passage through Shepherds Bush, I was imbued with an ominous sense of great forces at play. In fact, I was rather overwrought given ITV were trying out a new commentator. That was actually all it was.

John Degenkolb won the stage wearing the green points jersey. That, along with the German's furiously muscular head-bobbing sprint style made him mercifully extremely identifiable. Thank you, John Degenkolb! As a result of somehow managing to shout the right name at roughly the right time at my first attempt, my life changed. And, as a consequence of that, I have developed a strange affinity with the German: one that isn't necessarily reciprocated.

In a strange twist of fate, I would find myself two years later being helicoptered to an uninhabited island off the coast of Bodø within the Arctic Circle of Norway, and dropped off there in the company of John Degenkolb and the defending champion, Rein Taaramäe from Estonia. We were all there to help promote the 2016 Arctic Race of Norway, and for some reason this necessitated being dumped on a rock and left there while they went back to pick up a photographer. We stood and looked out at the helicopter flying back to the mainland over the pristine, mineral green sea. With a quite stunning lack of self-awareness, I chose that moment to tell Degenkolb that his victory on stage five at the 2014 Vuelta had been the first ever commentary I had done. The comment met with as profound a silence as hung over the open Norwegian waters themselves. The German winner of Paris–Roubaix and Milan–Sanremo stared ahead, unresponsive. After an agonising 20 seconds, I let my engaging smile fall and turned instead to Taaramäe, figuring, correctly as it happens, that the Estonian would be more open to conversing with a simple-minded enthusiast. 'Hi Rein!' I put out a hand.

A cursory check of the notes from that (for me) portentous day reminds me that for the majority of the 166 kilometres of stage five of the 2014 Vuelta, and for the entirety of the broadcast, until he was inevitably caught, Dutch journeyman Pim Ligthart was off the front on his own, his breakaway companion Tony Martin having suffered a mechanical and dropped back. The loneliness of Ligthart in the heat of southern Spain presented me in my commentary debut with another very significant challenge – and one which would by far eclipse any difficulties thrown up by the eventual bunch sprint. I had time, before I started to talk, to jot down three things I knew about Ligthart. I then had two and half hours in which to re-work and re-phrase the same paucity of information over and over again, to accompanying shots of Pim Ligthart from side on, Pim Ligthart from head on and Pim Ligthart from the reverse angle. I went to bed that night with two words lit up on West End-style mental billboards, the capital letters of the words fringed by the golden light bulbs of the mind: 'Pim' and 'Ligthart'. These are the profound psychological fissures that this job can force, as I had just discovered.

And so the time came for me to be unleashed on the viewing public. My co-commentator would be David Millar, a mere four months into retirement. David had never commentated before, not once, not even (as I had) for a try-out. So that seemed like a good plan.

* * *

All along, the unseen and unspeaking powers that be had been planning that David and I would become the next commentary pairing at the Tour de France. They knew, but we didn't. This new role obviously necessitated David no longer racing the Tour, which happened rather suddenly and not entirely of his choosing in 2014, when he was deselected for the team; a first in his career. That year he had joined us for the Yorkshire *Grand Départ*, working as a pundit in a hat alongside another prologue specialist, the less tall and less dandyish Chris Boardman, stoical in his beloved Rohan. Functionally dressed, Chris was never knowingly flamboyant on screen. He left that to others.

Then David was asked to come back to Yorkshire the following April to commentate with me on the inaugural Tour de Yorkshire, the short-lived, terribly named, rather wonderful race which exploded into life and then guttered out in scandal and ignominy all within the five brief, but eventful, years of its life. Perhaps the horrible hybrid of French and English incorporated into its actual name was a portent of its unviability. I remember on the eve of the race challenging no less a figure than the Director of the Tour de France Christian Prudhomme, whose company ASO were partners in the Tour de Yorkshire. I asked him who on earth had come up with the name. 'It was him,' Prudhomme said, pointing at Sir Gary Verity, a man whose meteoric rise and steep fall characterised the absolute zenith of cycling interest in the UK. Prudhomme smiled ruefully, shook his head and then wandered off. Verity was still holding court with some local TV crew.

Knowing that this would be my first ever commentary on TV, I did as much as I possibly could to prepare. In March, I even went as far as to borrow the empty house in York of a friend of mine who was away working overseas. I took my bike with me, determined to ride all three stages of the upcoming race by way of reconnaissance.

Blithely assuming that, without any training, I could manage three consecutive days of typically hilly Yorkshire roads, totalling 515 kilometres and well over 6,500 metres of climbing (all in the form of nasty, steep, little bastard hills, rather than gradual Alpine passes), I asked my Twitter followers if anyone would care to join me. Day one passed relatively serenely, accompanied as I was by a decent chunk of a local cycling club. Day two broke me, as we headed into the Dales and into a headwind that left me cycling along the tops at something less than walking pace. Day three simply didn't happen. I called it off, due to not wanting to suffer any further in the name of commentary research. I drove back to London a little wiser and 10 years older. Such diligence never returned.

So much for the course. The next vast unknowable was the riders' start list. For weeks prior to my commentary debut, I fretted about how best to assemble a database of knowledge that I could access instantly and on demand during the upcoming televised bike race. Eschewing the evidentially useful and well-proven invention of the computer, something deeply intuited from my childhood schooling steered me instead down to W.H. Smith in Lewisham. Perhaps mistaking stage one of the 2015 Tour de Yorkshire for my first day at secondary school, I bought myself a whole armoury of analogue stationary items, just stopping short of adding an Oxford maths set in a tin to my inventory.

The most significant of the items I did come away with was, naturally, a full set of highlighters. This much I knew. No commentator has ever been able to resist decorating a start list with correctly chromatically assigned embellishments, designed to draw attention to the most important riders in the race and their Top Trumps-style attributes. In the case of the Tour de Yorkshire, this meant that the sprinters got a green highlight and the GC aspirants (always a tough call at the Tour de Yorkshire, which featured lots of climbing without any climbs, if you see what I mean) were coated in a fetching light blue.

But the highlighter work, so totemic I now understand to the final preparation on any given day of commentary, could only be executed once the final, definitive start list had been published. This happened late in the evening on the day before the race. For weeks I had been calling up team managers and *directeurs sportifs* trying to divine, pre-empt or second guess the team selections, grilling them for background information, and then diligently filling out my index cards with information that I deemed might be useful. At the last minute, though, I would find that three of the seven riders Topsport Vlaanderen-Baloise had pencilled in for the race had, in fact, stayed at home and that three completely different, but mostly anonymous, young Flandrien all-rounders had made the unusual-sounding trip to Bridlington instead.

My rather analogue commentary notes for the 2015 Tour de Yorkshire.

I spent the eve of the race in a hotel lobby just outside York, index cards sprawled all over the uncomfortably low table in front of me, biros and highlighters cascading intermittently to the polished tiles below, Pritt stick and scissors in occasional use to cut and paste the faces of riders who I had never heard of on to cards, and an untouched beer growing slowly warm as I awaited with dread the arrival of the official start list. I was deeply anxious about how many late additions I might feverishly need to add to my ever-growing pile of hand-written sporting biographies.

At some point during this purgatorial stretch of time, David Millar ambled stylishly through the revolving doors. Flying in from Spain, where he lives, he had an expensive looking bag slung over his shoulder, his elegant head was topped off by an ironically perched trilby, from whose brim a single curl of black hair fell with insouciance across his un-furrowed brow. He strolled over to me.

'Nedster!'

I looked up. 'Hello, David.'

He grinned at me from his position of 6 foot 2 above the planet. He glanced down at my elaborate handiwork, disgorged across the surface in front of me.

'Who's in the bike race, then?'

I looked at him, scissors in hand, for a beat longer than he was anticipating, forcing him to turn his gaze elsewhere. Then I looked down at the froth of analogue information seething across the table in all directions. As if suddenly struck in the solar plexus by an invisible fist, I realised to my horror that I could not in that moment recall a single one of the 141 names I had been cutting and pasting on my silly little cards for weeks.

Overnight the rising panic had not abated; not at all. We had driven early to the seafront in Scarborough, which over the course of the all-too-brief years of the Tour de Yorkshire became the totemic finish line of the race, and we had breakfasted on TV catering, far removed from the cuisine of the Tour de France: flaccid, pinkish bacon slices, which, once exposed to the wind whipping off the North Sea, took no longer than a few seconds to cool to match the ambient air temperature. It didn't settle the nerves.

Then the race started and the rain set in, as forecast. A looping course up the coast and then inland and across the length of the North York Moors got underway, unseen by the television cameras. The first edition of the Tour de Yorkshire was only three stages long. And those three stages would only be visible for the final two hours or so of the race; a throwback to the days before flag-to-tape coverage became the norm for the broadcast of major bike races.

That meant that for the first half of the race we could only follow the events from the information that was relayed via race radio or intermittently tweeted by the PR operations of the various teams. What became evident, however, as the clock ticked down to our on-air time and the race grew ever closer to the finish line, was that it was out of control. The usual order of a small and manageable break-away, held at a comfortable distance for the peloton to pick off at will, had been usurped entirely. As the race hit the vast, brooding, heathery lump of the North York Moors, God's Own County did its very worst, blasting sea-frozen air skywards off the choppy breakers beyond the cliffs, and whipping the tops with a furious wind whose every moan and sigh brought with it a fresh inundation from skies as black as ink. It was awful weather.

But awful weather, in this most masochistic of sports, presents an opportunity. In the minutes before the final countdown, with the moto cameramen shouldering arms, trying vainly to hold a steady shot and wiping the lens clear of water as often as they could, and with the helicopter now angling its blades into the easterly above the riders to keep a position, the race simply blew apart. The clock counted down to zero, Gary, by now safely on dry land, had done his introductory spiel with Chris and then handed over to the 'new duo in the commentary box'. By this time, stage one of the first ever Tour de Yorkshire was shredded into tiny, incoherent pieces: 130 individual riders, all in identical black rain jackets, spread across the county, sometimes falling, sometimes staying upright, all suffering.

'Thanks, Gary,' I'd said, with a shred of irony.

As for the rest of the words which escaped me that afternoon... God alone knows. I have a vague memory of being flatly and correctly contradicted by David every time I attempted to offer any kind of rational explanation for the bedlam unfolding on our screens. The race, having somehow navigated Whitby, past the ghostly bones of the ruined Abbey, dropped down and then climbed up from Robin Hood's Bay, battened down against the storm, formed and re-formed, and then reached the Scarborough seafront. It was total chaos, picked out only through the rain-spattered de-focussed lenses of the long-suffering camera operators. At no point did anything make sense. It came to a thunderous close when the almost completely unmemorable Lars Petter Nordhaug became the first name I ever had to shout out loud, outsprinting Thomas Voeckler as he did so. And it was done.

My baptism in the commentator's chair had been every bit as chastening as I had feared. Once I finally took off my headphones and dropped my biro on a pad that had remained devoid of notes, I realised that I had not shifted from a rigor-mortised position at the very front of my swivel chair; that I probably hadn't blinked; and that I couldn't be sure I'd remembered to breathe. I glanced over at David, who was calmly doing some online banking. Then I stepped out of the truck and into Scarborough.

All around me there was activity: riders making their way to the team buses, TV crew darting about, commissaires and chaperones, organisers and police. And thousands and thousands of fans, standing in the wet grass of the bank which rose steeply up and away from the seafront where the race had just come crashing in. It was a vivid sight, which I, on wobbly sea legs, blinking at the unaccustomed daylight after so many hours in the dark, could only stare at in mute wonder.

A rider from Cofidis came past me, looking profoundly lost. At that point I realised two things: that I hadn't referred to a single one of my lovingly handwritten index cards. And that I would have to do it all again tomorrow. And the day after that.

This is how it all began – at the Tour de Yorkshire; a race watched for the most part by people in Yorkshire. My job change had started tentatively at best. I had found myself talking on air in a more or less muddled fashion, rather than actually commentating, something which would take me many years to figure out. And back then it seemed far from obvious that I ever would. I had only a brittle faith that I might ever succeed.

It would be no more than a year before I was thrown to the wolves and sent to commentate at the Tour de France.

4

A COLD COMING

I have learned to loathe the winter, with a passion that seems to gather fury with each passing year, to the point where my hatred for its desolation has started to infect even the summer months. No sooner has the Tour de France finished than I am dreading the relentless march of the months towards autumn. Must be an age thing.

This increasing anxiety has been exacerbated over the last years by the sad appearance of the horse chestnut trees on the Champs-Élysées. I think I first became aware of their infection in 2019, which, perhaps coincidentally, was the first edition of the Tour de France to have been prematurely decided by climate change, when Egan Bernal was denied his probable race-clinching stage win by a landslide. On arrival in Paris 48 hours later, I noticed for the first time that the leaves of the great conker trees on either side of the avenue had a brown, shrivelled look to them. I would later learn this was not the early onset of autumn, but the result of a bacterial infection called, rather darkly, *bleeding canker*.

Nonetheless, it upset me. Gone was the verdant green canopy, providing relief from the white sunlight which can make Paris an overwhelmingly bright summer landscape. Instead, the autumnal hue of the foliage suggested, slyly, that summer's days were numbered. And ever since then I have started to feel ever more keenly the onrushing autumn, nibbling back from October, through September and even biting chunks out of August.

I don't want to overstate this case, but the end of the Tour is the end of hope. What follows is merely an after-echo of the year's zenith; all sense of anticipation is replaced by dull dread of darkness and of winter. By November, when hardy folk start to pretend to get enthused by cyclo-cross, the foul mood is complete. And even the sudden new-year proliferation of riders posting selfies in their new cycling kits does little to allay the sense of loss.

* * *

And then it all starts again. Each cycling season trickles infuriatingly into life, dripping races of varying importance into the world until one day you wake and realise that road racing has started to metastasize, spreading its grasping tentacles far and wide. As if from nowhere, like a giant network of hidden fungal spores, the whole eco structure has burst back into life.

There is no grand fanfare day which is universally accepted as heralding the beginning of another year of pedalling and breathing heavily in skin-tight clothing. In fact, the very act of asking, and then attempting to answer, the question 'Which is the first race of the year?' is tantamount to firing the opening salvo of a culture war of a very specific road-racing variety.

Few heritage European fans, rubbing their chins sagely as they take a sip from a macchiato and look up from their battered second-hand copy of *Nous Étions Jeunes et Insouciants*, would ever claim that the actual first race of the calendar is anything other than a lurid irrelevance. The national stage race of Australia, the Tour Down Under, is, for the shivering North, a maddening reverse-engineered Fata Morgana, offering a distant mirage of incomprehensible heat, gazed upon in disbelief from cycling's heartlands: a wilderness of north-easterlies whipping in over the harbour defences of quantifiably awful places like Ostend.

The Tour Down Under, with its Chardonnay-yellow vineyard sponsors and entry-level kangaroo-themed logo, its questionable justification in a climate crisis whose effects routinely engulf the

Adelaide Hills in wildfires and its uniquely Australian nomenclature (Willunga Hill, Mount Lofty), is rightly celebrated by a home nation that has a small yet passionate cycling fan base. These hardy nocturnal souls deserve some recompense for their devotion throughout the rest of the year. They think nothing of staying up into the very small hours of the night to watch a stage of, say, the BinckBank Tour from the middle of a European afternoon and this is their reward: the chance to cheer on a decent peloton, encrusted with a top-level jewel or two, whose stars can enjoy the searing heat of an Australian high summer, while their teammates are left at home to trudge wearily to the utility room and pretend they are somewhere warm on Zwift.

It is a trip which my erstwhile Tour companion and commentary predecessor Phil Liggett still makes in a paid capacity and on an annual basis. In Australia Phil is worshipped, as he is in the UK, the USA and South Africa. There is no other way of putting it. In January 2024 he celebrated a significant birthday on the eve of the race and was presented with an improbably vertiginous cream cake. Two huge inflatable numeral-shaped helium balloons, an '8' and a '0', had been hauled into whichever hotel function room was being used and placed behind him. Our Perth-resident ITV cameraman colleague John Tinetti sent a picture of the celebrations to a WhatsApp group that David Millar and I are both in. David immediately posted:

'NUTS – that's like Ned still commentating the Tour de France in 2049?!'

Then he followed it up with a message of unalloyed positivity: 'You got this, Ned.'

That message didn't age brilliantly, David.

* * *

Another 25 years in the job, I thought to myself, as I strolled around the house that January morning, picking up socks that had fallen to the ground en route from the washing machine and sporadically clutching my back after another twinge entirely in keeping with the life choices of a fairly sedentary man in his mid-fifties. Phil's undiminished staying power is almost mystical, I mused as I stared at a single running sock. I made a mental note once again to catch up with Phil to find out his secret. The last time I had done that had been in Calais in 2022, when we went out together for a dinner of *moules-frites* and Sancerre. On that occasion, he'd managed to give the impression that he was treating me to dinner while deftly managing to avoid paying most, if not all, of his share of the bill: all with an irresistible twinkle in his eye. This was perhaps the secret of his legendary longevity. That and the wondrous oaky timbre of his voice, at once urgent and in command. I'd grown into cycling with it ringing in my ears. Most of us had. Still, I'd bought him dinner that evening.

At least Phil was actually *in* Australia, enjoying the cake and adulation. Other broadcasters could not have afforded to make the trip. My thoughts returned to Chris Boardman's brief stint as a Tour Down Under pundit back in January 2010. Team Sky had just launched and their first race was to be the Tour Down Under. Sky Sports had just woken up to the fact that cycling existed. The team sponsorship had nothing to do with the sports channel and everything to do with the corporation's marketing arm, who in turn had no understanding of sports and had acquired the rights to show the new British team that basically bore their name.

Then someone had contacted Chris to ask him if he wanted to work as a studio pundit on their live coverage, to which he readily agreed, as the terms of the contract involved the payment of money. What they also involved, and what 'Olympic Bloke' had failed to appreciate in his haste to sign on the dotted line, was that his working day would begin at around 2 a.m. And that no one would be watching. By 'no one', I think I may be exaggerating by a factor of maybe four or five. But I doubt they got half a dozen.

I tuned in just to be amused at the fact that the bags under Chris's eyes had once again overtaken mine in the race to be the baggiest eyes on telly, but by the time they actually handed over to Phil Liggett for him to say something like, 'So, only 96 kilometres remaining then…' I was fast asleep, dreaming of summer days rather than winter nights. So I missed André Greipel's bunch sprint victory over Gert Steegmans (blimey, how quickly these names fade from the immediate past and recede to somewhere sepia). I missed Greg Henderson recording Team Sky's first ever top 10, when he came fifth in the opening sprint. I slept through it all.

If truth be told, the Tour Down Under is not a race to follow on TV. It is a race to attend in person, by the side of the road, probably a little tipsy, as 1983 World Darts Champion Keith Deller never fails to enthuse when I am in his company. Deller, the Milky Bar Kid, as he was known, weirdly found himself the guest of some vineyard-type people one day in 2014 when the race had come by, 'not once, but six times!' Keith is a gentle soul, with inbuilt enthusiasm and a strong penchant for telling me the same story more often than is necessary for me to remember it. 'I couldn't believe it! I started supporting Movistar by the time they came round the third time, Ned.' This not totally sober encounter might be the only time that the Milky Bar Kid and Gorka Izagirre have ever, and will ever, lock eyes.

Night-time punditry was not a mistake Chris would make again. Indeed, it wasn't a mistake that Sky Sports would make again. They opted out of showing the 2011 Tour Down Under and every one since. Sky Sports then half-heartedly picked up the highlights rights to the Giro in 2013, when Bradley Wiggins failed to win it after his Tour de France victory, and were probably a little annoyed that Vincenzo Nibali won instead. They went back the following year to witness someone small and inscrutable called Nairo Quintana winning, after which they paid no further attention to road racing. Not so long after that the wider corporation packed up its interest in the sport altogether.

That exit in turn opened up the opportunity for Ineos to come fracking along en route to installing Dave Brailsford at Manchester United, which is rather a rapid summary of a decade-long process, but had with hindsight perhaps been the long-term objective of Brailsford all along. And I am only exaggerating a bit: starting in 2010, when the Team Sky launch on London's Millbank took place the morning after I had presented ITV's FA Cup third round highlights show, Brailsford never missed an opportunity to talk football with me, even when I made it clear that the only reason I was attracted to cycling was so that I didn't have to talk football.

* * *

Once the Tour Down Under and the Cadel Evans Great Ocean Road Race are done with, the attention of the cycling world switches mostly back to Europe as the season starts to flicker into life. On the island of Mallorca, a sequence of strangely named (the Mallorcan dialect can appear complex to the non-speaker of Spanish) one-day races all featuring the prefix 'Trofeo' herald the start of a confusingly profuse few weeks of racing across the Iberian Peninsula, from the Algarve to the Spanish regions of Valencia and Catalunya. Lots of the big-name GC riders make their seasonal debuts at this point and the sudden proliferation of so much high-quality racing after such a string of barren months is overwhelming.

For those of us at home whose fortunate professional duty it is to watch endless hours of televised cycling on streaming platforms, the concurrent welter of stages proves befuddling, to say the least. Never quite certain which riders are in which race being held in which country, I was for many years plagued by the conviction that Alejandro Valverde had probably entered all of them and would fancy his chances on any given day, at least twice a day, in a time trial somewhere built up on the coast, a bunch sprint near a castle and on a mountain top in Portugal. Most of these races are pretty insane and start with a solid mountain stage, instead of easing the peloton in. They are great.

But few really claim that those Iberian festivals of racing represent the actual start of the cycling season, because most of their winners are thinking about bigger, greater wins down the line. There's a grudging, tacit admission that the whole shebang obviously *must* have begun. But no one can remember why or when, a bit like the way it is with Ed Sheeran. I have seen the view expressed by one ultimate purist that no races matter until February's Étoile de Bessèges, a lovely low-key bike race held over a few days around the tiny town of Bessèges, which is venerable but not ancient, unless you think of 1971 as genuinely historic, which perhaps you do, because perhaps it is.

The Étoile used to be a fabulously parochial French affair, often contributing to the zenith of a French rider's career; the type you'd regularly see at the Tour who would just as regularly fail to win a stage on the biggest race of them all. That all changed in the re-jigged Covid calendar of 2020, when all of a sudden all the big names were turning up to anything in order to get the miles in before the start of the delayed Tour de France and, ever since then, the cosy little French traditional race has lapsed into the internationality of a greatly enhanced start list. Shame really. But to claim it somehow signals the start of the season is to pivot to a hipster stance that goes way further than even moustache wax and homemade kombucha.

The last opportunity to assert your greater understanding of the circadian rhythm of the cycling calendar is to contend with monotonous certainty that the Opening Weekend is the indeed the, well ... opening weekend. The two races on consecutive days towards the end of February are often bleakly frigid and upsettingly violent in nature. Belgium is at that time still submitting to an endless winter routinely inflicting its final few weeks of hailstones and biting gale force blasts from the Channel. I heard tell from some that were in the race that, on one occasion, Edvald Boasson Hagen finished in such thermal distress that he had to be manhandled off his bike and basically carted like an iced corpse into the shower. It took the Norwegian half an hour under scalding water before his customary vacant smile broke out once more across his fine Nordic face.

I have been to watch these races, simply as an observer, and I concede that there is some sense in seeing them as the starting pistol for real racing: these are the first notable, genuinely historic prizes on offer for the Classics riders at least: Kuurne-Brussels-Kuurne and Omloop Het Nieuwsblad are both very serious Flandrien cobbled Classics. The latter is a race which changed its name in 2008 only because the newspaper which has always sponsored it merged with another paper and changed its name from *Het Volk* to make it sound less Volkish and less 'anti-socialist', as it once proudly proclaimed from its title banner. It was first raced in 1945 and was thought of as a potential rival to the predominance of the Ronde van Vlaanderen, rather than the frozen warm-up act it now is.

It's at this point that my excessive TV viewing, and the piling up of an unfeasible mass of notes and tiny observations about riders which I can use later on in the year, becomes a form of personality disorder. Though I may have already dropped into a race in person to meet with a rider for a magazine feature (rare these days) or spent some time on the race for a podcast (less rare, but more fun), by February I am champing at the bit to get going. But my commentary debut every year is not up to me. That technicality sits squarely at the discretion of the race organisers and the TV executives who employ me.

* * *

For a number of years, my first race of the season was the ethically fraught Dubai Tour, which functioned for many a Classics rider, oddly, as a very warm warm-up race for the freezing cold warm-up race which is Omloop Het Nieuwsblad. At first, and perhaps before I even started to question the consequences of my actions, the opportunity to jet off to a completely reliable 25 degrees and sunshine, just at the point when winter was pressing hardest on the European spirit, seemed too good to resist. And so I went, laptop, notebook and swimming trunks in hand, to perform in front of the microphone in the playground of the global bourgeoisie, whose interest in the bike race almost ran into double figures of spectators.

My years commentating first on the Dubai Tour, then the Abu Dhabi Tour (which finished on the F1 motor racing circuit every year in a race of stultifying tedium) and then the merged UAE Tour were, with hindsight, both fascinating and the opposite of fascinating: I could never work out which. If I had to choose, however, I'd have to err on the side of fascinating.

This may come as a surprise, perhaps, to any readers who may have passed a few idle morning hours watching the proceedings of this most opulent and pointless of the desert races. To say that not much happens would be an understatement entirely out of keeping with the ethos of a nation state which has no word for understatement. The race passes beneath the shadow of the mighty Burj Khalifa (the tallest skyscraper in the world, because of course it is), alongside the sparkling coastline of the Persian Gulf, whose private beaches are encrusted with monumental buildings that have been translated straight into concrete from the fever dreams of the world's least restrained architects. It cuts straight lines through deserts, whose pristine dunes are flecked only with rich kids hammering along in sand buggies. They roll and meander as far the eye can see. But they are the only wrinkles: the race itself is far less contoured. A daily Playstation sprint unfolds, on roads which feature no bends for 60-kilometre stretches and are so wide that at certain points, if it were minded too, the peloton could probably stretch out horizontally and ride 136 abreast.

Thank goodness for Diego Maradona, then. He appeared, or at least a man who looked very like him, appeared at the finish line of stage two of the 2016 Dubai Tour which was placed right outside the colossally expensive Atlantis hotel, a luxury block built in an architectural style which pays five-star homage to a Bucharest housing development designed on the back of a napkin by one of Nicolae Ceaușescu's favourite nephews after a night on the țuică.

Elia Viviani won the stage, as I remember. Though that in itself was not a straightforward commentary to get right. 181 of the 183 kilometres of stage two were a formulaic procession along big wide roads bathed in warm sunshine. Then, with a couple of kilometres to run, and with the leadout trains in full flight, the race dived into a tunnel, and entirely out of view, leaving me and my co-commentator Magnus Bäckstedt to speculate about what might be happening in the underground bike race, until finally they charged out from the gaping mouth of the tunnel, turned right and Viviani won. I think I just about had time to shout his name before it was all over.

It was only as Magnus and I stood in the afternoon sunshine, admiring the complete lack of crowd at the podium as Elia Viviani popped up and down collecting a vast array of different awards and jerseys, that I noticed an unshaven man in a shell suit and dark glasses who kept photobombing Viviani's special memories. Just as I was wondering why Dubai's highly trained security operatives had not removed the interloper, a colleague from the Italian race organisers with whom I was working nudged me and said, 'He was the greatest, no? But of course I say that. I'm from Napoli.'

With sudden and renewed interest, Magnus and I gazed back at Diego Maradona, whose hand of God was by now pointing back at the hotel entrance, in which direction he was scuttling as fast as he could on those arthritic knees without being obviously disrespectful to the Dubai Tour. Whilst I cannot be certain of this, not having had the chance to interview him, I have a suspicion that the World Cup winner from 1986 had not spent the previous five hours glued to the television to chart the progress of the breakaway, noting which of the riders picked up maximum points at the hotspot sprints and when they might be caught. In fact, I think he'd just got out of bed, and was going back there now. Further enquiries among my Arab colleagues suggested that Maradona was a personal guest of Sheik Mohammed in Dubai, and, at this low point in his majestic and miscreant career, had been temporarily installed in the penthouse at the Atlantis free of charge. All that was asked of him in return was that he occasionally step out and perform a civic duty or two, which involved simply standing around for photos and looking like Diego Maradona. He managed to fulfil at least one of those functions from time to time; sometimes, on rare occasions, both.

So Maggie and I spent a week traversing the Emirate in a massive hired SUV with stickers on it. One evening, on a long transfer back from Hatta Dam on the other side of the peninsular, we actually ran out of petrol; quite a feat in a country which sucks 3 million barrels of oil out of the ground every day. Forgetting the sheer emptiness of the land, we were not remotely unsettled when the warning light came on, assuming that we'd be able to pull over and fill up long before it got critical.

Approaching the city of Dubai from the south, and almost an hour later, all conversation had long dried up. I gazed from the window, hallucinating petrol stations in the gathering gloom (night falls like an axe in the desert). And Magnus had gone into survival mode, piloting the car with all the skill he'd acquired from his years of working in the peloton. Like the sprinter that he had been, he spent fully 20 kilometres jumping wheels, figuring that the more we could draft trucks, the less energy we were burning. In a succession of manoeuvres which didn't feel especially legal from where I was sitting, the winner of stage 19 of the 1998 Tour de France flicked between lanes, accelerating with the briefest touch of the pedal to within a foot of the rear bumper of some enormous vehicle laden with rubble or goats, then almost freewheeling until another opportunity for an aerodynamic tow presented itself to his right and he flicked out again. I continued to stare out of the window, the knuckles on my right hand, wrapped round the door handle, grew ever paler. Then, with the finishing lights of a vast petrol station appearing on the horizon, and with 200 metres still to go, Maggie pulled out from behind his final leadout truck, touched the accelerator one last time and completely ran out of petrol. The Swedish man mountain stamped twice on a pedal rendered suddenly impotent. 'Yes,' he said, with a degree of Scandinavian understatement as we drifted silently on to the forecourt, victory secure. We sat in the car wordlessly for a moment or two while we savoured the sweetness of the win.

'Want anything from the shop?' I then asked and looked across at the 2004 winner of Paris Roubaix staring fixedly through the windscreen at the pump.

Not all the action at the desert races came from the drive to and from work, of course. I remember the sudden arrival of the lovably goofy Texan Brandon McNulty, who, as an unknown 19-year-old, nearly held off the world tour teams all the way to the steep finishing line at Hatta Dam. And when the wind blows, which it often does, the racing becomes instantly compelling, since there is no place to hide in the desert with its hundreds of kilometres of straight lines. It was in just such a moment that the Kazakh Andrei

Grivko, so infuriated with the way the German sprinter Marcel Kittel was behaving, rode up alongside him and threw a punch with such venom and accuracy that it split open the skin above Kittel's eye. To this day I cannot figure how you might be able to throw a punch from a bike travelling at 45 kph with enough force to split anyone's eye socket, let alone Marcel Kittel's, which was fashioned from Thuringian teak.

Standing with Matt Rendell and Pete Kennaugh at the top of Jebel Hafeet.

But the desert scenery, as barren as it is, can genuinely inspire awe, not least when we cross to the southern coast of the Arabian peninsula and enter the Hajar mountains for the annual set-piece (and very hard) summit finish on Jebel Hafeet, which either Adam Yates or Tadej Pogačar are contractually obliged to win. This range of jagged peaks rises as if from nowhere out of the sand and shoots skyward, bearing no vegetation, just honey-coloured rock glowing increasingly golden and then angry red as the sun sinks ever lower after the race is run. It can be a place of great beauty; in fact, it is. The TV pictures speak for themselves on the Jebel Hafeet stage.

In commentary, I was not encouraged to dwell for too long on the petrochemical might of the UAE. Nor was I to expect to see any shots of Dubai's most hubristic housing development, ambitiously called 'The World'. Built offshore, it comprises a series of man-made islands fashioned to resemble the land masses of Planet Earth and intended to be sold off, country by country, to billionaires and Gary Neville. Somewhere along the line, however, the islands never quite got completed and now The World sits there in a rising ocean, neglected, depopulated and slowly falling apart like an enormous, unwieldy metaphor.

Instead of passing any form of comment likely to encourage debate, I was instructed to focus on the wealth of cultural and leisure facilities in the Emirates. It is a popular race among the riders, and the limitless pockets of both Dubai and Abu Dhabi make sure it stays that way, flying in, paying for and accommodating a peloton which would not have looked out of place on the start list of a grand tour.

Mark Cavendish was perhaps the most loyal of all the attendees, often using the race to make his seasonal debut; a chance to get some tan line definition and also score a psychological point or two at the expense of some of his greatest rivals, since most of the best sprinters in the world would be present. So enamoured with the race was Cavendish that when interviewed ahead of a stage, his answers tended to dwell not on the race itself, but on the beauties of the corniche, the splendour of the country, and the warmness and hospitality of its people, as he waxed lyrical with uncharacteristic enthusiasm.

The Emirates want to be admired. They want you to come here, bring your money and then leave without it. The race is designed, however misguidedly, to nudge you along that course of action, as you gaze at the unbroken sunshine, mobile phone masts designed to look like palm fronds, and general unreal glamour of the whole setting. Since I was being paid directly by the race organisation, I was not really at liberty to express my own opinions, as I am on these pages. My unease with my role as mouthpiece of the tourist board began on one edition of the race when I was asked to attend a pre-race briefing with the man in charge of the Dubai Sports Council, which bankrolled the whole venture. Handed a lengthy, glossily produced brochure of the various landmarks which the helicopter would pick out during the hours of the live transmission, I was then schooled on what to say.

Hesitating slightly over some of the printed rubric, in particular the paragraph concerning the camel racing track, which informed me that the animals were no longer ridden by humans, but instead by 'tiny robot jockeys', I then turned to the page which announced the Dubai Labour Camp.

'Can I ask what this is?' I hesitatingly inquired.

'It's the Labour Camp,' came the straightforward answer. 'For the first time, we are routing the race through the Labour Camp to include our labourers and to thank them.' I had been to Dubai enough times to realise that there is an army of workers, often from South Asia, who are bussed in and out of the city from somewhere in the ragged, sandy outskirts of town every day to work on the innumerable construction sites; tired faces at dawn and dusk, pressed up against the windows of crowded buses, passing through but not in any way part of the city that they built.

'I see.' I wondered how to address this proposition in commentary later. 'May I suggest that you perhaps find another word for this compound? "Labour Camp" does not have a very positive association for an English-speaking audience.'

The boss looked at me for a second or two, a moment in which something not quite convivial hung suspended. Then he looked down and waved a hand airily at me, turned to the next page and muttered, 'Labour Camp.' I dropped the conversation but knew in that moment that I had some thinking to do about why I was there.

Things came to a head for me during the 2021 UAE Tour, by which time Dubai and Abu Dhabi, often rivals, had thrown in their lot together and would find a women's race the following year to match. We happened to be there, Pete Kennaugh and I, when Russia launched the beginning of its invasion of Ukraine and started to head immediately for the capital city Kyiv. We were thousands of miles away, of course, staying in a typically opulent hotel just up the coast from Dubai in Umm Al Quwain when the news broke, or at least I became aware of it, just after breakfast. Heading back to my room, I got into the lift with a Russian family. We all stood in silence as the lift ascended, revealing endless vistas of desert, sky and sea as it climbed. I got out, went to my room, changed and went out for a run to clear my head, which I singularly failed to do. On my return, I bumped into the EF Education Easypost *directeur sportif* Charly Wegelius, who I hadn't seen for a number of years, since before the pandemic. Dispensing with small talk, Charly spoke immediately about how he needed to get back home and make plans without delay to move house, to leave the country of his birth: Finland, he said with total certainty, would be next.

The last few days of the race passed slowly, but with one consistent feature. The sole Russian team at the race attacked every day to get in the day's breakaway, their riders already justifiably fearing that they would soon be disbanded and unemployed. Few other riders would go with them on these forays. On the penultimate day, three of their riders were among the four who stayed away all the way to the finish line. At around about the same time, the UAE was one of three countries which was abstaining from a UN resolution condemning Russia's aggression. I felt as if sport, caught up in geopolitics, and its core concern of money-making, had never felt so irrelevant. And besides, I was genuinely afraid I might not make it home before the worst imaginable outcome.

My relief came when the race finally ended and, with the most cursory Covid test I have ever been subjected to (the nurse barely even touched my upper lip with the swab), I was fit to fly home and put it on record that I would never return. That race and I were done.

So now, instead, I sit at home and gaze at the images from afar, wondering why cycling, like no other sport, balances this sense of colossal importance with an equal and opposite impression of total irrelevance.

Every year, no one is quite sure what to think. Which races matter? Which do not. I follow them all with growing interest watching the procession of winners celebrate either with a shrug of their shoulders or a full-blooded roar of delight. But by April this ambiguity will have started to dissolve, by May it all matters, and by July tears will be shed by the winners and the losers alike.

As for me, I just want to get started.

5

THE VICTORIAN DESK CLERK

There is a fat chunk of Tour de France history, in the middle of the 2010s, which I suspect will recede into the background as time marches on. It was during these uncelebrated years that I made the switch to commentating. I don't know really how they will be remembered, but I know this much: for a man with remarkably little sense of the history of the sport, Chris Froome chose an ornately gilded edition of the Tour to make his mark on the great race.

Maybe it was the final stage of the 2013 Tour de France Haussmann had in mind when he sketched the geometric architectural drama of the Paris he rebuilt. Maybe he had, on some deep metaphysical plane, foreseen the advent of Chris Froome, but I doubt this. It was the 100th Tour de France. The Champs-Élysées was lit up with the honeyed evening light that the high-minded architect had dreamt of when he sketched the avenue into existence and swept away all that lay in his path in order to satisfy his grand creative urge.

It was the first time in its history that the race had finished so late in the evening. And as a consequence of the late hour, deliberately envisaged by the image-makers and marketers of the Tour de France brand, the sun began to set behind the Arc de Triomphe's marble bulk with mathematical precision, just as the podium ceremony got underway. Ever since its inception 100 editions before, in 1903, the race had been on a century-long mission of self-aggrandisement. The Tour de France was celebrating itself in the customary manner, by ladling out great dollops of grandiosity.

It was a curiosity then, given the epic quality of the setting, that the rider about to step up on to the top step of the podium was perhaps the first in all those long years to have grown up thousands of miles away and without the faintest notion of the history that he had just become a part of. Chris Froome might as well have come from the moon. Certainly, he looked completely out of place on a bike; awkward, head-bobbing, legs whirling, elbows jutting out like a Victorian desk clerk working late hours to please his boss. He was different to any rider who had gone before. Even LeMond and Armstrong had grown up following the sport from afar. Froome hadn't.

I stood at the side of the small walkway between the marquee in which the riders were corralled, and the podium that the organisation had wheeled into the very centre of the self-styled 'most beautiful avenue in the world'. I was part of a select phalanx of media allowed this close to proceedings, while at the same time held back by a rope, as if we were gawping at the antique furniture in a stately home. In this case the valuable objects were the jersey winners and podium riders of the 2013 Tour de France.

From this vantage point I watched Chris Froome go about the casual-seeming business of winning the Tour de France. I had been watching him off and on for five years already. It was a curious thing. There was a direct line and unchanging connection between the 28-year-old in the yellow jersey, smiling his muted smile, nodding his assent, meekly posing for pictures and signing stacks of replica jerseys, and the character who I had first met in 2008, in a low-key, quiet hotel in Brittany: the unknown Kenyan on a South African team, racing under a British licence. Back then he struck me as no different, in the wrinkled polo shirt of Barloworld. He weighed his words; was neither ebullient nor overly reticent; was cautious, but not shy. He was hard to pin down. It was only later, heading away from that first encounter, when I had interviewed him merely out of professional curiosity (who was this 'Brit?'), that I found out he had lost his mother to cancer only a matter of weeks before his debut at the Tour de France. And it was later still that I realised he was effectively estranged from his father and that I had been talking, to all

42

intents and purposes, to an orphan about to tackle the greatest physical challenge imaginable.

But in the afterglow of his first Tour victory in 2013 I could see no change in him at all: nothing but the same hard-to-grasp combination of elusive characteristics, even though everything had changed around him and everything had changed for him; even though he had changed the race, or at least was about to.

* * *

The transformation of his fortunes had begun a little while before this coronation, of course. But not that much earlier. I had first made contact with Froome during that 2008 Tour; contact that was sporadically renewed throughout the three weeks of the race, every time his team were in the news. Unfortunately for him, they often were. Their main GC hope Mauricio Soler crashed on stage one. Moisés Dueñas tested positive for EPO, prompting the police to raid their team hotel. Three more riders crashed out (two of them into each other) and Froome's teammate John-Lee Augustyn almost disappeared entirely into a ravine descending the Col de la Bonette.

It was after that stage that I remember interviewing Froome outside the Barloworld team bus, while his teammate Robbie Hunter leered through a window from the inside of the bus, pulling a finger across his throat and pointing at me. I still don't really understand why the South African sprinter wanted to have me killed and, all these years later, despite the occasions when he's joined David and me in commentary, I keep forgetting to ask him. But the point I am trying to make is that 2008 was a deep dive into the Tour de France for the young Froome. Barloworld were, perhaps not unsurprisingly, not invited back to the race. But it didn't matter to Froome, because by then he had agreed to join Team Sky. And though neither he nor they knew it, a startling future was being charted.

A year and a bit on from Froome's first Tour de France, I found myself in Turin. This was in the line of football duty. Back then, in the spring of 2010, I was still some way off winding down my first sports career with ITV as a pitch-side reporter at football matches. But already my interest in football was starting to wane, as the grip that cycling exerted on me grew ever stronger, to the extent that the two aspects of my professional life were starting to overlap in unexpected ways.

On the morning of some Champions League match, I went on a long walk across Turin from one branch of Avis to another to pick up a hire car I had booked. It is a city I know well nowadays from covering bike racing. Indeed, in 2024, I went there on four occasions, simply because of racing. But back then it was my first visit and I got very lost. This was a pre-Google maps age and getting lost wasn't as easily avoided as it is now. What made this increasingly fraught traipse still more memorable was the fact that I was accompanied by Gareth Southgate, recently relieved of his duties by Middlesbrough FC and still three years from joining the FA en route to becoming one of England's most successful managers of all time. I don't know why he decided to come on what turned out to be a three-hour yomp. Perhaps he was bored. But for whatever reason, this long schlep around Turin has stuck in his memory and to this day, when our paths cross, however tangentially, he will remind me of its epic nature.

'What do you need a hire car for, Ned?' asked the man who missed the penalty at Wembley, niftily avoiding being wiped out by some particularly aggressive driving as we crossed yet another road. We were heading for the branch of Avis which actually had my reservation, rather than the branch which didn't, to which I had dragged the former Aston Villa skipper. 'Where are you off to?'

'Tuscany,' I said. 'A little place called Quarrata. There's a cyclist there I'm going to talk to.'

'Anyone I've heard of?'

'Who've you heard of?'

'Lance Armstrong,' Southgate replied. 'And… Cavendish…?'

'It's a bloke called Froome. He's riding for the new team, Team Sky.'

During his playing career, especially when he was at Middlesbrough, Southgate had often asked me about the Tour de France. The club's physio at the time, as well as one of their press officers, were wildly interested in the Tour de France, so when I turned up at the club he'd often had to sit patiently and listen while we all discussed the latest doping scandal. On that walk in Turin I was pleasantly surprised at Southgate's persistent curiosity. But then again, he'd already told me that after a lifetime of kicking a ball around it was simply refreshing to talk about something, *anything*, other than football.

'Is he any good?' he asked me.

'Not sure, really.' I answered as honestly as I could, as we finally reached the correct hire car branch. 'I doubt it. But he's quite interesting.'

The next day, after completely underestimating the distance between Turin and Tuscany, I arrived in the main square of Quarrata, the home of the British Cycling academy and where many of the pros still lived, including Cavendish, Thomas, Swift and Cummings. Rather than give me complicated instructions as to how to get to the house he was staying in, Froome had suggested I park in the square and he'd come to pick me up. He arrived bang on time, pulling up in a slightly battered, blue Volkswagen, which had cassettes and empty bidons falling all over the passenger seat.

Froome was staying in a little spartan apartment that belonged to Pete Kennaugh. Pete was off at a training camp and had let his team-mate use his place as a base to get in some long, lonely miles. I spoke to him at length as he sat at a low table on the tiled floor, recovering from what had surely been another monster ride. He ate no more than an apple while I was there and looked significantly thinner than how I remembered him. I made some notes at the time, which I used for an article I later published in the *Cycling Anthology*:

That day he told me that he wanted to become a GC rider. I was surprised by how confident he seemed. He wanted to compete for the biggest prize in the sport. And he thought that one day he'd be good enough. I wished him well and left him to it. He struck me as lonely and perhaps misguided.

That was wrong on two counts. He was neither lonely nor misguided.

The 2013 race started well for Froome and finished in triumph, of course. It was the moment that he emerged alone and victorious from the chaos of his relationship with the management of Team Sky, and his (at that point) still entirely broken relationship with Bradley Wiggins, the man who would still probably maintain he had the beating of in 2012, had he been protected and allowed to ride for himself.

* * *

The newly knighted Sir Bradley Wiggins was unhappily back at home, no longer the road rider he had been in 2012, un-selected for the Tour de France and starting out on his extended run of entertaining public appearances in which he developed the habit of airing increasingly profane public grievances; some devoted to Froome, others to Dave Brailsford, still more aimed towards Shane Sutton and then whatever he had left directed at whichever moving targets he could find.

I, like many others, did not escape his sharp tongue, though many years later he would seek me out to apologise for some of the choicer insults that had come my way. I had always felt with Brad that relating to him was like standing on shifting sands. One minute he was railing against dopers in the peloton, as when his Cofidis team was summarily thrown off the 2007 Tour de France (David Millar actually lent him a Saunier Duval tracksuit so that he could travel incognito to the airport, such was the vitriol). But then, years later, embroiled in the tortuous web of the endlessly complex 'Jiffy bag' affair, he would be full of praise for Lance Armstrong and take to task anyone who raised an eyebrow (me), calling us 'arsewipes', which I acknowledge is an amusing insult.

'I'm not going to change my story just to appease people like Ned Boulting. I know far more about the sport than he does and I'll challenge him on it,' Wiggins would later tell his audience during his 2018 theatre tour. I wasn't for a second going to contest this claim, as Brad Wiggins had been thoroughly steeped in Tour history since childhood and had literally won the race. I, on the other hand, was a converted football reporter who had written a book called *How I Won The Yellow Jumper*, which specifically set out to document how little I knew. On the charge Brad levelled at me, I was bang to rights.

The last few times we have seen one another, when Wiggins was still working at the Tour de France and the Giro on the back of a motorbike, we have been on good speaking terms. I don't know about him and Froome, but it wouldn't surprise me if they will have somehow contrived to end up friends, now that they have nothing more at stake. The kinship of having won the Tour must mean something very profound after all. Perhaps they had more in common than they might have thought or have been obvious to the outsider. Bike racers are a very particular breed, after all, and very separate from the remainder of the human population.

* * *

Of course, 2013 was just the beginning of the Froome domination at the Tour and it ushered in an era which changed the sport forever, but whose absolute predictability and partially tarnished legacy mean that it will perhaps not be remembered fondly outside a rather small constituency of support. This is not an observation born of any personal grudge. It's just the way it is. This is what you will hear, without fail, if you spend time talking with cycling lovers and Tour aficionados across a range of countries which have traditionally produced the winning riders in the biggest race of them all. The cold reality is that the Froome years are not widely celebrated. Some of this is fair, some of it is not.

Though he crashed in the 2014 Tour de France with the number 1 on his back and climbed off in the pouring rain the following day on the cobbled stage, he was back again in 2015, repeating his successes of 2013 in even more emphatic manner. But still, for most cycling fans the comeback story left them cold. It was perhaps hard on Froome, who was much more of an instinctive racer than the machinery of Team Sky's tactics allowed us to understand. In evidence to support this claim, I will never forget David Millar's delight in commentary next to me in the ITV booth when he realised that, far from going for king of the mountains' points over the top of the Peyresourde in 2016, Froome had bluffed. He attacked on the descent and won the stage by 13 seconds. He also told me once that he liked to suggest he's suffering badly on climbs, only to come roaring back. He even confessed that there is a secret sign he has which only his wife Michelle knows, which he signals to her when the camera is alongside him to reassure her that he is not suffering, that it is just a bluff. I never did manage to find out what it was.

In the early Froome years I was still deployed on the ground, there at the start of stages to ask the yellow jersey what he thought was likely to happen and there at the end of them, too, to talk to him about what did just happen. It followed a certain script, albeit a slightly porous one. Chris Froome, increasingly able to front up, and confidently bat away, the perfectly justified questions about Team Sky's ethics and anti-doping credentials, nevertheless had certain intriguing difficulties when it came to discussing the actual race and his principal rivals. In the early years of his winning streak, he would sometimes refer to his most dangerous adversary, Nairo Quintana, as 'the little Colombian'. At first I took this to be a power play of sorts, deliberately affecting not to know his name and therefore not deigning to acknowledge him as a person. But, increasingly, I became aware that he just wasn't good with names. I noticed a hesitancy every time he talked about certain rivals.

'Hey, Ned,' he interrupted me just before we were about to conduct one of our many interviews about his increasing stranglehold on one edition of the races he won (I forget which one; they tend to merge into one in my memory). 'Just remind me... which one is Bardet and which one is Pinot?'

It was not the first time he had asked me this. 'Pinot's the guy in blue. Bardet's the really skinny one.'

'Ah, OK.' He looked up and his lips moved imperceptibly as if repeating the names to himself and committing them to memory. 'Thanks.'

The truth was that, unlike the duels which went before, even in the Armstrong years when the American despatched with ruthlessness the challenges of Marco Pantani, most notably Jan Ullrich, but also Tyler Hamilton and Ivan Basso, Team Sky's primacy under the bobbing, nodding influence of their unlikely-seeming destroyer-in-chief was never remotely threatened, at least not at the Tour de France. In the immediate years before their assumption of control, there were interesting duels between Contador and Schleck. And in the subsequent generation we have witnessed Jonas Vingegaard and Tadej Pogačar write chapters of Tour history that will stand comparison in the fullness of time with the great rivalries of the post-war years. But Froome rode his races alone and according to the Froome method. This was enough to win him four Tours, mostly by a handsome margin.

* * *

It was after his second victory in 2015 that he signed a contract with ITV to tell his *Life Stories*. This documentary formed part of a strand which included a string of big-name sports stars, some still active, others retired. I had contributed to the making of the films on Didier Drogba and Kelly Holmes, among others. Then I flew to Johannesburg to spend a few days with a film crew in the company of the two-time Tour de France winner.

Our short stay in the Froome household was interesting, in a low-key, very Chris Froome kind of way. A considerate host, he invited us into his home and into his life, even stopping off at a drive-through Nando's to buy food for everyone and guzzle a stunning amount of it himself. But his house was bare. It was well appointed, as you'd imagine; he had, after all, earned a substantial seven-figure salary for the previous three years, so it was pretty luxurious, but it was devoid of personal touches. No paintings on the walls. No photos on display. No books, save for a Chris Carmichael coaching manual which he jokingly removed with faux embarrassment from the shelves when we walked through his exercise room (Carmichael having been Armstrong's cycling coach).

Froome's prodigious strength of character was deeply sunk into his personality, to the point of inaccessibility to others. It's not that he was distant, not at all. He was alert, engaged and sometimes curious about others. But there was something about his even-temperedness that made him hard to get a handle on. Even today, when I hear tales (true ones, as it happens) of him storming on to the Astana team bus and pinning Vincenzo Nibali against the wall, I can't square such aggression with the Froome I thought I knew. A childhood which had turned him in on himself no doubt contributed in part to this guardedness. But for the larger measure, I suspect it was just the way that he was wired. His middle name, after all, is Clive. Again, I think of a desk clerk.

During those days of filming in South Africa, it drove his wife Michelle mad that, whenever the cameras were on, he'd drop back into standard 'TV interview' mode. This version of Froome involved a lot of polite nodding and deferential comments, the very essence of non-committal. For anyone who watched the Froome years on TV, this blandness will be deeply familiar. From the back of the car, as we were filming a chat with him on the way to a training ride, she'd suddenly interject, 'There you go again, Froomey! You're doing your TV voice!' From her back seat she reached over and clipped him playfully, I think, around the ear. 'We talked about this!'

Before arriving in South Africa, Michelle and I had discussed a way of de-Frooming Froome, in the nicest possible way. Because, even if it was understated, there was a lot of depth, warmth and complexity to the tall, skinny champion we had both known in our different ways for a long time. I would still struggle, when challenged, to articulate that any more exactly, but I would also vouch for its existence, as would many riders who have raced with and against him, shared teams and shared rooms.

Peter Sagan had, and as far as I know probably still has, an enduring affection for Chris Froome. I would often witness Sagan in those years, perennially in green while Froome was so often in yellow, pass behind or alongside him in the media zones as the race leader was patiently fulfilling his obligations to the press. The Slovakian could never resist addressing him in his unmistakable squeaky tones, half teasingly, but with affection. 'Hey, Froomey!' I swear one time he goosed him. But that may have been my imagination.

How to show this likeability, this subtle richness of character on camera? How to break down the Froome façade? It wasn't straight-forward, but Michelle and I hatched a plan for the Froomes to host a *braai* (a South African BBQ) one evening during our filming sched-ule. She invited his best friends from school; the same little gang who had travelled to Paris in 2013 to be there when their unassuming schoolfriend won the Tour de France for the first time. They had then set off on a riotous few days with their newly minted champion pal as he went from one paid appearance to the next at post-Tour criterium races, cashing out around €50,000 for each evening's work.

They were a nice enough crowd, who had all made their way in the world in solid if unexciting trades. They drank a fair bit and, as the sun started to dip down to the horizon, the roof terrace of Froome's house filled with laughter, Chris's included, as they recounted stories from his past, both recent and more distant. As the star of the piece receded into the background, so his personality was revealed; a strong sense of groundedness, a quietly articulated but unshakeable ambition and a great sense of purpose, all wrapped up into the well-rounded, but decidedly different, set of characteristics which made up Chris Froome: one of those kids who you might point at in your old school photo and struggle to remember anything about beyond his name. Someone who fell through the gaps.

It was an interesting experience to accompany him on a visit back to his school in Johannesburg. Though Froome had spent the major-ity of his childhood living in financially straightened times with his mum in Kenya, his estranged father later paid for his education at an exclusive boarding school called St John's College, a grey-stoned, rather austere late Victorian institution which has produced a welter of influential South African politicians, actors, businessmen and sports stars, only one of whom went on to win the Tour de France four times. In a sports-mad country, St John's website lists a total of 12 sports which can be practised by students, not one of which is cycling.

Pulling up in Froome's sponsored Land Rover outside his old school, to be greeted by the head teacher as we disgorged from the vehicle with the cameras rolling, it quickly became apparent that Froome's celebrity in 2015 was wildly at odds with the curious lack of an impression he made while at the school some 15 years earlier. Very capable, if not hugely academic; liked, but not one of the cool crowd; a cyclist, and not a rugby player or cricketer. We strolled from room to room, and along stone and wood-panelled corridors, with Froome making pleasant if stilted conversation for the benefit of the cameras with a head teacher who was trying to make the most of a few biographical scraps which he'd pulled together by way of remembering Chris Froome.

'And here's where you would have probably done your homework.'

'Yes, I think so.'

'We've extended it now, built a new common room.'

'Yes, it looks a bit different.'

This was probably not a verbatim exchange from the film, but serves as a useful approximation of the kind of slightly awkward absence of any spark. At one point, I wanted to pep the conversation up. I suggested that Froome relate the story which he tells in his ghost-written autobiography about how he used to sneak out of school with his bike to go for long rides before dawn. He would bribe fellow boarders to sign the breakfast register for him by smuggling porn magazines back into the school, which he had purchased in Johannesburg, rolled up and somehow concealed in the hollow tubes of his handlebars.

'And what was it you used to bring back into the school, Chris?' I ventured, in an attempt to get him to embark on one of the more interesting tales from his book. But Froome blushed slightly and looked at me with that panicked expression people adopt when they simply want you to shut up. The head teacher too pretended that he hadn't heard. It was only later, when I asked him why he had shut me down, that I discovered a bit more.

'The thing is, Ned,' he told me, with the hint of a playful smile, 'it wasn't porn mags I was smuggling back into the school.'

'Oh,' I said. 'I see,' I added, not really seeing.

'Yeah,' he continued, a little cryptically. I nodded along, like I understood. It wasn't the first nor last time in my association with Chris Froome that he had surprised me. Then we changed the subject and moved on.

* * *

During the course of making the film, I cajoled him into re-telling the story of his famous 2012 'attack' on Bradley Wiggins on the Alpine slopes of La Toussuire. It was a story he had recounted fairly often; how he'd 'not intended' to put Wiggins into difficulty, but rather he'd been trying to make back the time lost on stage one to Seraing, when he'd punctured and been left without support. But also, of how he'd resented being called back on the radio when he had attacked on that final climb and how dysfunctional the atmosphere was back at the team hotel: the two riders not talking to one another; Wiggins threatening to leave the race; the staff uncommunicative. After all, it is one of the most compelling tales of rivalry within a team with two potential Tour de France winners in its ranks. Not since Hinault and LeMond had such a situation played out so wildly.

Froome's assertion that he expected shared leadership is one thing. But what lies beneath it all is pride. The pride related to his belief that he could have won the race. It's impossible to know whether he would have, of course. But it's very hard to claim with any certainty that he wouldn't.

* * *

Of course, money also plays a central role in every rider's career planning. In that, Froome is not unusual, even if in his case it's been a larger amount over a longer period of time than almost any other rider. Perhaps the roots of this overweening concern might have lain in his childhood, and how his family's fortunes took a nosedive when his father upped and left their Kenyan home, taking his money with him. Maybe Froome was always on a mission to shore up his financial future as best he could, for which he is in no way to blame. But it has shaped his career, for better and perhaps for worse.

In a sporting sense, Chris Froome's narrative ended with his three, amazing, successive grand tour victories: the 2017 Tour and Vuelta, followed up in the spring of 2018 with his final race win of any description, which was simultaneously his greatest: the Giro d'Italia. That his participation at the Giro was in doubt right up until the eve of the race getting underway in Israel is easy to forget. Caught up in a scandal that related to abnormal salbutamol levels, he was only cleared in the days running up to the Grande Partenza. Convinced of his own propriety, even if his many doubters would never fall into line, Froome doggedly kept at it, until he was able to deliver that final death blow to his opponents, when he attacked over the Colle delle Finestre to wrench the race lead from Tom Dumoulin and win the Giro. It was his greatest single ride and his last ever win. Even though he is still racing, I say that with confidence.

Though he very nearly managed to win the 2018 Tour, denied instead by his stronger teammate Geraint Thomas, the following year would change everything. His crash at the 2019 Dauphiné nearly cost him his life, could have cost him his leg and almost certainly did cost him his career as a winner. The injuries from which he had to return presented an insurmountable hurdle, even for a man with as much mental tenacity as Froome. He could only do so much.

Though that was the end of the winning, it was not the end of the racing. Froome was released by Ineos, but signed an eye-watering deal with Israel Start-Up Nation and raced on for another five years. As I write these words, and perhaps as you read them, he is *still* active in the peloton. As business acumen goes, a five-year, multimillion-pound salary for a rider already well into his thirties and coming back from a potentially life-threatening injury is smart negotiating.

I remember flying to Gran Canaria in late January 2020 to spend time with him at a solo training camp as he had started to resume his work. He could scarcely walk straight. His body was buckled; broken by a crash whose violence was borne out by the scarring he showed me. Barely a single part of his skeleton had escaped trauma. That afternoon, just before the pandemic added further disruption to his rehabilitation, I said goodbye to him as we exited a lift.

As ever, he was curious about what I was up to, genuinely so. He always was, when we met, which by now we had done over many years; years in which his greatness came and went, to a great extent overlooked by a large section of the sporting public. Our paths have crossed a few times since, but he has grown distant, less responsive to my messages. 'Been blue-ticked by Froomey' is something of a catch-phrase that we throw around in the car when we are on the road for the Tour de France. These days he has withdrawn still further and that blue tick has become a grey tick.

He remains something of an enigma. Under-appreciated, unconventional, undemonstrative, Chris Froome represented a period in the history of the Tour whose passing few outside the handful of Sky/Ineos superfans will mourn. Admiration for his dominance is certainly warranted, but it's something of an intellectual exercise, rather than one built on the emotion that this sport is designed to engender. His career was as peppered with iconic moments as those of any other champion. Think of that day he was left without a bike on Mont Ventoux and started running. But somehow I have a feeling his legacy will not endure in anything like the same manner as the other multiple Tour winners.

This all seems a shame. Because as I stood by the side of that first podium in 2013, microphone in hand, I thought I was watching the beginning of a Tour myth, a fairy-tale career. In the end, it was a story that somehow stuck in the telling and never really reached a satisfactory conclusion. And saying goodbye in a mirrored lift in Gran Canaria certainly wasn't it. That was the last time we met.

6

FIELDWORKERS OR LIVESTOCK

The year of Froome's bikeless ascent of Mont Ventoux and his auda-cious attack on the descent from the Peyresourde – 2016 – was the first year that David and I were sent to commentate at the Tour. It was, for the most part, pretty excruciating. But the awfulness did not endure forever. I can't remember when it was, but there was one day at work a year or so later that went rather well, which came as a pleas-ant surprise.

For a couple of years we had been feeling our way into the job, trying to establish voices that were both authentic enough to our true natures and therefore not phoney, but also clear and polished enough to try to make sense of a race well known for the opacity that in turn lends the Tour its grace. That balance had taken time for us to achieve, as we unconsciously turned from people just talking about bike racing into people commentating instead. There is a difference; a hard one to define, but one that matters. Either way, I remember leaving the commentary booth that day after a few hours of ever-increasing concentration, peaking out with the drama of a bunch sprint and feeling like something had clicked into place. To my amazement, because it's not always the case that our thoughts and feelings are aligned, David felt the same.

'We sounded like commentators, there, Ned.'

I paused, the door to the commentary booth half open as I made for the exit. I looked back at him and smiled. 'Yeah,' I said. 'Maybe we did a bit.'

* * *

The Booth. Let's give it a capital letter; that's the least it deserves. The Booth is where it all happens, where I live for at least three months of my professional life every year. The first definition in the dictionary for this commonplace, but still surprisingly specific, word that so permeates my working life reads: 'A temporary shelter for fieldworkers or livestock'. That's us.

The work of a commentator at a televised road race differs from the experience of most other practitioners of this laughable, perhaps unnecessary and certainly niche occupation. Those who provide the words alongside the action at say, football, rugby, cricket, athletics, tennis or any other of the much, much bigger and more lucrative sports benefit in one peculiarly meaningful way: they can actually see what they are talking about. In road racing, we can't.

Perched at some propitious location mid-way up the raked seating, offering up an overview of the whole sporting arena, most commentators need only look down to see the exact, yet indefinable moment that, for example, Usain Bolt accelerates away on the track beneath them to devastate his rivals once again. From the press box at Lords, they can actually feel the might of that Ben Stokes shot, see the onrushing cricket ball getting bigger. It sails through the very same summery air that they are breathing. Thud. It might land just outside their booth.

Not so with road racing. When the action gets underway, we're normally 200 kilometres away. Where the riders are smiling for the cameras as they roll off the start line in the warm sunshine of Pau, we might as well be in a different time zone, experiencing an icy shower at the top of the Tourmalet and turning up the heating in the back of a truck, listening with awe to the force of a Pyrenean storm thundering on the metal roof above our heads. The notion that in a few short hours they will pass right by us seems fanciful. And when indeed they do, we are so absorbed in the minute but intense drama of the final moments, that we scarcely know where we are, so focussed are we on the screen in front of us. In our booth.

* * *

There is an important distinction to make, of course, between road and track cycling. I mean, there are other differences, of course, like gears, brakes and mountains. But here I want only to focus on one, since it relates to my lived experience, which unfortunately is what this book is loosely based on. If you *really* want to learn about track, then I suggest you get hold of one of the many, many autobiographies by the stars of the golden British generation of medallists, from Hoy to Pendleton to the Kennys. You will gain no such insight here.

But that isn't to say I haven't dabbled in a bit of turning left, turning left, turning left and turning left again. I used to 'race' with the veterans at Herne Hill velodrome for a few years, learning that there are thousands of ways of losing and perhaps two or three ways of winning, at most. I put the word 'race' in inverted commas, because to a pro, what I considered racing was almost as far removed from their experience as chess is from boxing. I remember once talking to a highly decorated ex-Paralympic swimmer who was working as a pundit when I presented the IPC World Swimming Championships. He told me that what most people do in the pool is just 'fast floating', not 'swimming'. So, that's the difference between our racing and what the pros do.

At the track, I was known throughout the cohort of white middle-aged men (and one woman, Catherine, who was by far the best of us) for my heroic and completely doomed propensity for attacking impossibly far out. I was, in many ways, the Pierre Rolland of our little group, without any of his talent, charisma, race craft, courage, ability or achievements. I did this until age and wisdom caught up with me, arriving in a dead heat for last place in the great repêchage of life.

But I have also, on a few occasions, been booked to commentate on the arcane and confusing world of the velodrome, presumably because the gene pool of cycling commentators is so small that eventually even people like me squeeze through the gaps and end up trackside at some major event, poised with a microphone in hand.

I did a stint at the Birmingham Commonwealth Games (the track was in London, not in Birmingham), at which I sat at the mic and watched in absolute horror as GB rider Matt Walls was catapulted over the railings and into a row of spectators at 60 kph, only to walk out of hospital later that day with a few scratches. That was a new way of hurting yourself as a bike rider – and endangering spectators in the process – that I had not seen before. But the fact that it happened immediately in front of me, and not hundreds of kilometres away, gave it a shocking immediacy.

I most recently commentated at the newly revived 'six-day' track event which went by the name of 'London 3 Day', because cycling does this kind of silliness and doesn't seem to care what anyone thinks, which is one of the reasons why I love it. Other than that isolated experience, for which I still haven't yet been properly paid, because the organisation didn't settle its bills (another endearingly familiar feature of working in bike racing), my most prolonged spell of commentary was at the not-quite-as-short-lived Six Day London event, which was genuinely six days long rather than three and to which Covid put a premature end.

The staple of six-day racing is the Madison event. To those of us (99% of Planet Earth) who have never really bothered trying to understand the Madison, there is categorically no more confusing sporting spectacle imaginable than the Madison bicycle race, which involves pairs of riders repeatedly flinging each other into the action by reaching out an arm and slinging their teammate at warp speed down the track. It is a furious, two-wheeled particle accelerator, an entire reception class on a playground roundabout without a teacher, the contents of an overloaded washing machine drum with five sets of trainers and 20 pairs of brightly coloured pants, the visual articulation of a walk home after nine pints of Stella Artois, all set to the title track from the final album of a free form West German jazz quintet from 1972 entitled *What Happens When Things Collide Or Don't Collide*.

To make matters still harder on my Madison commentary debut, the usual data screens which might be used at official events like the World Championships and the Olympics, and which offer indispensable information in the chaos of such a complex race, were deemed an unaffordable luxury by the organisers of Six Day London. I could only guess that that line of the budget had gone instead to the excellent DJ Martin 'Two-Smoove', whose barrage of beats throughout hours of racing was met for the most part with a wall of apathy by the predominantly middle-aged audience in the arena.

No information screens, coupled with a scoring system that made Duckworth-Lewis seem like the two times table, was bound to create a frisson of unpredictability for any spectator, especially when all this incipient chaos was supposed to be being made comprehensible by a man (me) who had never watched a Madison before. My co-commentator for this job was the wonderful Rob Hayles, with whom I had often worked, but on road racing, naturally. Rob, apart from being one the finest men I've ever met and a much-underrated bike racer to boot, was also a former World Champion in this exact discipline: the Madison. On the first evening, for the first race, we were to be joined by the rider with whom he had won that title in 2005, a bloke called Mark Cavendish.

Of all the many years that I have been broadcasting, I have never known stress like this. Flanked on either side by Rob and Mark, adrift in a sea of scribbled results and loose calculations-on-the-fly, I tried to keep track of where exactly on the track the front of the race was in a bunch which had atomised, leaving isolated riders all over the place. When the furore of the race was all over, 45 long minutes later, Mark took his headphones off, gently placed the mic down and turned to me.

'I don't know how you did that,' he said. Which was not at all the comment I was expecting.

'I have no idea either,' I replied, wiping my forehead and collecting up the scattering of paper and pens that lay like a crime scene at anarchic angles across the desk. Some of the writing had been blurred by salty drops. Sweat had been forcibly exiting every pore of my body. It had pooled in unusual places, like behind my ears and in the crook of my elbows. It had collected in my socks. 'Thanks Mark.' I walked numbly away, my feet squelching as I went.

Incidentally, the stress of that encounter with Cavendish was only matched a couple of years later when he was actually racing at Six Day London. This time, rather than commentating at the race, I was the paid fool in the track centre, who had to announce the events to the live audience at the track and interview the riders. One of my main functions was to oversee the draw for the derny race, in which riders slipstream behind a pacing motorbike. Now, it is worth saying that six-day racing has a long and ' honourable' tradition of being fixed; or if not fixed, then certainly manipulated, which is a posh way of saying fixed. There is nothing wrong with this, though. It is deeply part of the history and culture of six-day racing, most of the crowd are in on it, and in no sense is it anything other than just part of the fun. Nonetheless, there is a clandestine ritual to it which has to be cloak and dagger. That's half the fun, too.

The object of the fixing is to produce a close contest, deliver drama and allow for a thunderous finale with the right outcome. It's entertainment delivered with skill. In London, this probably meant Mark Cavendish winning, but only by the thinnest of margins, in the very last race and on the sixth day. Of all the events on the programme, the derny is the most fixed, because it is also the most fixable. The derny pilots often decide in advance what will happen in the race. The riders have little say in the outcome. On this occasion, Mark had got wind of which derny was going to win.

Sometime before the draw to determine the pairings of riders and derny pilots, conducted live on stage in front of thousands in the velodrome, Mark came up to me and my co-host backstage.

'Hey guys,' he said, with that characteristic disarming smile he uses to great effect when he wants something very specific to happen. 'Can you put the 8-ball in a freezer?'

'Sorry, what?' I said. He explained that it would mean he would know to pick out the cold one when he reached inside the bag.

I explained, hesitantly, because I couldn't quite believe I was having this conversation, that we didn't have a freezer in the middle of the velodrome. He cast a mildly distrustful eye around the stage in the middle of the track, as if he might spot the freezer that we claimed we had no knowledge of. Undeterred, Mark then asked my co-host to lightly grip the 8-ball at the bottom of the bag, so that when he reached in, he would be able to figure out which one it was. The plan was hatched. All that remained was the wait for its execution, in which we rehearsed our part in the deception and then went silent, like a bomber crew at dawn before take-off in some East Anglian airfield in 1942.

A short time later, I introduced him on to the stage for his part in the draw. In front of thousands of wildly cheering fans, the Manxman strode up to us, thrust his hand into the velvet bag, never once lowering his eyes from us, and...

...drew out the 8-ball. I exhaled. The minutest smile played over his unshaven features as he turned, waved to the crowd again and exited the stage with a wink in our mostly dumbfounded direction.

* * *

But so much for my limited experience of working at the track. I need to return to the different rigours of the road. But let's stick with Mark Cavendish. In the early years of my experience at the coal face of the Tour de France, and long before David Millar and I took over the reins of commentating for ITV, Phil Liggett and his late friend and co-commentator Paul Sherwen were in charge of finding the words to match the moment. When, in 2008, Cavendish announced his arrival with an uninterrupted string of successes that endured for half a decade and then more, they were on hand with the superlatives. Of course, Phil and Paul had been doing it for far, far longer than that. In Phil's case, his association with the Tour went back to the very early 1970s.

What I found astonishing was how ridiculous Phil and Paul's usual workplace was at the finish line. I would occasionally visit them in those early years, either to film an interview with one or both of them or to simply say hello. Every time I marvelled at how cramped it was, how unfit for the purpose of broadcasting the Tour de France to a global audience of millions. On the ground floor of a double decker truck specially adapted for TV commentary, they occupied a tiny booth, hemmed in by partition walls on either side like a railway compartment for small children. On the other side of those walls were all the other broadcasters from the many nations at the Tour, mostly shouting. Basque voices would be raised to the left, Flemish from the right. Somewhere above them an Italian was getting worked up about Mario Cipollini.

But, and I used to think that this was a significant 'but', they had a window that faced on to the road. On a normal flat stage, if either of them had been minded to, they might have been able to crane their necks around and gaze perhaps 300 metres up from the finish line. Realistically, they could only see the final 50 metres of the race clearly. Travelling at the speed of an average bunch sprint, the winning rider (let's call him Mark Cavendish) would perhaps be visible outside their window for around three seconds: three seconds in a commentary that might have lasted for four or five hours. Perhaps long enough for Phil to shout 'It's Cavendish!' and to see him with his naked eye, but not much more than that. The rest of the race he would have been, well, watching telly just like the rest of us.

There are times, very few and far between, when something happens *right* outside the commentary window. The day of Phil's famous commentary from 1987 was an example of just this, when Stephen Roche appeared out of the mist on his decisive Tour de France ride. 'It's Roche! It's Stephen Roche!' yelled Phil in disbelief at what he was witnessing, quite ignorant of the notion that 25 years later his words would be immortalised and then monetised via a range of T-shirts and other merch by the growing armada of Liggett fan franchises. As soon as he crossed the line, Roche collapsed and slumped against the wall of the commentary tribune, right in front of Phil's position. Sensing an opportunity, our hero commentator prised open his window and dangled a microphone into the face of the asphyxiating Irishman as he was having oxygen administered to him.

And even I have had the odd occasion where an actual window on to the actual world has come in handy. Away from the Tour de France, when I am working with Matt Stephens in Italy at the Giro d'Italia, we are also consigned to a double-decker commentary truck similar to the one which is still used at the Tour, albeit much less heavily populated (the Giro being a tiny media concern when set against the behemoth that is the Tour).

At the end of a series of torrentially wet stages at the 2023 Giro, the race finished in Salerno, to the south of Naples. That was the day where Mark Cavendish performed the greatest feat of acrobatics, when involuntarily dismounting a bicycle, that I have ever seen from him, which is setting a high bar for a rider I have witnessed catapulting himself on to Yorkshire high streets and French barriers, Italian roads, road signs and even into the back of a car in the desert of the UAE. In Salerno, in the closing couple of hundred metres, he opened up his sprint on a wet white line on the road, lost traction with his rear wheel and with it temporary control of his bike, veered right, taking another rider into the barrier, swung left, definitively lost control and, as his front wheel went off at an angle all of its own, Cavendish was launched vertically, but upside down as if he were a gymnast on a pommel horse, and then slammed into the tarmac like a ragdoll from a height. He slid the rest of the way, still holding on to his bike, to finish fourth on the stage, but not riding it. I am not exaggerating when I say that I thought he might be dead.

He slid as far as our commentary truck. From our window, we watched on as medics rushed over to him. Gradually we watched him come to consciousness, sit up and, after a few minutes, walk away from the scene of the crash as if nothing had happened. Later that afternoon Matt exchanged messages with him. The gist of his reply was, 'I'm fine.' To this day, I don't know how he walked away from that crash.

* * *

Seven years earlier, and on the day that Cavendish claimed his only yellow jersey, David and I took over our new duties at the Tour. In the planning for the 2016 race, we took the collective if ground-breaking decision to withdraw from Phil and Paul's overheated commentary Truck of Babel (for the use of which, incidentally, the race organisation charges a small fortune to the broadcasters) and establish an adapted commentary area in the back of ITV's own rather battered, multipurpose lorry.

Already stretched beyond the capacity of any other truck in the TV compound, our knackered lorry carried all the equipment which needed to be unpacked every day: the set, the cameras, the lights, the cables, as well as a multitude of road bikes and Bromptons which the crew used on a daily basis. Once unpacked it became a sound-mixing studio, a vision gallery, a kind of makeshift edit suite called an EVS, a satellite uplink operation, plus an office for Gary, Matt and Chris to work in, or in the case of Chris fall asleep in while Gary hand-ground his bespoke coffee beans and began to boil them, and Matt ran a pencil across the pages of *l'Équipe* occasionally and sagely muttering 'Aha!' to himself.

It was like a Tour de France universe in truck form, a veritable wonder, to the extent that it was pointed at and giggled about by all the other, much better equipped TV networks at the race who arrived with all manner of specially adapted vehicles that variously unfolded and raised themselves up on hydraulic stilts to perform a bewildering variety of functions for which they were specifically and expensively designed. The longer this went on, the more stubbornly we clung to our old truck, which had become a point of pride, a ragged statement of difference. It was all a bit Brexity, on reflection.

Now the truck suddenly also needed to facilitate a commentary booth on top of all the other requirements. Ingeniously, David and I were placed in the back of the truck, from which all the technical equipment had been emptied for use during the day. This empty space then converted into a desk with three large monitors and two swivel chairs, which had a habit of collapsing and/or rolling downhill on the many occasions when the truck had been parked on a slope at the top of a mountain. A network of bungee straps was then deployed to prevent David and me from drifting to the side wall of the truck.

One of our more precious stipulations, which was hotly contested over a protracted period of months leading up to the 2016 Tour, was our rather twee desire for a window to be cut into the side of the truck, so that we could at least let some French daylight fall into our space and be reminded that we were actually on top of Alpe d'Huez/ in a car park in Mâcon/by the amphitheatre in Nîmes. We won the debate, though it was hotly contested at the time by the late Steve Doherty, the programme's long-standing director.

'You won't ever see anything out of it,' was his deflating contention. 'Just a row of toilets or whatever.'

Annoyingly Steve was mostly right. It was mostly toilets that greeted us every morning through the window. We had a tiny little red-checked curtain hung in front of it to make our space a little cozier. It wasn't until the middle week of the 2018 Tour that we got payback, when we opened the silly little curtain on race day to reveal an astonishing vista of sun-kissed snowy peaks on the day that Geraint Thomas rode into the yellow jersey at La Rosière. The same day, incidentally, on which a disconsolate Mark Cavendish finished the race alone, outside the time limit and effectively (so we thought at the time) signing off on his Tour de France career. I will remember for a long time sitting at my desk in the booth making notes for the stage to come, having ridden to work up the climb with David and another former *maillot jaune* Rolf Sørensen, with a shaft of warm alpine sun falling on my notes from our little window to the world.

* * *

To say that this area was a bit haphazard in its design would be an understatement. Even in the last years of its functioning life before an upgrade came to the rescue in 2024, our commentary area retained a sort of awful charm. Charming if you were a kind of dewy-eyed luddite nostalgist for things which should have long since been put out of their misery. Awful, if you looked at it with any degree of sanguine analysis. And evidentially awful when, parked up at the finish line of stage four of the 2023 Tour, which happened to be the paddock of Nogaro motor circuit, a large section of sharp-edged aluminium framework suddenly swung like a guillotine from the ceiling above my desk as I was preparing my notes and struck the back of my hand, leading me to stagger out of the side of the truck, half blinded with pain, bleeding profusely, swearing extravagantly. I was really very brave and could tell by the barely suppressed smiles of my colleagues that they thought so, too.

One of them fetched water and urged me to sit down on the damp tarmac against a set of shelving on casters. I did what I was told. No sooner had I leant back than the shelving tipped out its contents of cables and plugs on to the top of my head, adding comedy to injury. That was the morning when I discovered, for the first time in my 21 years at the race, that the Tour de France *zone technique* has an actual doctor in attendance. As he stitched the back of my hand, we discussed Tadej Pogačar's chances of unseating Jonas Vingegaard in a form of French that contained unusual accents at sudden moments when he pulled the thread tight. 'Je CROis que le DANois van gagNER!'

Perhaps the final nail in the coffin of a facility which had served its purpose for eight solid years was the sight of our array of illustrious commentary guests having to make do with our third chair, which would be placed at an angle to the desk, too far from it to be of any use. What notes they might have brought with them would have to be held on their lap as they either couldn't reach the desk or could find no room among all our bits and pieces. But the real insult was the nature of the chair itself. First purchased by the production company in around 2006, it was the kind of white plastic chair that you might normally expect to find abandoned in the corner of a pub garden, upturned and pooling water on its mouldering underside into which cigarettes had been stubbed out. It must have cost about £10 when new and had steadily dropped in value ever since.

It was the sight of, in sequence, Cadel Evans, Australia's first ever winner of the Tour de France, followed by Marcel Kittel, one of the race's greatest ever sprinters, and then the reigning World Time Trial Champion (and incidentally seven months pregnant) Ellen van Dijk, all forced to sit in the chair of shame, that finally did for it. They all put up with the indignity with tremendous humility, but it was wrong in every sense that I towered over Kittel at the desk, the bulky German having collapsed the chair's overly flexible legs, meaning that his knees shot up in the air and his handsome chin was now at desk height. A similar fate befell Ellen, at which point it was no longer up for debate that something had to be done. Her suffering had to be taken seriously, even if Marcel's was still somehow funny and Cadel didn't seem to notice the indignity (which was true of almost everything which Cadel could have complained about, to be honest).

Strangely, we were so used to the somewhat haphazard nature of our surroundings by this point that we never stopped to question the appropriateness or otherwise of the collapsing pub garden chair. Indeed, the evolution of our Tour de France coverage followed a stop-start trajectory, rather than a steady curve. We tended to settle into an unchanging pattern of dysfunction for a decade at a time until someone suddenly questioned it. Only then did we realise that it was mad. But then there are many things at the Tour de France which are. Take the publicity caravan, for example. Total insanity.

One such minor revelation came about in 2023, the same year as the collapsing Kittel-chair and the near hand amputation. We suddenly realised that we were the only production company on site not to bring a coffee maker for the production crew to the race. This prompted David and me to go halves each on a Nespresso maker from a branch of Carrefour near the finish line of some forgettable second week stage, which we jealously guarded in our commentary booth and only *very* reluctantly shared with any of our colleagues, Pete Kennaugh included. The only problem we found was that we could only run the machine during commercial breaks, as it made a thunderous clattering noise, lasting minutes when

David was making a coffee as he used upwards of three pods for each cup. Fortunately ITV4 had an unlimited supply of extremely long commercial breaks for donkey sanctuaries, so there was never any great rush.

* * *

The closest the booth ever came to a terminal technical melt-down, however, came on stage 15 of the 2019 Tour, when Simon Yates was off the front on a descent into Bagnères-de-Bigorre, having attacked in a group with two other riders, but then 10 kilometres from the finish line all our monitors suddenly went blank. Power to most of our truck had failed. The lights went dim on our commentary units. We looked at one another blankly. Then, seconds later, the truck burst into action. Back-up microphones appeared in our hands, hastily thrust there by Mike, our technical supervisor, who made an urgent gesture which implied 'Keep talking!' But about what? While the race was in full flight, we could see nothing.

For complicated reasons too hard for me to grasp, the audience at home in Derby, Islington and Cheltenham were entirely unaffected, save for the slightly odd pause in the commentary. Steve had rushed through in the meantime and whispered in my ear, 'Keep going, I'm on the phone to London. They've got pictures and can tell us what's happening.'

What followed was a form of TV insanity, with a Houdini-like ending. One of our London producers, sitting in a studio in Ealing where the highlights shows get edited, could still see the live feed. He relayed the bare facts by phone into an old Nokia pressed to Steve's ear. Steve then waited until David picked up a sentence, before relaying to me in an urgent whisper what he'd just been told from someone in London watching the telly without commentary.

'The three are still together, 7 kilometres to go.'

'So then, the three are still together,' I'd confidently repeat to the TV audience, all of whom could see what I couldn't. 'Around about 7 kilometres to go.'

David then picked up, with his eyes closed, to analyse a race that was playing out entirely in his imagination. He was uncannily accurate, it seemed. I have often wondered since if he is some kind of spiritual totem for the bike race or just a bit odd. We carried on in this vein until close to the final kilometre, when Mike appeared at the back of the truck holding a heavy monitor on his head and crouching down in front of me, David and Steve, so that it appeared at roughly the correct height. He had legged it to the Norwegians, plugged into their kit and run a cable across to our truck, just in time for us to see Simon Yates take the win and for me to call it over the line without guessing. Then Gary appeared at our side, pressed up against us and sharing the same microphone. The entire ITV presentation team now occupied a space not much bigger than a telephone box.

'Over to you, Gary,' I said, delighted to absolve myself of any further responsibility. And then I literally handed him my microphone and tried to crawl under the cable to exit the over-crowded corner of the truck we all found ourselves stuck in. 'Thanks Ned,' Gary began in unruffled fashion, as I somehow clambered free of all the carnage and almost ran from the scene. I looked back and the last thing I remember seeing is poor Mike, with the telly still on his head, crouched on the floor, as a replay of Simon Yates punching the air played out above him like a Tour de France-themed moving crown, while Gary and David summed up the stage – over shots they would only be able to watch as long as Mike's trembling thighs held out.

The most chastening realisation came later. Apparently, no viewers had noticed what was going on behind the scenes during those long minutes when I had been literally commentating blind. It seems no one could discern the difference in quality between me with my full array of senses and me with my eyes shut. What could that mean?

7

AN AGE OF WONDERS

A Tour de France I remember with almost nothing but joy is 2019. It exists in my memory as an untroubled, golden expanse of time. Maybe it's because of what happened next to the world and how it's now changed into something at once familiar and unfamiliar. Perhaps the act of looking back means sometimes that we brood with too much affection on the way things were. But in this case I make an exception.

It could be that some of 2019's importance can be attributed to the fact that it coincided with a very significant birthday. I turned 50 that summer and was not immune to the accompanying emotional punch to the soul and metaphysical stock-taking that goes hand in hand with completing half a century spent meandering around on this planet.

But then again, it might all be simpler than that. It's possible that 2019 burns so brightly in my imagination because of a human bicyclist called Julian Alaphilippe. I think that's right. I think he had a lot to do with it. And when I read my commentary notes back, I can confirm that impression. His name is scribbled all over them, on every page, often in capital letters. Even before Alaphilippe strode on to the stage with his particular dash of bravura, like a laminate-flooring-sponsored Robin Hood, this particular race already felt special.

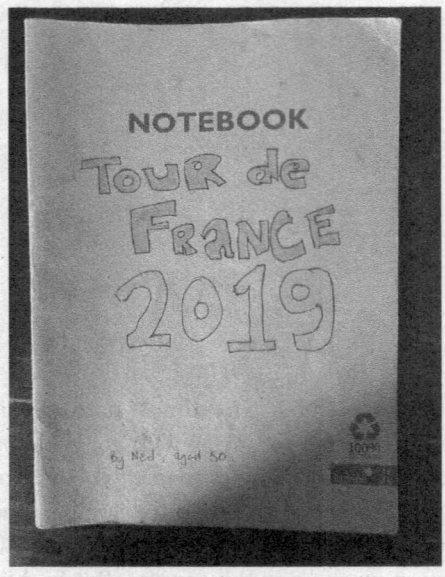

My commentary notebook from the 2019 Tour de France.

The race got underway in Brussels. And it did so for as profound a reason as any I can recall for a *Grand Départ*: Christian Prudhomme had chosen to bring the Tour to the Belgian capital to mark the fact that 50 years had passed since Eddy Merckx first won the Tour, in 1969. It was Merckx's first attempt at winning the race he would go on to dominate as the 1960s gave way to the 1970s. He took the jersey on stage six and held it all the way to Paris, winning on 20 July 1969 with a margin big enough for him to have sat down to a bowl of *moules-frites* and a Trappist beer before watching the next man come in. The Belgian had been nearly 18 minutes ahead of Roger Pingeon.

On that very day, somewhere back in Hampshire, as family legend has it, I was lifted gently from my cot and brought through to the living room to watch the telly. It was my ninth day on the planet, bawling infant nonsense into the world, unaware that the unformed vowels and embryonic consonants gurgling from my mouth would eventually form into words like 'Egan Bernal', 'intermediate sprint' or 'general classification'. I am led to understand that I was placed in front of a rented television set with a fuzzy bluish screen and told to watch. Not the Tour de France, however. That wasn't on. Instead friends and family had gathered around to watch Neil Armstrong cautiously descending a ladder backwards like a middle-aged man whose sudden zeal for home maintenance had seen him shinning up the side of a house to clean the gutters and now wasn't sure how to return to the surface. At pretty much exactly the same time, the 1969 Tour de France had come to an end in Paris, not that we knew anything about that in Hampshire.

The whole 'giant step for mankind' was having a knock-on effect on the post-race protocol at the Tour de France. All the lunar excitement meant that Eddy Merckx had to wait patiently in the Belgian TV studios for the moon thing to be over when the presenter could finally return to the subject of the Tour de France he had just won. It took an event as important as a man landing on the moon to keep Eddy waiting. But personally, I love the fact that the two events coincided one July afternoon in the final year of the Swinging Sixties and that I was on the planet at the time. Just.

* * *

I cannot re-invent my story. I came to cycling late and so can lay no claim to having been aware of Merckx's greatness and aura until long, long after he had stopped winning every race he entered. Introduced to his personality and career by retrospective immersion, though, it didn't take long before I could *feel* the weight of his legend. In a curious way, the fact that I had to educate myself post hoc lends my discovery an even greater poignancy: I missed Merckx when he was still racing and regret that.

That said, from the very first time I was sent to cover the Tour in 2003, I had grown accustomed to noting his imposing physical presence around the margins of the sport, occasionally moving into centre stage and at other times going about his business with a curious anonymity. Eddy was, back then, the only cyclist I had heard of, apart from Lance Armstrong, and even then only because a friend of mine back at home had ridden a Merckx bike. None of us had a clue, though, who that difficult-to-spell foreign-looking name referred to, except for some vague memories of hearing it spoken aloud every now and again on *Sports Report* on the radio.

I was fortunate enough to have shared a stage with Eddy Merckx at the first of London's very successful Rouleur Live events, which seek to give a platform to the great riders of the sport. Often when I am interviewing legends of any sport, I am not aware in the moment of the true stature of the character I am talking to. Sometimes that understanding only emerges later. Not so with Eddy. Separated by no more than a slight language barrier (his English can be hesitant) and 15 centimetres of space between our knees, I was completely attuned to the fact that here was a man whose place in the history of the sport is forever uniquely safeguarded (or so I thought – Pogačar was not yet a thing). He was honest in his answers, full of subtle swagger and, to the delight of the audience who were equally stunned to be sharing the room with him, pretty adroit with his jokes. He was funny, which is something I hadn't been prepared for.

A year or so later I hosted Eddy on stage at a similar event in Birmingham. I remember less about that, since it was completely overshadowed by the fact that we had gone to lunch together with a handful of others at an Italian restaurant around the corner from the venue. I had sat next to him as he emptied a couple of glasses of Barolo and generally held court. We spoke almost not a word about cycling. He wanted instead to tell me about his grandson Luca Masso, who was about to represent Argentina in field hockey at the forth-coming Rio Olympics, his daughter Sabrina having emigrated and married an Argentinian tennis player. His pride was self-evident and yet no different from the warming joy that any grandparent would display, watching the following generations forge a path in life. Then he lost me on the tactics of hockey, which he was just beginning to take an interest in, to the extent that I think he thought he under-stood everything about it and would probably have won everything in it. Once a Merckx, always a Merckx, I guess.

As I ate with him, I was reminded of a story told to me by my friend and colleague Matt Rendell, who had been at a similar trade fair in the autumn of 2013, after Chris Froome's first victory at the Tour. For convoluted reasons lost to me now, Matt had found himself in the extraordinary position of having to babysit both Eddy Merckx and Chris Froome as they killed a few hours backstage between media commitments.

'Shall we go for lunch?' Matt had offered, more for something to do with them than actual hunger. Both agreed and so this strange trio of diners sat down at a restaurant in Monaco. Quickly it became apparent to Matt that Froome and Merckx were meeting one another for the first time and that, as a result, neither man being exactly garrulous, the responsibility for keeping the conversation ticking along was down to Matt.

This wasn't a straightforward task, as Eddy appeared to be in rather a taciturn mood. So, he was relieved when Chris Froome, the most recent winner of the Tour de France turned to the former five-time winner of the Tour with a question.

'Eddy,' he ventured, articulating the great Belgian's iconic first name with his slight Southern African accent. 'You won the Tour, right?'

Merckx, Matt later related with delight, raised an eyebrow, put down his soup spoon and simply nodded, after a significant pause.

'How many times?'

There followed another almighty pause, while the greatest rider in the history of the sport tried to decide whether to answer this skinny lad sitting opposite him or maybe plant a giant Belgian fist through his face.

'More than once?'

Merckx eventually nodded, though the detail of how many 'more than once' his actual 'more than once' was remained hanging in the air, unspoken. Apparently, Chris Froome had been impressed by the encounter. The record books show that Froome subsequently set off in valiant, if ultimately just unsuccessful, pursuit of Eddy Merckx's record at the Tour de France, pulling up one Tour de France short when he had to concede defeat at the hands of his teammate Geraint Thomas in 2018.

So that was the context of 2019. Froome was recovering from his devastating injury, Egan Bernal was now leading the newly named Team Ineos and everything had changed. Everything except Eddy. There he was, the Cannibal, smiling with what looked like genuine delight at the huge crowds of well-wishers. They had packed out the streets of Brussels for a glimpse of the man who was the standard bearer for a patched together country emerging into the late 20th century in search of a unifying identity. Without wishing to overstate the case, Merckx played his part in Belgium's own sense of nationhood.

All this is by way of saying that the start of the 2019 Tour de France had an emotional context that few *Grand Départs* can boast, not least because Merckx was there in person to soak it all in and lap up the rightful adulation that came his way. The sight of him emerging into the brilliant sunlight of Brussels' Grande Place, its mercantile glory and intricate facades facing on to a cobbled square stuffed to the gills with tens of thousands of well-wishers, was one of the most moving I have seen in my many years of reporting and commentating at the Tour.

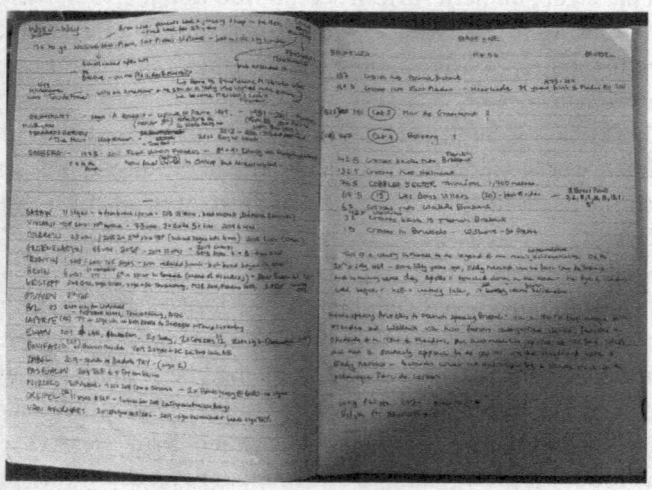

Notes from stage one of the 2019 Tour.

Looking back through my commentary notes on stage one, I discover a lot scribbles about the passage of the race through the Brussels suburb of Woluwe-Saint-Pierre, in which Merckx had grown up. And, in anticipation of the rather formal moment that would define the start of this and every edition of the race, when Gary Imlach hands over to me and David for the first time, I had scripted a little introduction:

> This is a country in thrall to the legend of one man's unparalleled achievements. On 20 July 1969, some 50 years ago, Eddy Merckx won his first Tour de France and on the very same day Apollo 11 touched down on the surface of the moon. The Age of Wonders had begun. Half a century later, it all seems barely believable.

* * *

The 2019 Tour got underway with a stage finish in the park which surrounds the royal Palace of Laeken. It had started in the southern part of Brussels, near Anderlecht, then passed in a long loop through both Flanders and Brabant before approaching the finish line again via the south of the city. Gary, David, Matt and I were all in our usual places at the finish line, making our final preparations for the start of the race. We were also waiting for the arrival of a new member of the ITV team.

This was the year that Pete Kennaugh had announced his sudden retirement from the sport, mid-Bora-Hansgrohe contract. He'd had enough and urgently needed to escape the rigours of this most demanding of sports for the sake of his own mental wellbeing. It was both a brave and an honest move. It was also, very fortunately for us, a decision that meant the 30-year-old Olympic Champion and once great hope of the British cycling establishment would be free to join us as part of the ITV Tour de France panel.

He was called in as a direct replacement for Chris Boardman, who had announced his first retirement after a 15-year, post-racing career stint at the Tour. This stepping back came in 2019 before he subsequently announced in 2020 that he would be un-retiring. Chris stayed unretired for the next three years, before retiring again in 2023. As I write there is no immediate prospect of a change of heart, although history would suggest that, like Halley's comet, it is imminent and mathematically predictable. Maybe that's why ITV dropped the rights; to end the speculation.

Pete arrived in Brussels in a flurry of excitement. Free from the shackles that had constrained the way he had lived his life since his teens, he was a simmering samovar of enthusiasm, eager to experience everything and anything that didn't involve suffering on a bicycle. His last race had come in early March that year at the UAE Tour. His last ever professional training ride had been enormously long, at a wet and cold training camp in the spring. That had been the point beyond which he no longer wanted to go. He had simply stepped off and into a bright new sparkly world full of different experiences and new friends he probably didn't know he was about to make.

Though of course we'd been acquainted with Pete for a long time in our different ways, neither David nor I would have claimed to have known him particularly well before our Baptism of Kennaugh in 2019. I remember meeting him briefly when he was barely out of his teens, during the initial recruitment of Team Sky. He graduated to their pro ranks straight from his bedroom in the academy in Quarrata, whose walls were festooned with literally hundreds of photos of riders torn from the pages of cycling magazines. He was the one, so we were often briefed, on whom hopes of a 'British winner of the Tour de France within five years' were founded and not so much Bradley Wiggins. Things, of course, turned out differently.

I next encountered him in the apartment on the Côte d'Azur which he shared with his partner Lauren and her son. That was in 2013, by which time he'd already raced the Tour, in winning support of Chris Froome. He struck me as extremely serious minded and teeming with unfulfilled ambition. That impression was only reinforced when he was overlooked for Tour de France selection in 2014. Later that summer he raced and won the Tour of Austria. Back home in Nice, and obviously still annoyed about his non-selection, he rang into our live coverage and had his say on air. Being unwaveringly forthright is also a Kennaugh trait.

But not half as much as being Pete Kennaugh is a Kennaugh trait. What that particular trick involves is hard to put into words, but since this is a book, I'm going to have to try. While I think about it, here's a picture of Pete from 2019.

Pete, newly retired and enjoying life.

He is a determinedly restless soul, but not remotely in the pejorative sense in which that description is sometimes deployed about people. I simply mean to say that Pete is always on the lookout for how to make things better, whether that be his hair, his commentary (which he takes very seriously), his fitness, his devotion to his family, his considerable network of friendships, his appreciation of the world and his place in it. If the given day is a Thursday, Pete will be thinking hard about how to make it the best Thursday.

He is curious about things to the point of taking delight in almost any given object or experience, however grandiose (to coin a Millarism) or mundane. In 2019, he started carrying around a little notebook that we bought for him, into which he wrote words that he claimed not to be familiar with, like 'topography'. *Pete's Words* became a source of constant addition and discussion. His some-times-faux naivety was often counter-balanced by an actual naivety, as he began to explore the endless world beyond racing bikes that had always been there, but which had remained inaccessible to him for so long. His journey of discovery was a constantly joyful renewal for us all, as we saw the job through his wonderfully fresh pair of eyes. And it was, for him, revelatory; even if it got off to a bumpy start on the very first morning of his new broadcasting career.

At our production meeting on the eve of the race, our producer asked Pete to be on site an hour before our on-air time. It was to be the job of Garry Beckett (a former *soigneur* on a number of pro cycling teams) to drive him there. It was also Garry's first day ever working for a TV production at the Tour. And that was how the problem arose.

Given that there were probably a combined 250 Tours de France that had been notched up by the members of the small but very experienced ITV crew, the notion that things needed explaining to outsiders never crossed our minds. In other words, no one ever actually made it clear to Garry and Pete that the broadcast operation sets up every day at the finish line and not at the start. Naturally, since both men were fresh out of the racing scene, they jumped in the car and set off, as you would do, to the start of the Tour de France, not thinking for a second that they should head to the finish. After all, what sense would that make?

Somehow realising their mistake, Garry seemingly executed a handbrake turn and drove hell for leather to the finish line. Pete arrived with minutes to spare on his broadcast debut, managing to appear miraculously unflustered alongside Gary and able to articulate some impressively cogent thoughts about the coming race. If the start and the finish that day had been 200 kilometres apart, rather than 25, then they'd have stood no chance. But the trauma of his just-in-time arrival, coupled with the fact that no one had bothered to tell him otherwise, still sits deep with Pete and will surface in unexpected ways from time to time, even now. We all found it simply very funny, which was hardly supportive of us, but quite irresistible.

That unexpected start to the day set the tone for a race that crackled with unpredictability from the moment I shouted, with unnatural confidence, 'Wout van Aert!' as Jumbo Visma's Mike Teunissen won the first stage and took the yellow jersey. Van Aert had been leading out Dylan Groenewegen, who had crashed, an incident the cameras had caught only fleetingly and that I had not noticed. I mean, it *should* have been Van Aert. But it wasn't, which is I suppose what matters more.

I spent the rest of the afternoon trying to work out how many of my international colleagues had been similarly deceived and was horrified to discover that a good many of them *hadn't* got it wrong, which did nothing to assuage my filthy mood. Correctly calling home the first *maillot jaune* of the Tour seemed like an important thing to get right, because that's exactly what it was. I had failed to live up to the moment.

* * *

My spirits were slightly lifted, however, by our warm, summery commute back to our Ibis hotel in the lively, tatty streets near the Gare du Midi. It was time for another new experience for Pete: the Brompton. David's CHPT3 brand has a collaboration with the folding bike company going back to 2016, when we made our commentary debuts. That year, and every year since, Brompton have kindly equipped David and me with bikes for the Tour de France. They have become completely interwoven into the fabric of our experience, saving us from traffic jams at the end of mountain stages, providing us with a means to get around the finish zone without breaking into a sweat, allowing us to embark on reconnaissance rides up the final climb or along the closing 20 kilometres of the stage and, more importantly, have enormous fun, as Pete was about to discover.

'It looks well weird,' he stated, staring at the bike that had been placed in front of him in its partially folded state. Its rear wheel had been flipped in, so that it sat next to the bottom bracket and pedals. 'How does it work?'

Remember, this was a young man who had both enormous and yet very limited experience of the world as many of the rest of us know it. And with that he tried to jump on it and ride off, without unfolding it.

'Pete!' David took on that exasperated tone of older cousin for the first time that year. It would be a syllable we would hear repeated in 2019 and in the years to come many times over as David delighted in gently correcting Pete's thrilling combination of enthusiasm and innocence. 'Let me unfold it first.'

But once we got going, we raced downhill towards the canal that bisects the capital. It took Pete a few pedal strokes to adjust to the weirdness of sitting on a saddle that perches at the top of a metre-high seat post and to the fact that his wheels were smaller than the circles his feet were now wildly describing. And then the sheer joy of it started.

Piqued by the sight of an ex-rider 12 years his senior accelerating away from him, Pete stepped up to the challenge, putting me into immediate difficulty on the technical section near the Church of Our Lady of Laeken and setting off into an improvised aero-tuck in an attempt to peg David Millar back. The two former racers arrived many minutes ahead of me at the Ibis, where I found them giggling like schoolchildren, Pete fairly red in the face and David pretending manfully that he wasn't screaming inside, teaching Pete patiently and ineffectually how to fold a Brompton. It was stage 16 before he was even remotely competent in this important life skill. This was the 2019 Tour called to life one warm Brussels evening and toasted later with beers in an atmosphere of anticipation for all that was to come. Little did we know just how good that would prove to be.

Through Belgium we ran over the next two days, before crossing the border to the motherland, where, once back in France, the race started to develop an edge of excitement that few had anticipated and which kept it crackling right up until its torrential conclusion three weeks later in the high Alps.

On the morning of stage three I rode the final kilometres of a beautifully designed course that cut through the Chardonnay vine-yards of Épernay, the little town famous across time and space for its association with some of the oldest, most prestigious and most stuffy of Champagne houses. Labouring my small-wheeled way up some of the steeper climbs, I remember thinking, 'Either I am even more unfit than I thought or these are actually quite hard.' In the end, both these things proved to be the case; I was painfully slow to the point of torment, and also they were rather nasty hills.

In pain on the road to Épernay.

It was on these very climbs a few hours later, on a humid afternoon, that Julian Alaphilippe started to… happen. I can't think of another word for what came next. Alaphilippe *happened* that year.

* * *

It's true to say that he'd already shown amazing form in the 2018 edition of the race, but the 2019 Tour was where his brief but brilliant tenure as the Most Exciting Rider in the World started, before coming to an abrupt halt just three years later with a crash at Liège-Bastogne-Liège. His broken bones in 2022 not only rounded off a series of astonishingly glamorous crashes, but also seemed to spell quite a sudden end to a dazzling career which had yielded in no time at all a Monument, multiple grand tour stage wins, two World Championships and a long, fascinating spell in the *maillot jaune* in 2019.

His short-lived, explosive dominance began as he crushed the opposition in Épernay, shooting his arms out crucifix-like to take a landmark victory by 26 seconds to a distant chase group containing what were considered to be the strongest riders in the world. Gosh, we all thought, or words to that effect. This was not very French.

Alaphilippe had already staked a claim for being one of David's and my favourite riders for a couple of reasons. In 2016 he'd been part of a remarkable two-man breakaway with his Quick-Step teammate Tony Martin. They stayed away longer than anyone thought possible, the little Frenchman sitting for 99% of the time in the wheel of the German, simply praying that his teammate stop and that they could just drop back to the bunch. It was genuinely funny, but also full of crazy from both riders and it resulted in them both being awarded the Prix de la Combativité at the end of the stage.

Two years later, Alaphilippe started to win stages at the Tour, albeit from breakaways. He was so strong that on both occasions, one in the Alps and the other in the Pyrenees, he found himself dropping his breakaway companions too far out. His indecision over whether to wait for them, or push on solo, was marvellously comical to observe; you could see the thought process play out in every twitchy pedal stroke. It was during that edition of the race that David and I coined the expression 'waiting really fast' for the way Alaphilippe rode to victory. I think that was perfectly matched to the man and the moment he found himself in. In 2018, he ended up winning the king of the mountains jersey outright and you might be forgiven for thinking that was probably going to be a career high-tide mark. That was also the year that I first started to refer to him as Begbie, Robert Carlyle's psychopath from *Trainspotting*, again because it was a perfect match, both physically and psychologically.

Now suddenly, in 2019, he was winning from the GC group, taking not the polka dot but the yellow leader's jersey. Gathering together my notes and leaving behind the commentary position that afternoon in Épernay, I found myself riding back into the heart of the old town from the elevated finish line set slightly apart from the Champagne houses. A hot sun was starting to drop with syrupy languor over the gnarled outlines of the vines, in full leaf and starting to bear fruit. It was a scene that seemed created to fit a remarkable moment in the race, promising ripeness, joy and fulfilment. But what neither we, nor Alaphilippe, nor France knew was what would happen next.

For 14 days Begbie held the jersey in two stints, interrupted only for a couple of days when Giulio Ciccone kept it (extremely) warm on his behalf; 14 days which eclipsed even the Voeckler legends of 2004 and 2011. Those two years had been underscored by a sense that no one really believed that Voeckler would actually go on to win the bike race; not least Bernard Hinault, the last French Tour winner, who almost burst out laughing when I put it to him that Voeckler might be the next. The Voeckler years were a wonderful consolation prize, but no more than that really.

This one, however, threatened to become something very different altogether: credible. It slowly started to dawn on us that France might actually win the Tour de France in 2019, if not with Julian Alaphilippe, then perhaps with Thibaut Pinot: a two-pronged assault. Pinot's challenge was probably more real, in fact. But we will never know, which is a huge sadness to anyone who has followed Pinot's career. His real challenge was undone by a knee injury that forced him tearfully and publicly to concede defeat and abandon a Tour he might indeed have won. And what might that have meant to France if either man had done it? I cannot imagine. Never before nor since have I witnessed such an awakening of belief across the land.

But all that came after two weeks of self-discovery for Alaphilippe, whose crowning glory came one glorious sunny July day in Pau, one of the eternal touchstone locations of the Tour de France. It was the individual time trial; a day on which the Frenchman, most decidedly not a TT specialist (far too emotional a rider for all that 'pacing' stuff), was expected to relinquish the race lead in favour, probably, of

Geraint Thomas, looking to win the race again after his 2018 victory. But that's not what happened.

Instead, Alaphilippe won the stage and increased the strength of his grip on the lead. The sight of him tearing up the final steep ramp that led to the finish straight, roared on by the kind of French crowd I had never seen before, was not one that I will ever forget. The fans screaming at him from behind the barriers believed that anything was now possible; that Julian Alaphilippe could actually win the Tour de France. What a paradigm shift for France! What a sight to witness. It was unrestrained, unexpected, exuberantly nerve-touching in the best way that racing can be when it is laced with meaning, as this was. It was by some margin one of the finest moments I can recall in two decades of watching the Tour.

But it couldn't last. By the time the race reached its rainswept deluge of a climax in the Alps, which produced the Pinot tears and swept Egan Bernal into the yellow jersey, Alaphilippe, holding on for as long as he could, felt his fingers prised loose. His grip on the lead failed at the last, but he rode on determinedly to finish fifth, a small detail that does him great credit, because it would have come at a terrible physical and mental cost; gut-wrenching effort merely to finish just off the podium after holding the nation, and the broader cycling world, in a charmed state of growing incredulity for two solid weeks.

* * *

Less publicly but almost as agonisingly, there was a race within the race that David Millar had been quietly designing. Anticipating 11 July (my 50th birthday), which happened to be the day the race finished up the now iconic Planche des Belles Filles in the Vosges mountains, he had been setting off on secret little trips of his own to branches of the famous French retailer Decathlon.

David's love for this shop knows no bounds. For those who haven't yet fallen under its spell, it is a giant warehouse of cut-price sporting apparel and equipment; the kind of place you might go into simply for a pair of socks and leave with a canoe, some roller blades and an ice pick. But my co-commentator was highly targeted in his purchases; scouring the athletics aisles for the most egregious kit he could find, spending hundreds of Euros personalising the matching singlets and shorts with our names and respective ages, David was ensuring that we would look the part for the sporting challenge he had decreed would happen on the morning of my 50th birthday: The Plank Attack.

David, Pete and I prepare to run up a mountain.

The idea was breathtakingly simple, almost beautiful in its purity of purpose: we should run to work up the famous 6-kilometre climb to the very top of the mountain. It should be a handicap race in which we would be accorded a minute's head start on Pete (the scratch runner) for every year of our lives. That meant I had eight minutes to defend against David and a mighty 20 against Pete.

That morning, before descending to the perfect breakfast of fresh bread and homemade jams laid out by the hosts of the immaculate Maison d'Hôtes du Parc, in which we always stay when we are in the vicinity, I opened a birthday card from my oldest child, which I had been carrying in my suitcase all the way from London, and burst into tears. I did not realise, as I wept profusely on the hotel balcony into the chill morning air in the shadow of Corbusier's famous Notre-Dame du Haut chapel, that this was not in fact destined to be the only emotional trauma of the day.

That would come when I had completed the distance, physiologically destroyed from the moment I was told to start; a revolt of the body and mind that merely grew in ferocity all the way up the final tortuous 250 metres of gravel road to the finish line, hounded by David Millar who had caught me in the final kilometre and then pretended that he couldn't beat me, so as not to ruin my birthday.

The cognitive dissonance he demonstrated by not realising he'd done that already was of great psychological interest to me. Or at least it would have been had I not been on the point of complete biomechanical collapse, my lungs heaving as I bent double over the barricades. Minutes later Pete came roaring up the finish line, having damn nearly caught us both. What it is, I thought, not to be 50.

Slowly my body regained some of its usual functions: the heart began to relax; lungs eventually remembered how to breathe without signalling imminent risk of suffocation; all the soft organs which had shrivelled up inside my abdomen for the duration of the effort, like shaved hedgehogs in danger, began to unfurl and resume their jobs, the pancreas being the last to kick back in. My eyesight returned.

I looked back down the hill to the distant village of Plancher-les-Mines, trudged off to do battle with the portable shower block and its terrifyingly unreliable appliances and thence to the commentary, where I would later witness Giulio Ciccone relieving Begbie of his yellow jersey for a couple of days. This was indeed a beautiful race. Despite everything.

Merckx and the moon landings were a golden echo from the past. Another Age of Wonders had just begun, for better and for worse. The next year Pogačar would make his debut at the Tour, in the middle of a pandemic.

8

HOPPING MAD IN KENT

It's curious. I remember the end of that day's broadcast like it was yesterday. I can't say the same about all of the other 483 days (508 if you count rest days) I have spent working on the Tour de France. In fact, thinking back, there are probably more than 300 days which I have completely forgotten and which will most likely never return. Not so 20 October 2020.

Reluctantly, in order to place that day in some sort of context that makes sense, I have to return to that first year of Covid restrictions, which impacted us all in so many ghastly ways. The last World Tour race on the calendar had been Paris–Nice, which came to a premature conclusion in early March. With hindsight, and even with nearsight at the time, it was preposterous that the organisation even considered ramming the race through against the growing tide of panic that the incoming tsunami of Covid had already induced in us all. But that's cycling. There's always an edge of desperation to its functioning, like a spinning top starting to lose speed and beginning to wobble, although it somehow never falls over, defying all laws of physics and logic. A bit like riding a bike itself.

There were only 137 starters at Paris–Nice that March after several teams had the good sense to withdraw before things even got underway in the wild and windy conditions in the inappropriately named little town of Plaisir. It was the day when the German Max Schachmann (a commentator's dream to identify due to a physiological quirk that means his head nods like a Churchill car insurance dog) won from a small late breakaway. Schachmann went on to claim overall victory a week later, as the race pulled up a day shorter than originally planned. At some point, when there were still 112 riders left in it, France introduced a new law, a stepping stone towards full lockdown, which prohibited public gatherings of more than 100, prompting us to note in commentary that there'd have to be a breakaway of more than 12 or the peloton might be arrested. Gallows humour. Only 61 riders completed the race; most had already slipped on face masks, jumped in cars and driven hell for leather to get home to be with loved ones before the world shut down around them.

David Millar, Gary Imlach and I had gathered for the Last Race Before Everything Changed not in Plaisir, but in Ealing. For the week-long stage races Paris–Nice and the Critérium du Dauphiné, ITV had grown accustomed to sending our reporter Daniel Friebe out to France with a camera crew, but retaining the rest of the staff back in London, in a kind of scaled-down operation that resembled the Tour de France production in the same way that Blackpool Tower has the same vibe as the Eiffel Tower. David and I commentate for highlights only. This normally means that we sit there simply watching the race without commentating for at least an hour while not much is happening, baffled at how strangely disembodied the experience is of watching cycling without either listening to or doing commentary. Then we burst into life. For around 45 minutes. That's the entirety of my working day and shortly afterwards I ride home across London. Don't scoff.

That year, when we all pitched up at the studios for our first get-together of the season, I remember our innocent enjoyment, sprinkled over with a topping of bewilderment at the Covid protocols which were already in place. There was elaborate social distancing in corridors, huge semi-circular arcs of skirting-one-another manoeuvres. There was the new and exciting way of greeting colleagues by trying to bump elbows without missing. There was the sudden appearance of tubs of disinfectant and wet wipes in every room; the whole studio stank of TCP. It was rather amusing, but also strangely upsetting.

David and I were kept in completely separate but adjoining commentary booths, visual contact facilitated by a double-glazed window between our rooms. The sound-proofed glass was engineered to such a high specification that it was almost impossible to communicate between the booths. Beating both fists on the window to get David's attention, fixed solely on his monitor, as he was emphatically and consistently misidentifying the many mis-identifiable riders from B&B hotels, or simply imagining that Ben O'Connor was in the race (something he often hallucinates), was rendered futile by the industrial-standard glass. It was like screaming in space.

When the race inevitably fizzled out, one day short of its envisaged finish line in Nice, it seemed scarcely possible that we would be reconvening to cover the Tour de France that year. Indeed, I remember feeling a strong sense that nothing would ever return to normal, which, arguably, it hasn't.

For four months, nothing moved. Riders were confined to barracks, even in Monaco, where Chris Froome was among a number of riders advised by local police to turn around and stay at home. Behind the scenes, cycling's stakeholders were frantically trying to rescue their devastated season; forcing as many races as they could into the second half of the year. Eventually, restrictions across Europe eased sufficiently for the races to begin once more. But everything was topsy-turvy; races in the wrong month, time was disjointed.

In August I found myself boarding a flight to Florence. Having barely left the house for months, it was a surfeit of experience to find myself heading to Italy to commentate on Strade Bianche, the first World Tour race in the forthcoming mangled assembly of fixtures, since the post-lockdown resumption of racing. Normally the race is held in the bright chill of a Tuscan March, not the searing heat of high summer in Siena.

Our flight from London was all but empty. My passage through the Italian border was exclusively facilitated by RCS, the organisers of Strade Bianche, as well as the Giro d'Italia, for whom I would be working. It seemed that in Italy, the profession of cycling commentator qualified as an essential worker. Not an argument that would have held much sway at Heathrow's border control, I suspect.

Siena, largely deserted in 2020 for Strade Bianche.

On 1 August I was in Siena where the famous Tuscan race finishes, spending fully three days in the Renaissance wonder of a city, for one summer only, almost totally devoid of tourists. Sitting next to the recently retired Steve Cummings, from our post in the heart of the Piazza del Campo I watched in wonder as Wout van Aert destroyed the field, as had Annemiek van Vleuten before him in the women's race. Then I travelled on to the outskirts of Turin to commentate on Milano–Torino, which ended in a bunch sprint outside the ludicrously opulent baroque hunting lodge of Stupinigi, also deserted.

A few days later I was in Sanremo for an edition of Milan–Sanremo that would mark the high tide mark of van Aert's stunning progression as a one-day racer. Perched in my commentary booth in the Via Roma, I looked down on the podium celebrations, breathing in the heavy, sticky scent of the cheap sparkly wine brand that sponsors the Italian races. As the bubbles frothed and flew, and for the benefit of no one except an isolated TV cameraman and one or two photographers, I looked along the length of the finishing straight and saw nobody. The carabinieri were ensuring that people were kept at arm's length. Stay at home, they were told. And stay at home they did.

* * *

In the background to all this, it had been announced that the Tour de France would begin in Nice on 29 August, two months late. ITV were preparing for the broadcast, considering various different options as the regulations shifted, including a quite horrifying proposal that we all 'work from home'. In the end, they opted to drive the big truck that normally rumbles around France to a car park in Maidstone and leave it there, immobile, for the three weeks of the race. The production company then looked for accommodation near to the surprisingly well-appointed Maidstone studios, which ITV often use for major sporting events. Somehow they managed to persuade the extraordinary Leeds Castle to let us live there for the duration of the race. The moated chateau, normally accustomed to hosting extremely posh weddings, had been starved of income by the pandemic, and was just re-opening for trade. It was that brief, mad summer of 'The Rule of Six' and 'Eat Out to Help Out'. The hospitality business was limping back into life, navigating the ever-changing regulations that no one seemed fully to understand. Apparently, the negotiations had gone a bit like this:

'Hello, it's ITV, here. Would you like a block booking of 15 rooms for three weeks?'

'Very much. We can offer you a significant discount. How about each room for £200 per night?'

'Hmm. £75?'

'Done.'

Or rates to that effect.

So it was that we were all handed ancient bedrooms which we could only access during the day by lifting up the red ropes that marked the limits for the visiting public and entering parts of the castle normally reserved for, among others, foreign dignitaries negotiating government treaties (the Good Friday Agreement was hammered out, for the most part, behind the thick stone walls and deep moat of Leeds Castle).

Fish and chips in the grounds of Leeds Castle.

The weeks passed like a kind of extended black and white fever dream from a bygone era. Waking to the sounds of water fowl skimming the surrounding waters to get airborne into perfect late summer skies, we would congregate briefly in breakfast rooms usually used by tourists for afternoon tea and sit, one to a table, in splendid isolation, tapping our way into boiled eggs and engaging in staccato conversation across the considerable empty space of the vaulted hall about Julian Alaphilippe, while waiters from the local villages busied themselves around us, bringing coffee and clearing plates. After breakfast, we would variously saunter the three miles into Maidstone, almost all of us on bicycles, like a squadron of fighter pilots heading home for leave in a second-rate Battle of Britain war movie with a young Richard Attenborough playing me, Edward Fox as David Millar, and James Mason as Gary. No one wanted to ride with Chris, because of his propensity for riding quite fast and talking. And Matt Rendell often ran, instead of riding, for reasons of eccentricity and stubbornness.

* * *

The race got underway in Nice, whose mayor had just raised the Covid alert level and urged spectators to stay away. We were all taking bets on how many stages the Tour would last before it collapsed under the weight of positive tests and government restrictions. Chris and I scoured the regulations to establish how many stages they would have to complete for any kind of a result to stand, and found out that there was no such regulation. It would, in classic cycling fashion, be made up on the back of a Gitanes packet. So, they lined up for the first neutralised roll-out of the race, with a brass band from the gendarmerie alongside them, blasting their trombones and euphonium exhaust pipes right in their faces, ensuring that Covid droplets were projected as efficiently as possible across the peloton. It was surreal, and darkly comical, and the day ended in a tempest of rain and crashes after a detergent brand in the publicity caravan had rather thoughtlessly hosed the roads outside Nice with washing up liquid, which they thought might be a bubbly and eye-catching stunt. What a weird way to get the race underway, two months late and thoroughly out of whack. Alexander Kristoff won the sprint in the pouring rain.

Deprived of any sense of a journey, as that dystopian, late edition of the race unfolded and we stayed put, we all set about rapidly taking leave of our senses. The ever-evolving Covid restrictions were one thing. The constant testing, the ubiquitous tubs of disinfectant, the discarded face masks, and the sense of dislocation between the race, our isolated community in our castle accommodation and the car park from which we broadcast were another. It felt like a distant echo of the vibrancy of the normal Tour experience. Only Daniel Friebe and his small team made the trip to France. For the rest of us, it was an unreal sort of routine; horribly disconnected.

In between commentary shifts, before we started for the day and after we came off air, David, Pete and I played 'wall ball' obsessively: smacking a little pink ball against a studio wall until our hands were bruised into submission. The school playground game became a passion of ours, which endured for a few years afterwards and then fizzled out. But when we returned in 2021 to Maidstone for the second year of Covid-enforced remote commentary, we shared the studios with the ITV Football broadcast team, who were working on the delayed Euro 2020. Leeds Castle was not available, sadly, so we shared a Marriott hotel with them, too. It was strange for me to have two of my broadcasting worlds collide, football having been for many years my primary concern.

One day we were offered some sage words of advice by Roy Keane, as he pulled up in his Range Rover alongside our wall ball court. Dismounting the car, he briefly stopped to watch me and David lolloping around, commented that he used to play that as a kid at school, then wandered off towards the football studios with the warning, 'Don't put your backs out now lads. You're not the youngest.' Two days later I had put my back out and needed physiotherapy in a nearby village.

On the first rest day of the 2020 Tour, Pete Kennaugh, David Millar and I played golf. Golf, for God's sake. Pete decided we all needed to look like proper golfers, so spent a whole morning trawling the charity shops of Maidstone to find a series of comfortable nylon slacks, salmon-pink polo shirts and lemon-yellow sleeveless pullovers. Then we proceeded to take hundreds of wildly uncontrolled shots and three hours over nine holes of Leeds Castle's golf course, dissolving into uncontainable laughter at regular intervals. The sight of two of Britain's best cyclists of recent years making such a total arse of another sport had me helplessly amused. Staggeringly, I won.

On the second rest day, keen to avoid golf, I cycled alone to Whitstable where I ate a lunch of potted shrimp and Dover sole. On my return, passing through Kentish country lanes, I stopped on a couple of occasions to scrump apples, as if I were living in a chapter of *Cider With Rosie*. I might as well have worn plus-fours and a flat cap.

Rest day ride to Whitstable and back.

The whole affair, broadcasting the race from Kent, had me on the horns of an identity crisis which resulted in me no longer knowing what was happening or why, save for the growing understanding that whatever it was, it was decidedly not the Tour de France as I knew it. In fact it was very far from it, despite it being only just over the English Channel and even though the crowds still turned up despite the advice of the authorities. But not being there made it feel unengaging as an experience. That intangible difference that *being there* makes: when it is removed, its importance comes to light. Those occasional interactions with riders, snatched conversations with locals who knew the roads better even than the teams, breathing the same air, feeling the same rain fall. When all that is taken away, so much colour and texture goes with it. Thank heavens, therefore, for the actual race, which was the only point of sanity in one of the weirdest three weeks of my life.

* * *

Before the Tour had got underway in that filthy deluge in Nice, a conversation had broken out between me and Chris Boardman in the temporary production office that had been erected in the Maidstone car park. Chris had been asked to write a script for the opening show, in which he outlined the favourites for the 2020 race, detailing their attributes. Having cycled into the office on a gravel bike that bore his name, he changed from one set of performance cycling attire into an equally bland set of performance punditry-wear, and was now huffing and puffing over a keyboard, trying to wrestle with his prognostications. Having already picked the low-hanging fruit of Egan Bernal, Richie Porte and Primož Roglič, and plucked the unlikely French fancies of Thibaut Pinot, Romain Bardet and Julian Alaphilippe, the Man from the Wirral was now casting around for a hipster pick.

'Does this sound about right, Ned?' I looked up from my notes and smiled at Olympic Bloke with my best listening face on. He read from his laptop screen, in his TV voice:

'And then there's the young Slovenian, Taddedge Podgy-car…'

'Tadej Pogačar,' I corrected. 'Like today, except with an 'A', then pog and archer – Pogačar.'

'Pagg-orchar. Podg-iracar…' It was clear to me by now that Chris was saying this name out loud for the first time in his life. He might even have been reading of his existence for the first time in his life. The millionaire and active travel tsar Chris Boardman was a busy man back then, with little time (unlike me) to sit and watch the Tour of California. He carried on with his script, 'So much talent. But will his youth and inexperience count against him?'

I remember raising an eyebrow and venturing a mild corrective. 'I think he's really mature actually, Chris. He's genuinely race-smart. I think he's ready.'

Chris deleted a few words, and then read his final draft back out to me. 'And then there's the young Slovenian, Tadej Pogačar. So much talent, and despite his youth and inexperience I think he's mature beyond his years, and could surprise us all.'

He flapped shut his laptop with a sense of satisfaction and went off in search of some junk food, as was his wont. I still don't know if Chris knows that David and I call him the Magpie. If you leave anything shiny lying around, like a fact or a well-founded opinion, he'll pick it up with his beak and you'll see it coming out of his mouth on the telly moments later. If he doesn't know, he will if he reads this. But he won't read it, so I should be OK.

* * *

Pogačar, tuft of hair sticking cheekily out of the vent on his helmet, was all of those things we had hoped he might be. Save for one stage, when Peter Sagan's Bora-Hansgrohe team shredded the race and then shredded themselves, and Pogačar found himself out of position and isolated, losing a chunk of time to the increasingly confident Roglič, he raced with real potential. On the second rest day of the Tour, we spoke to Chris Froome via Zoom, at home and still recuperating after his serious injury of 2019. Despite the fact that Roglič now led Pogačar by 40 seconds, Froome predicted that this would change.

'Rog or Pog, Chris?'

'Oooh. Tricky one. I'd have to say Pog. I think the kid'll do it.'

And so it came to pass. The final individual time trial, the one with the long, flat approach to the wonderfully named La Planche des Belles Filles and then the brutal final climb produced a reversal which none bar Pogačar and a very few of his inner circle had seen coming. By now, the 21-year-old had fully 57 seconds to make up on Roglič, a specialist time triallist. What transpired that day instantly entered into Tour history. It was one of the greatest reversals of all time.

Commentating at my side, as ever, David Millar picked up on what was actually happening earlier than any. He sensed, with a time triallist's empathy, the respective directions of travel for the two Slovenian rivals. Roglič, the last rider off, had scarcely started the final climb when he called it. 'The Tour de France is getting away from him. This is going disastrously wrong for Roglič.' And David was, as he often is, quite right.

By the time Pogačar was at the top, Roglič's reversal was significant enough for me to call Pog the winner of the Tour, despite the fact that Roglič was yet to follow him over the finish line, by which time the *maillot jaune*'s helmet was pushed back on his head at an undignified angle and he was utterly, and very publicly, defeated.

Unprepared in any sense for this outcome, I had in that instant to find the words to best sum up what we were witnessing. A historic upset, caused by the bravery and brilliance of the youngest winner by far in the modern era; a race that would be remembered a century hence – all of that in a five-second soundbite to coincide with the final few metres of Pogačar's violently brilliant time trial that forced Roglič into painful submission.

'History is being written in the present tense!' was the best that I could muster to match the moment. It was all I had in my head and would perhaps look better on the printed page than it sounded when I shouted it into my microphone. But there you go.

When I now reflect on the particular challenges of my work as ITV's lead commentator, I do think that this rather wordy phrasing best sums up the task at hand: it is the responsibility of the commentator to witness in real time events being forged in front of our eyes, and to find accompanying words that explain the moment, that describe the size of it, justify the swelling of emotion in the viewer, that will stand the test of time. And all that improvisation has to take place in the very instant that the Future flits through the Present and takes its place in the Past, where it sits in a sequence of recorded events, locked into finality. For ever.

This was, is, my job.

But it wasn't always. The journey to get to this point had started a long time ago, yellow jumpers and all. Before anyone had heard of Tadej Pogačar, while Primož Roglič was still a child dreaming of becoming a ski jumper and Jonas Vingegaard was getting ready for a life of toil in a fish factory. Before a pandemic turned our world upside down. Before I'd ridden into a ditch and ended up walking into Maidstone General Accident and Emergency, shaking with cold and pleading for morphine in the middle of a global health emergency.

I've just remembered that *How I Won The Yellow Jumper* also started with a visit to A&E. What is it with me? Or rather, what is it about me and bicycles?

9

COME PRIMA

There is a hotel in Sanremo which often features in my dreams. Each year I become more and more resentful of the slowly passing UK winter and I tend to sulk. February refuses to give way to March, and even when it reluctantly does so, March refuses to offer comfort. The whole thing is unnecessarily drawn out.

That's when I start to find my inner eye shuttering the shafts of light which fall from the Ligurian waters of the Sanremo coast and into the marbled foyer of the Hotel Paradiso; warm, lemony rays that pass through palm fronds swaying from side to side, untroubled by the kind air creeping softly up the hillside. Normally, this is my first overseas commentary trip of the year: La Primavera or Milan–Sanremo.

The Hotel Paradiso is the kind of place which Italy has developed solely to make British visitors of a certain disposition weep on account of its sheer, fussy, stuffy Italian-ness. Its staff are dressed in serious black suits with waistcoats of light grey. They are serious about their work, receiving, photocopying and then handing back passports over the counter at reception with a snappiness that comes from the confidence of having observed decades of quiet apprenticeship. The keys hang on hooks embedded in old oak fittings, and are handed over with a slight flourish of the wrist and the ghost of a professional's welcoming smile.

The key fobs comprise a massive brass weight on which is stamped the made-up-looking name 'HOTEL PARADISO', as if to impress on the visitor that what they are experiencing is not real. It is a trick of the light, a sleight of hand, a thing dreamt up: not a three-star lodging which prosaically accepts vouchers from Booking.com. To complete the illusion, you should perhaps only be able to settle bills by signing a traveller's cheque with a fountain pen, or by counting out sheets of crisply folded lira banknotes dusted over with a sprinkling of tiny coins. The very name of the hotel, Paradiso, seems to trap the imagination of the itinerant guest in the not unpleasurable sense that they are not actually at work and about to commentate on the longest bike race of the year. They are, in fact, a minor character in some long-forgotten drama set in the Italian riviera that aired briefly on ITV in the early nineties, starring David Suchet and Glenda Jackson before she became an MP.

* * *

All this is dreaminess in keeping with this race. Milan–Sanremo, run for over a hundred years in late March, is unlike any other on the calendar. It is a luxury item, a bauble, a dangly shiny thing hanging off the handbag of the season. It is a sudden and almost jarring injection of Mediterranean glamour into a grey world; an open-topped cabriolet, hair-flowing freely in the sun, when everything hitherto has smelled of mould and embrocation. You don't have to *pretend* to like it, as some do at other races. It's simple to fall under its spell.

This first of the season's Monuments works to a set of rules which are the opposite of the Belgian Classics. Instead of the violent unpredictability and stomach-churning chaos of the cobbles, this formalised transit up the Ligurian coast takes on a ritualistic function, until the final ascent of the Poggio. Until that moment, Milan–Sanremo is less a 'bike race', more a tradition, a marker of the changing season, a touchstone in time and space. It is almost liturgical, its participants riding in response to a command from the pulpit, raced by a congregation of the willing, who know what it means, who do this every year, who understand and comply.

I'm being pompous, of course. But, in my defence, many of these thoughts have been slowly worked on, often over a luridly coloured glass of Aperol spritz, iridescent in the setting Mediterranean sun, or over a perfectly formed plateful of *spaghetti alle vongole* and a glass of white wine, crisp and cold.

Villa Nobel in Sanremo.

Still more potently than that perhaps, I have often meditated on the eternal-seeming nature of La Primavera while heading out on my pre-race jog along the seafront, over the Poggio and back into Sanremo. The route takes me past Alfred Nobel's elegantly painted retirement house with its genteel gardens and large windows that gaze out across the water. My run follows the course of the southward-snaking cycle path built along the now redundant railway track that was constructed by the 19th-century engineer Giovanni Marsaglia. His bronze bust stands on a marble plinth at the top of the Poggio, perfectly placed to watch the riders at the front of the race make their moves and plummet left-handed and down to sea level and Via Roma. I run past Giovanni every year, having struggled my way happily up the climb, passing vines coming into leaf, church bells calling the kilometres and quarter hours, flower-forcing greenhouses twinkling in the sudden profusion of light that rises and rises without end into the unnatural blue above. My thinking has been addled by the accompanying poetry of this unique bike race.

Mine is not an uncommon affliction. In 2024, the day before the race, more than one international media outlet visited the same left-hand turn at the top of the Poggio to talk to locals visiting the café or the pharmacy about the removal by the Italian Telecom company of the famous and much fetishised red-painted, glass-windowed telephone box, which used to stand sentinel at the most important left-hand turn in Italian cycling culture. From the telephone box onwards, the race can be won with an attack on the descent, so close to the finish line. Unsurprisingly, the locals, if they had noticed at all that it had gone, had little to offer by way of poetic insight to suit the agenda of the poetry-thirsty media.

'Do you have any particular recollections of the phone box?'

'Recollections?'

'You know, funny stories, interesting anecdotes...' the increasingly desperate reporter persisted. 'Anything.'

'Niente.'

The headline in *L'Équipe* was unambiguous and strident. 'THE END OF A WORLD', the newspaper trumpeted. 'The telephone box at the top of the Poggio, the lighthouse of the race, has been removed. Sacrilege!'

* * *

But then, I suppose reality always finds a way of biting. We get up early in the morning on race day and walk briskly from the Hotel Paradiso, down past the old railway station; a platform with no tracks and through which no trains have passed for decades. Past the fishing boats, the still-shuttered gelaterias, and the bike hire guys setting their stalls for the day's trade to come shuffling past in search of mild exercise and gentle adventure. Past the cafés coming to life, the rough sleepers waking up or being woken by the police and now shivering on street corners. Other handsomely jodhpur-sporting officers are advising people already that they may not pass in the wholly unnecessary yet time-honoured tradition of bike races around the world. This is normally the point at which my good friend and co-commentator Matt Stephens will start to talk about the need for coffee and some peaceful time with a highlighter and a start list.

For years, I have been working the Italian races with Matt. Handily, he is around about my height, my age and my degree of cheerfully disposed, which means that we are well matched. We generally chip along extremely well together, pleasantly and conversationally, for thousands and thousands of Italian kilometres, year in, year out. In fact, the only time I can recall Matt genuinely losing his temper was when he was trying to buy a house during the Giro, and was making long and complex phone calls to solicitors in the UK. This necessitated urgently uploading documents from the passenger seat of a Fiat 500, which I was driving in the dead of night across the Campania Apennines, with at best intermittent phone reception and, at worst, none at all. And even then, his bad temper was quickly erased when I resorted to my favourite joke in such circumstances: I waited until a very long and fraught-sounding phone call had come to an end, then turned to Matt and simply asked, 'Wrong number?'

Where Matt and I differ is in the paths we took to this point in our lives. He, in a long career which saw him juggling working periodically in a supermarket, as well as for Cheshire police force, was an extremely talented British professional road racer, a former national champion. Had he been born half a generation later he would doubtless have been rewarded to a far greater extent than he was: his professional career was, ultimately, an extreme act of faith. A victim of the scandalously sudden demise of the Linda McCartney team, which signed a bunch of riders and then promptly left them hanging without pay, Matt had to bend to blow the embers of its viability from year to year, which he did with great dedication. In short, I like Matt. And I think he likes me, although he did once turn to me in the hire car, a few stages from the end of the 2023 Giro d'Italia, and declare that I was 'a very odd man'. He didn't explain his reasoning. There was no need.

We drop our notebooks, laptops and assorted snacks in the commentary truck, where Italian colleagues from RAI are still scrabbling around with increasing urgency under the desks, lifting the floor up and threading the baffling tangle of cables somehow needed to make a simple-seeming broadcast work. At Milan–Sanremo, our 'world feed' commentary booth is a grand double decker unit, placed there by Italian TV and used by the race organisation for whom I work, providing English language commentary for distribution across the world. It used to be parked up around 10 metres from the finishing line, with a view across the Via Roma to the town house on the corner, with its baroque balcony that fills up with guests as the race draws near, towards late afternoon. This exceptional balcony is prime cycling real estate, matched perhaps only by a place on the barriers at one of the Tour of Flanders' mythical *bergs*.

Sadly, the last few editions of Milan–Sanremo have seen a repositioning of the commentary truck, as RAI has now requisitioned the spot on the finish line to set up their enormous, brightly lit, moulded-plastic studio on to which an endless parade of the Italian peloton's alumni will process throughout the morning and into the afternoon. This has led to our commentary truck being moved to the back left-hand corner of the TV compound in Sanremo, with an uninterrupted view of nothing more baroque than the temporary toilet block. Certain Scandinavian TV companies, having shelled out tens of thousands of euros to the Milan–Sanremo race organisers for their commentary set-up, have been mutinous on discovering the reality of their somewhat less than glamorous position. 'What's the point? We might as well be in Oslo!' they opine, understandably miffed and articulating a very valid point, which I try not to amplify given that it might spell the end to my endless months of accidental tourism.

Matt and I retire to a café on the Via Roma which serves tiny, bitter coffees topped by tiny clouds of hot milk froth in cups whose handles are too small for anyone other than Action Man to grip. We lay out our start lists and begin the process of inventing reasons why anything other than the Absolutely Inevitable might occur. We look at the weather along the coast road, after the riders have passed the midway point and dropped down to sea level from the Passo del Turchino with its bleak fortress; the mountain top that divides winter in Piedmont from spring in Liguria. If there is a tail wind, we will suddenly become enthused by the absurdly unlikely possibility that a strong breakaway (there is never a strong breakaway) will be able to stay away (they never stay away). Perhaps it's the caffeine that makes us lose our minds.

But it won't stop there. 'I tell you what,' Matt will say, as he reaches with a sudden urgency for one of my more unusually coloured high-lighters (I am particularly proud of my lilac ones).

'Vop's vam?' I ask at exactly the moment I pop an entire mini crois-sant into my mouth. 'Sorry. I mean, what's that?' I repeat, wiping a buttery flake from my lips.

'How about XXXX XXXX [insert second string rider's name here]?' Matt looks up from his work and stares intently at me, his eyes all a-sparkle with sudden and deeply felt meaning. Again, this may only be caffeine-induced mania. He points to the name on the start list which has been highlighted. 'If he decides to go long on the Cipressa and takes a good couple of riders with him, they could be hard to catch.' The Cipressa is the first of two climbs in the closing kilometres of the race. But neither are especially hard.

Artwork greeting the riders on the Cipressa climb.

'You're right!' I enthuse, grabbing back the lilac pen and scoring purple lines through five or six riders' names, building up a very accurate imagined picture of this completely fanciful late breakaway. 'XXXX and XXXX could go with him. And XXXX.'

'And XXXX XXXX.'

'Yes, and XXXX.'

We both pause for a beat and sit fractionally back in our chairs to admire our newly annotated start lists. At exactly the same time, the hard reality seeps back into our consciousness that such a scenario has never played out on the Cipressa and it will never play out.[1] It is just wishful thinking and we know it. Such euphoria is followed hot on the heels by a sense of deflation.

'Time for another coffee before we head back?'

Matt glances at his wristwatch. 'Go on, then.' And I stick another mini croissant in my mouth.

* * *

And so Cycling's Longest Day starts to take shape. The 300 kilometres of the year's first Monument, plus what used to be an extended roll-out through the streets of Milan, as riders dodged tramlines and an early exit from the race, will probably take us six and a half hours. And that's not all. After the finishing line has been crossed, we will have to stay in our seats for at least another half an hour to complete the podium celebrations and to hear from the winning rider. And all this without the commercial breaks which viewers detest so much on ITV4, but which serve the twin purpose of paying for the coverage and allowing us to walk at a normal speed to the loo. At Milan–Sanremo, if such a convenience stop is taken at all, it is at a flat-out sprint.

We try to postpone the moment that one of us reaches for a Haribo. To pop a Tangfastic into your mouth before the flag has even dropped

---

[1] This book was drafted before the astonishing 2025 edition of the race, in which exactly that scenario *did* occur. Pogačar, van der Poel and Ganna went clear on the Cipressa and came to the finish line together. History can be a terrible disrupter, sometimes. It never stays still.

and the correct number (seven) of Italian riders from second tier teams, plus one from Astana, have attacked, is to flirt with a gelatine-enhanced sugar black-out. I can usually ignore the urge to delve into the sweets for a good length of time, secure in the knowledge that Matt will at some point dive out of the commentary truck (well, not dive so much as scuttle like a tumbling crab down the external staircase at the back of the lorry) and return cradling a very small coffee with a foil lid that has absolutely failed to keep it warm.

He will also bring with him a couple of vast cannoli, each one at least as big as an adult human nose. The substantial, unapologetically sweet pastry will sit in front of me, slowly starting to run in the direct afternoon sunlight flooding our booth, until the race is over. Though Matt has eaten his, I will not have touched mine, for the simple reason that I absolutely detest cannoli. The problem is that, in the confusion and excitement of the Cipressa and the Poggio, the glory of the Via Roma and the podium, I forget that I should really mention to Matt my unchanged dislike for this most iconic of Italian sweetmeats. This issue gets lost in the drama of the race and its aftermath, resulting in me sliding the by now warm and semi-liquid confectionary uneaten into the bin, along with my commentary notes. During our post-commentary, post-race debrief over a beer, it has never once occurred to me to register my distaste for his noble gesture. I simply forget.

'The way Mohorič attacked on the descent!'

'Unreal. They knew with 400 metres to go that he wouldn't be caught and they all started racing for second place!'

'But how about that ride up the Poggio by Jasper De Buyst for Caleb Ewan. How can Ewan be so good at this race, without ever quite winning it?'

'Oh, by the way, never bring me a cannoli again. Ever.'

And that is how the subject never gets raised and then another year passes and it is once again too late to address it. There is the cannoli once more, sitting threateningly on a paper tray and placed next to my laptop.

* * *

Milan–Sanremo sweeps the day along with it and out the other side with an imperceptible, but then irresistible, kind of energy. Nothing can survive it, not even a strongly held view about cream-filled snacks. And that has to do with its design, topography and its traditions.

It may be true that the Apennines have to be crossed, but the Passo del Turchino is the most benign ascent imaginable, its metres of climbing spread so thinly as to be largely irrelevant over the best part of an hour of gradual altitude gain. And the one hundred-and-something kilometres that lead the race to its base are equally without complication. The descent off the climb can sometimes look stressful. Julian Alaphilippe, for example, somehow contrived to crash near the top of the Turchino in 2023, then proceeded to weave back through the convoy on the steep and technical descent to Savona. It was a hair-raising few minutes of arguably completely unnecessary risk-taking that spoke to the heart of Alaphilippe's complicated charisma.

But once on the coast road, the script has been written, given a legal read, signed, sealed, delivered to all the relevant parties and then enacted. The breakaway will fall apart on the Tre Capi (the series of three reasonably nasty headlands which have to be ridden over), the peloton will sweep up the front of the race in the charge for 'positioning' (I could, and perhaps will one day, write a whole chapter dedicated to this word) into the Cipressa, where the racing abruptly stops. That repeats itself on to the 5-kilometre Poggio climb, where the big players, those entirely predictable rivals, will only show their hand perhaps a kilometre from the top, at which point the ACTUAL race begins, around 290 kilometres after it started and almost within sight of the finishing line.

It is the ultimate bike race. In many ways, it is an event so puritanical as to be almost absurd; a lie detector designed to trip up the casual fan. For if you can genuinely sit through an entire edition of Milan–Sanremo and find the experience edifying, you will have won road racing outright. Yours is the Crown of Deferred Gratification, since the Poggio is only a truly electrifying spectacle if you have served your time admiring first the spires and domes of Alessandria, the Golden Madonna of Tortona, the first glimpse of ocean and then the colonnades of Imperia. If you have accompanied the quintet of hapless breakaway riders on their five hours of pyrrhic suffering. If you have breathed in and out in time with the waves lapping the rocky coastline of Liguria. If from your couch in Leicester or Dumbarton you, too, have followed with your eyes the sweeping arc of the sun across the plains of Piedmont to bedazzle the waters of the Med, then you have earned your right to stand and cheer when the winning rider makes their move with the bust of Giovanni Marsaglia in sight. Yours is truly the victory on the Via Roma.

Each edition of the race produces a differently sized and uniquely composed group of riders who contest the race win. My years of involvement in the race started with Vincenzo Nibali's last victory; one that nearly provoked a wave of cardiac arrests from the hordes of Lycra and bandana-wearing septuagenarian Italians who cycle to Sanremo in their hundreds. To these veteran *tifosi*, standing with their wrinkled brown skin pinched by the tight fit of their replica kits, the sight of Nibali, the last of an old school Italian tradition, was the culmination of all their many years of patient observance behind the barriers of the Via Roma. It might indeed have finished some of them off. More recent editions, though, have produced other, yet quite different, solo winners. And others still, as in 2024, have resulted in a chaotic cascade of attacks from which a final podium of a GC champion, a puncheur and a true sprinter emerged, forming a potpourri of rider characteristics only possible in Milan–Sanremo.

That barnstorming win for Jasper Philipsen was, once again, the fastest edition ever of the race, despite the fact that there was only a very light tailwind. But that still meant Matt and I had somehow contrived to natter without cease about Milan–Sanremo from 9:50 a.m. to around 5 p.m., long after the podium champagne had started to grow sticky and aromatic on the confetti-strewn tarmac of the Via Roma, which already echoed to the clatter of barriers being manhandled on to the backs of lorries by tattooed men with baseball caps on the wrong way round.

The race was evaporating. Sanremo was starting to grow dark and chilly as we eventually wandered back to the hotel for a dinner of *risotto alle gamberi* and *fritura*. At times, over our food, we paused, only to gaze across the table, unfocussed and somehow still subliminally aware of the sound of rotor blades. A commentary shift of that length unsettles the psyche, wobbling the synapses in a way which resembles a form of very low-key but insidious concussion.

In 2024, even the next morning, when Matt and I dropped our bags into the tiny boot of a Fiat 500 and set off for Milan airport, retracing the race in reverse, we were still not quite right in the head. Four hours of driving lay ahead of us, much of that along the astonishing motorway south towards Genoa, which shoots straight through mountains and across tight, steep valleys on concrete supports that look like the legs of a Salvador Dalí elephant, while over your right shoulder Liguria falls into a twinkling sea.

We started to play car games to keep us from boredom, all of them related to cycling. At first this involved assigning a professional rider to each car we passed, according to its characteristics and nationality. Thus was Cesare Benedetti deemed to be a Fiat 500, Clément Champoussin some sort of Citroën, and Lennard Kämna a Mercedes Benz that overtook us at 200 kmh. Our next game was more nuanced and ridiculous still.

'Matt, which rider in the professional peloton most accurately mirrors the vocal style of Annie Lennox?' 'I Saved The World Today' by Eurythmics was playing.

'Oooh,' Matt said, earnestly considering the challenge. 'That's a tough one. Is it Jonas Vingegaard?'

I snorted my derision. 'No, it's Michael Mørkøv.'

'Of course it is.'

Thus was Julian Alaphilippe paired with Meatloaf and Fernando Gaviria with Lemmy out of Motorhead. When Apple Car Play launched into Cat Stevens, we fell silent at last and gave up the game.

By now we were dropping out of the Apennine spur which protects the Ligurian coast. It was a glorious day, piling soft white warmth on to the new green of Piedmont's rice fields and vineyards. Mist still clung to the river Po as we crossed it. Ahead lay Alessandria, Tortona, Pavia and then Milan. The talking was done and La Primavera was over for another year.

Standing at the finish of Sanremo on the Via Roma.

10

STRAYING FROM THE PATH

It was in the winter of 2010, just after I had submitted the draft of my first book, *How I Won The Yellow Jumper*, that I started to do a thing called podcasting.

It was rather new at the time and now it has taken over everything, reaching like audio ivy into every gritty corner of human experience. Podcasts are both an immense triviality and something that have mysteriously taken root in the lives of many, giving pleasure to both the creators and the listeners. At their best they can be benign, fun or even mildly life-affirming. At their worst? Well, you can just not listen – and there are plenty of people who do that – but over the course of the last 15 years I have spent a lot of time extemporising into a recording device, which is all you need, really. That's the joy.

I can't recall now whether it was my idea or the brainchild of my ITV colleague Matt Rendell. But I remember the location. Matt and I were both sitting on a bench in London's Green Park on one of the coldest days of the year (we couldn't think where else to go), holding a recorder between us and starting, very hesitantly, to record a short-lived podcast called *Real Peloton*. This podcast could have been the making of us both – or the absolute ruin. In a remarkable turn of events, so shoddy was it that it succeeded ultimately in achieving neither outcome. After a couple of years we had it taken out the back and humanely put down, like a long-suffering family pet that had never really settled into the house.

The idea had been born out of our work the previous July, when we both reported for duty for ITV at the Tour de France. Someone at the new-fangled-seeming 'digital' bit of ITV had asked us to produce a daily *ITV Tour de France* podcast, which had very quickly gained a significant following. Mostly this consisted of me, Matt and Chris Boardman standing in a huddle, trying to remind Matt to move the single microphone, often by grabbing his arm and directing it for him. Matt had a stubborn, but fatal, flaw for a nascent podcaster in that he tended to hold the microphone towards whoever was *not* talking. The quality of the recording was, at times, offensively bad. And that was not all.

I say that we were 'talking', but what I really mean by that is 'failing to remember anything' about what had just happened. It's a curiosity of the way intense short-term memory can function that recently generated impressions, so vivid in the moment, can fade into obscurity with equal speed. This phenomenon explained why there was often a telling pause before any of us could remember who had just won the stage we were trying to discuss and which had only finished a matter of 40 minutes previously.

Added to the patchy quality of three men in early middle age scratching heads and staring blankly at one another was the chaos of the setting. Invariably the podcast would be recorded in some unloved corner of the *zone technique* at the finish line, which would start to be dismantled for its 250-kilometre onward journey the minute we opened our mouths and pressed record. As a result, our sage words would often compete with the clatter of toilet blocks being hoisted on to flatbed trucks, the rough language of Norwegian riggers and the warning alarms from oversized French lorries trying to reverse vast pieces of machinery through impossible-seeming gaps, only made possible by a series of resounding collisions that cleared the way.

After the Tour de France one year, Matt and I noted that cycling also happened in August. And, come to that, September, October, January, February, March, April, May and June. Freed of the strictures of the broadcast calendar, we spread our wings far and wide, finding multiple ways to lose money in travelling to events to produce the podcast and not one viable way of making any, save for the one time Matt's friend from Colombia flew into London with a suitcase full of *Real Peloton* socks, which we hawked liked two podcasting Del-boys. The podcast boom was a couple of years away still. We were a couple of pioneers, making it up as we went along, having fun and failing to sell many socks.

We even dabbled in strange winter activities, on more than one occasion heading up to the Manchester Velodrome for some track meeting or other. In fact, I happened to be there on the celebrated and painful occasion when Malaysian star sprinter Azizulhasni Awang was stretchered from the track centre with a 20-centimetre splinter of Siberian pine stuck clean through his left leg, from one side to the other. I missed it, obviously, as I'd gone to get a burger and a pint. *Real Peloton* was never knowingly on the spot when it mattered.

But, in a curious way, it was occasionally on point. Its brief-lived tenure as the only cycling podcast on the market (the benchmark *Cycling Podcast* was still a couple of years away from launching) coincided with the outcome of the Operation Puerto investigation. Matt, with his intimate understanding of doping culture born of his authorship of *The Life and Death of Marco Pantani* and his war chest of contacts on the inside, was on a mission to shed light on the murky depths of the predominantly Spanish doping scandal. This centred on the malfeasance of a certain Dr Eufemiano Fuentes, a master in the extremely effective, but also deeply revolting, art of the autologous blood transfusion.

As a result, over a series of episodes variously recorded in my brother-in-law's pub in Farringdon and my kitchen in Lewisham (we abandoned the park bench studio after that one chilly outing), Matt took Alejandro Valverde to task, lapsing into a series of dog barks whenever his name was mentioned. This he did in reference to one of the blood bags found at Fuentes's premises, labelled 'Piti', which just happened to be the name of Valverde's pet dog. This Matt found to be enormously funny. So did I. And so did our one or two listeners, who somehow found us online.

Valverde came to be the first name consigned to our ground-breaking podcast feature 'Sod-off Corner', a segment introduced by a clip from quirky Icelandic crooner Björk singing the English profanity 'sod off' with surprising passion. A few years later this rather firm position with regard to the future World Champion would be tested *in extremis* by Matt's appointment as press officer to Valverde's Movistar team. Matt, forever on the lookout for a viable career that did boring things like pay money into a bank account, had taken a really grown-up job, requiring diplomacy and finesse. But this new position pitched the nascent podcast host into direct and daily contact with their star rider, Valverde. *Real Peloton* was duly wound up and a silver stake driven through its heart. And anyway, Matt was dismissed from Movistar after about a year for being far too much like Matt Rendell. I have no idea who they thought they'd offered the job to.

Besides, the writing was on the wall well before we both got cold feet. Each episode was produced at the cost, born entirely by Matt and me, of £200. We paid this money to licence the specially composed theme tune and for someone to upload the podcast to the internet, something so mysterious and dimly understood back then that it necessitated the hiring of a professional consultant. We recorded dozens of podcasts over the course of a year or so. But with a revenue of zero pounds it was clear that, business-wise, *Real Peloton* was built on shaky foundations; a fiscal analysis that we didn't even have to pay a financial adviser to come up with. That stark reality was added to the imminent threat of legal action from any number of sources: Armstrong was still in denial; Valverde was a decade and more from retiring; and Contador was still contesting everything that related to dodgy steaks and mysterious trips across the border during the Tour de France. And all three were regular visitors to 'Sod-off Corner'.

* * *

But if *Real Peloton* had been strangled not long after birth, podcasting itself was just hitting its stride. In 2013, my friends Lionel Birnie, Daniel Friebe and the late Richard Moore launched their definitive and outstanding *The Cycling Podcast*, at which point everyone else should have packed up and gone home. To this day, but tragically without Richard, they continue to produce the most complete content out there in podcast form, across the season, year after year.

And yet, for many years the *ITV Tour de France* podcast limped on, stumbling blindly through events, still forgetting who'd won, tripping over cables and creating daft strands like The Thomas de Gendt Game, which was a direct copy of Radio 4's Mornington Crescent, except using the names of riders in the Tour de France. Seriously, it was that desperate.

It was around that time, and I forget the precise sequence of events since they hardly matter, that Matt was goaded into creating the iconic character known to *ITV Tour de France* podcast listeners as 'Scouse Nairo'. Because the Colombian spoke no English, and podcasts are an exclusively audio format, his interviews, which were often spliced into each episode, could not for obvious reasons be subtitled as they would be in the TV highlights show. Quintana's voice therefore needed to be dubbed and his good friend Matt stepped up to the task. I can't be sure, but I think it was Chris Boardman who first suggested that Matt adopt a scouse accent when dubbing the words of Nairo Quintana. To my astonishment, Matt acquiesced and thus created one of the most enduring characters in *Tour de France* podcast history (a very niche area of human endeavour).

Matt's curious interpretation of a Liverpool accent was a thing of wonder. Raising his pitch offensively high, cycling's most erudite academic and one of the most gifted linguists I have ever met would launch with gusto into a frankly remarkable form of human vocal communication. It teetered around a tiny pinhead of identifiable scouse, yet seemed uncontrollably to swoop around the country, nay the entire English-speaking world, scooping up vowels and diphthongs from an impossibly wide number of different dialects.

No amount of offsetting his variations with the injection 'well' (the only scouse-sounding word in his armoury) compensated for the scattergun extravagance of his display. Within seconds Chris and I would be helpless with laughter, which only seemed to further encourage the now peacock-like Matt Rendell in his glorious silliness. Podcasting allows professional broadcasters to drop their guard and escape the sometimes suffocating strictures of making TV. However, the *ITV Tour de France* podcast took this to extremes. And it wasn't the only one.

With *Real Peloton* now defunct (was it ever actually funct?), the opportunity presented itself for something else to appear on the by now massively overcrowded podcast market. No one wanted it, but it happened anyway. One day, preparing to commentate on the Vuelta from London's Ealing Studios, appropriately enough the famous home of 1950s comedies, David Millar and I launched a daily accompaniment to the race: a podcast called *Revuelta*. I think this means, among other things, scrambled eggs in Spanish. Once our commentary duties were done, we'd pick up another set of microphones and discuss the stage all over again, but this time adding in extraneous details.

Since David and I weren't actually in Spain but in London, we soon found that this extra content was very, very far from the matter at hand: namely the Vuelta a España. One episode was prompted by our brief interest in astrophysics after we had read about plans to deflect asteroids which threatened the planet. On another occasion, I set about trying to understand the importance of Ludwig Wittgenstein's *Tractatus* having happened upon the blue memorial plaque at Guy's Hospital which records his time spent working as a porter there during the London Blitz. The connections with cycling were vague at best. In the first instance, we interviewed a leading astrophysicist from the USA, John Noonan, who just happened to be a very proficient amateur racer in Texas. So *that* was our justification to include the material in what was ostensibly a cycling podcast. And in the case of the Wittgenstein diversion, well, I'd made my discovery when *cycling* back home via Guy's Hospital from Ealing. So that was also fine, according to us.

Revuelta lasted a year or so, before that podcasting behemoth made way for a re-branding. David and I were so enjoying our diversions into worlds we only dimly understood, like poetry, philosophy and science, that we wanted to carry on after the Vuelta had ended with Chris Froome/Alberto Contador/Fabio Aru on the podium in the Madrid sunset. And in this manner *Never Strays Far* was born: a cycling podcast with a title that doesn't make sense and also makes no reference to cycling. This was a sure-fire winning move from two clued-up media operators.

* * *

David and I began our haphazard and homespun approach to podcasting, and long journey into huge diversions, at the 2019 World Championships in Harrogate, with some excitable finish line commentary and discussion, which we recorded at some volume in the VIP tent at the finish line, to the annoyance of all the paying guests.

For much of 2020 Covid kept us apart, and without much racing to speak of we dealt almost exclusively in tangents for months at a time, meeting online every couple of weeks to maintain a trickle of non-racing material, because there was no racing. We reviewed the contents of David's bookshelves. I told stories about my childhood. During the first Kent-based Tour de France we did an entire episode of commentary on a village cricket match. But by 2021 we were tentatively back in the game, then spiralling out of control with seemingly wilful abandon.

That year I went to the Giro to commentate daily with Matt Stephens, while David remained at home in Spain. Every morning I would set my alarm for 6:30 a.m., wake up in a state of disorientation, instantly dial David up on a Zoom call and, without any preamble, start to record a podcast. By now, rapidly democratising technology meant that it had become easy enough even for me to master without needing any support. Podcasting had become everyone's favourite hobby. I don't know whether it was a function of that specific edition of the Giro (won, you may remember, by Egan Bernal, the almost forgotten superstar who was only a matter of month's away from a terrible, career-threatening injury), but, that May, I was particularly psycho-active.

Every night I dreamt with an uncommon intensity, often waking with some deeply affecting dream still trailing through my blurred consciousness. It quickly became a habit for me to relate my dreams instantly to David before they evaporated. And David, to his surprise, as well as mine and our increasing number of listeners, realised that he had a natural talent for classic Freudian dream interpretation.

One morning I'd be telling him about my primal fear of dogs (something that aligned closely with my lived experience while out for my daily morning runs) and the next day I'd be recounting a particularly vivid dream in which I kicked an orange football by mistake into a huddle of podcasters, who turned out to be Daniel Friebe, Richard Moore and Lionel Birnie of *The Cycling Podcast*. Quite what any of this had to do with Peter Sagan's stranglehold on the points competition at the 2021 Giro was anyone's guess, but my sequence of dreams revealed little more than an entrenched imposter syndrome. It all seemed to strike an unlikely chord with our small but growing listenership, catapulting our strange little podcast up the iTunes charts. David's status as dream guru endures to this day. Only this morning did I awake after a dream involving a leaking roof and a trampled garden and wondered if it had something to do with my imposter syndrome as a cycling commentator and podcaster. Most things do, according to David.

At this point we also started to experiment with re-naming the already confusingly named podcast, according to where we were in the world. This began with calling our Giro podcast *Never Strays Farfalle*, which almost worked. But then the concept overreached itself again and again. By the time we finally gave up on the confusing re-branding, we had dreamt up *Never Strays Fahrrad* (Germany), *Farl* (Ireland), *Fata* (Turkey), *Farmyard* (cyclo-cross), *France* (France) and *Farthing*. This last variant was for the Tour of Britain, which I had originally wanted to call *Never Strays Farage*. David didn't think this was quite as funny as I did.

* * *

What then turbo-charged *Never Strays Far* to reach a different level altogether was ITV's inability to find a sponsor for the 2022 edition of the Tour de France podcast. It was the first post-Covid race and would see our crew return to the roads of France, as well as Denmark, where the race began.

With an alacrity of strategic thinking quite unusual in David and myself, we suggested that *NSF*, as it was now rather cutely being abbreviated, stepped in to fill the breach. We decided to produce daily podcasts from the Tour, recorded in the car as we drove in the evenings to the next destination. With an unerring sense for marketing, we called this strand *Never Strays Car*. Again, not only did the title now not make any syntactical sense, it also failed to mention cycling or the Tour de France.

Pete Kennaugh then joined in the fun. He had little choice, given that he was sitting in the back of the car, faced with the prospect of either joining in or having to listen silently to us babble on without him.

With Pete's arrival, *NSF* took another definitively weird turn. Pete is simply unable to keep his true nature concealed, which is one of the reasons why we and our listeners love him so dearly. Pete is a wonderful, living and laughing, bundle of contradictions; a kind of *tableau vivant* of all the emotions a human can be subjected to within seconds of one another. He is a 30-second snippet of a Wagner aria on repeat. To listen to his surprising passions, his constant state of bewilderment and deep enthusiasm not just for cycling but for the sheer fact of being alive, is to be invited along on a very special journey; one in which the most complex thing can be rendered beautifully simple, and the opposite. Pete can also inhabit a world which mystifies him at every turn, even when the object of his wonder is as banal as a haybale.

'What I don't get with haybales is, are they just a Tour de France thing?' he asked, microphone in hand, during one of our earliest episodes of *Never Strays Car*. We were driving through Picardie alongside a field of neatly ordered haybales, which Pete had been gazing at for some time while the question germinated. And now, finally, it had seized him.

'What do you mean, Pete?' asked David after a very long pause, too long perhaps for a podcast.

'I mean, do the farmers just put them out in the fields when the Tour's coming past?'

The car fell silent as we wrestled to get on to Pete's very particular wavelength. No one spoke, until Pete broke his own hush with an amazing follow-up question. 'And where do they put them afterwards?'

The car erupted. To this day, I have a picture of Pete Kennaugh, racing for a decade, summer after summer, frowning in confusion at the millions of haybales he must have passed that had been deliberately placed in the field to honour the passage of the race.

One summer we were joined on the ITV team by Lizzie Deignan, heavily pregnant at the time with the Deignans' second child. Told that she would also be travelling around in our, by now, massively overcrowded hired car, the former World Champion had similarly little choice but to join in the podcast; a task to which she warmed immediately. It took the plain-speaking Yorkshirewoman no time at all to settle into her role as the eye-rolling grown-up in the room, bitingly funny and almost always right in a podcast that literally only knew how to be wrong. In short, she was so good at podcasting, that it was humbling. Listener feedback instantly propelled her to the status of everyone's favourite, which was galling for those of us who had been slowly building the podcast over many years. It was completely understandable, but still hugely annoying.

* * *

The following year, a trio of other guests joined us in the car for the duration of the 2023 Tour de France. Cadel Evans, the first bona fide Tour de France winner ever to have graced our vehicle, was the first to be initiated. I had not seen Cadel since he had retired some years previously. Prior to that, our encounters had been restricted to the usual routine of 'niggly journalist meets wary athlete'. I can remember the sometimes fractious figure who I found myself inadvertently upsetting from time to time during his marvellously resilient victory at the 2011 Tour de France, when Cadel was often uncomfortable in the public eye. That was the year he presented an awkward, unusual figure to the world's media, flinching when touched by an ASO chaperone, parading a tiny pet dog through the mixed zone and threatening to chop the heads off journalists. Pete and David also agreed that he was a rider they, too, had singularly failed to get to know during their time in the peloton. Now here he was in our car, looking angular, cleft-chinned, tanned and very much like a slightly older version of Cadel Evans, which is exactly what he was. It took a bit of adjusting to.

But very quickly, it became apparent that Cadel was nothing like the man that any of us (didn't) know him to be. Asked, I think by me, whether or not he'd like to take part in the podcast, he at first answered something self-deprecating like, 'Aw, I can't see why anyone would be interested in what I have to say,' before readily accepting the microphone and being at once engaging, funny, decidedly original and really rather emotional.

Almost overnight, Cadel decided that he would use the 2023 edition of *Never Strays Car* as a kind of group therapy session. When the little red lights on my recorder lit up as it slipped around in the back of the car, often sliding off my lap as David took a corner slightly too fast, Cadel opened up about things that had wounded him, amused him, perplexed him, left him with grudges or things that were said which had simply driven him on to even greater heights of performance. And often this had nothing remotely to do with cycling. Cadel, safe to say, and in the uniquely crowded field of complex bike rider personalities, is one of the most engagingly extraordinary men I have ever met. But what went way beyond that surprise was the much more pleasing realisation that I really liked him, that he was a warm, funny, generous man with whom we could share the adventure.

Cadel Evans, beer in hand and smiling.

Very early on in our 10 days of podcasting together, Cadel likened the strange mobile society of Pete, David and myself to which he had just been invited as a kind of monastic brotherhood. It was nothing of the sort, of course (as our diet would attest), but the point remained: Cadel felt a surge of kinship with us and we felt it with him.

I am sure that no interactions with the media had ever presented him with the opportunity to be so authentic and the tone set during our recordings continued when we were simply driving along without a mic in hand, or checking into a hotel, or having breakfast, or, as we once did one glorious night in the Pyrenees, wallowing in a hot tub with a plate of charcuterie and a bottle of wine. Cadel's stream of conscious, glass of Nuits-Saint-Georges in hand, was as unbroken for 10 days as the stream of emails and text messages he received from the baggage handlers at Bilbao airport who had mislaid his luggage. For almost two weeks he uncomplainingly got by with a newly acquired toothbrush and David's donation of a bunch of CHPT3 clothing he'd brought along for the ride.

The 2011 Tour de France winner was only reacquainted with his luggage when we dropped him at some appallingly dangerous-looking motel near a French provincial airport so remote I can't even recall where it was. But Cadel wasn't remotely fazed, put out or complaining. He just chirruped and chuntered his pleasant way through a series of man hugs and farewells as we left him at the side of the road and roared off into the night. Later that evening we all received a series of messages from the former World Champion, in which he wished 'Brother Ned, Brother David and Brother Pete' all the best and thanked us all greatly for the opportunity to podcast. Frankly, we were stunned. No one had ever thanked us before.

* * *

Slotting straight into the spare seat vacated by Cadel Evans came the more familiar figure of Marcel Kittel. Actually, that's a slight untruth. Cadel had a habit of moving rather fluidly from seat to seat, and not staying firmly put in any one position in the car, which rather shook us up and knocked us off guard. This was not the case with Marcel, whose blond bulk never once moved from front right passenger seat, which he expanded to fill with muscular ease, reducing in an instant the car seat to the size of a child's chair on the back of a bike. Marcel, who I already knew much better than Cadel, having visited him in his home town of Erfurt a full decade earlier, was a more predictable podcasting presence: laid back, the right type of opinionated, inclined to a sunny disposition and just happy in an infectious, uncomplicated way.

After a few days Marcel seemed increasingly to exhibit an almost psychopathic solidity of purpose in his podcasting. Once installed in his front row cockpit, he would turn to face either Pete or myself when we were speaking from the rear seats, twisting his giant torso around to stare intently and directly at the talker, rather than just aimlessly facing forwards, gazing out of the windscreen. Not only would he fix you with an unwavering stare, he would also eat Pringles, his hand moving unsighted from tin to mouth. This combination of highly focussed human behaviours meant that the episodes recorded with Marcel in the car exhibited a higher than average degree of nervous energy. He was the kind of Übermensch podcaster that Nietzsche would have admired, if the German philosopher had known the first thing about podcasting.

And then, finally, one year on from Lizzie Deignan's presence in the car and on the podcast, her equally pregnant teammate from Lidl-Trek and reigning Time Trial World Champion Ellen van Dijk was propelled unwittingly into the Evans/Kittel vacancy for the final week of the race. This was different in a number of ways, since neither Pete, David nor I had ever once met Ellen before and she had never met us. We set about instilling a rapport; a process that took us about 22 minutes, at most. Like Cadel and Marcel, Ellen seized the microphone with both hands (benefitting no doubt from the fact that she co-hosts a podcast in the Netherlands).

Faced with our three different, and by now in the third week of a grand tour, increasingly ragged psychopathies, and with the added disadvantage of having to slot into our frankly bizarre quirks and foibles in a second language, Ellen came into the podcast family, settled into her chair and took total ownership of the situation. She was a joy, despite what Lizzie Deignan implied in her acerbic WhatsApp message to our group (which we instantly showed Ellen) that simply said, 'Bitch better not get too comfortable. That's my seat.'

Ellen van Dijk in the Never Strays Car.

Within a day, Ellen had become Sister Ellen and the monastery of *Never Strays Far*, identified a couple of weeks previously by Cadel Evans, had ceased to be an all-male institution. And it was all the better for it. She even embraced our habit of assuming, appalling stereotypical Dutch accents to intone our erstwhile catchphrase 'It's normal, eh?' Only when Ellen did it, it was show-stoppingly funny, as was her love for inventing terrible imaginary hashtags, like #RunYourDreams for David's latest athletic target.

As with Lizzie the year before, when we finally parted company we did so only after wishing her all the best with the birth of her child, but slightly annoyed that she, like Lizzie, seemed intent on return-ing to the peloton, rather than pursuing a much more interesting, if totally unpaid, career as a podcaster. Who did they think they were?

* * *

And who, exactly, did we think we were? The 2024 version of *Never Strays Car* saw the fulfilment of a long-standing dream of David's and mine. For as long as either of us could remember, we have shared a similar obsession with those in the media who come to the race with giant stickers of their own faces on their cars. I even wrote about this in *How I Won The Yellow Jumper*.

There's Dag Otto, from Norwegian TV, who drives a car with his own face all over it. We teased him once on the way to the car park: 'Which one's yours, Dag Otto?'
'That one over there.'
'Really?'

Teasing Dag Otto about his car.

Well, many years later, David, Pete and I set off from Florence to Nice via three weeks of racing in our own stickered car with our giant faces all over it. The thrill of joining the likes of Dag Otto Lauritzen, Richard Virenque, Greg LeMond and Laurent Jalabert in this particular vanity was unlike anything I can describe. So proud were we of our newly liveried car, that one day we deliberately parked it in front of Tadej Pogačar's team bus, for maximum kudos. Our little podcast had arrived, or so we felt. It had been, one way or another, 15 years in the making.

The Never Strays Car blocking Pogačar's team bus.

What I hope is revealed by these ad hoc recordings which have proliferated over the years is our sense of wonder and privilege. At its core, there are three men of different ages and backgrounds, two ex-racers and a journalist, all of whom are experiencing the shared journey intensely, but differently. I would hope that if one thing emerges from the chaos of the podcast, when it is distilled down to its essence, it is this: that what we have been lucky enough to experience is simply the stuff of life. It is, when all is done and then is said, just a pleasure to be on the road, on the move. Not much more than that. But that in itself is quite something.

11

LE PLAT PAYS

Belgium, and Flanders in particular, has played a big part throughout my adult life via the various different guises my so-called career has assumed, and even before such a thing as a career had even reared its head, the best part of a decade after it should have done.

My first visit to Belgium was as part of a troupe of student actors from Cambridge University, touring a production of *The Taming Of The Shrew* across Europe. It goes without saying that we displayed a curiously toxic mixture of post-adolescent arrogance coupled with Oxbridge's unique sense of entitlement, all wrapped into an evening of wild over-acting conducted under the inherently erroneous belief that we were somehow any good. After a forgettable night performing no doubt to the annoyance of the audience at the University of Canterbury's Gulbenkian Theatre (which I would visit on my own theatre tour 35 years later), we boarded our tour bus and headed for Belgium, and a two-night sojourn as guests of the English Faculty at the University of Leuven, half an hour to the south-east of Brussels, in the province of Flemish Brabant, the gateway to the Ardennes.

It would of course be decades before I had any notion of the famous Flèche Brabançonne (AKA the Brabantse Pijl). That said, it would be a further 20 years until the prestigious warm-up race to Liège-Bastogne-Liège switched from its traditional start in Alsemberg and then Zaventem to its current *départ* in Leuven, in the shadow of the colossal, borderline ridiculous, neo-gothic town hall with its terrifyingly steeply pitched roofs, numberless windows and unnecessarily over-embellished stonework.

I had not heard of Milan–Sanremo winner Jasper Stuyven back then. Stuyven is one of Leuven's most famous cycling sons and comes from one of the town's most prestigious chocolatier families. My ignorance of him was based on a generalised ignorance of the entire cycling world, coupled with the salient fact that he wouldn't be born for another four years.

But the proudly mercantile, archly Catholic and deeply hedonistic Leuven marked my introduction to Belgium, a country which hitherto had held no interest for me. I, like many millions of others of my ilk, had been weaned on a flavourless and insipid English diet of petty prejudices, most of which were reserved for the lampooning of our nearest neighbours: the Italians, the French and, *of course*, the Germans. Somehow, Belgians had slipped through the gaps of my pig-headedness. I had no particular reason to find them either untrustworthy, devious, smelly or psychotic, attributes which I was led to believe by most sit-coms of the early 1980s applied to most inhabitants of countries outside of Great Britain. Terry and June had a lot to answer for.

The rather odd Jacques Brel statue in Brussels.

133

I was even, as yet, unfamiliar with the hilarious 'Name a famous Belgian' joke, to which the follow-up to the obvious answers (Tintin and Poirot) is 'Name a famous Belgian who actually exists.' It would only be later that year that I was introduced, via a more educated fellow student, to Jacques Brel, for whose sinuous, impassioned music I have an infatuation that has only increased with the passage of time. Fifteen years would elapse before I got in a lift by mistake with Eddy Merckx (an encounter, both banal and other-worldly, which I recall in unnecessary detail in *How I Won The Yellow Jumper*). Indeed, 25 years would pass thereafter before I could, without recourse to Google, confidently and accurately spell the name Merckx, as I just have.

Having given my Lucentio in *The Taming Of The Shrew* (a characterisation that involved having a lisp. That was it. That was the whole characterisation), we were invited out by our host students to a night on the tiles in the historic and, funnily enough, tiled centre of old Leuven. It was an evening of riotous good humour as we sallied forth, and in and out of homely, lively Flemish buildings, delighted by their red bricks and exposed beams. It was also my introduction to the nefarious, occult world of Duvel, one of Belgium's most violent but also drinkable beers. It is, to repeat a phrase first coined by Chris Boardman, nursing a similarly potent Affligem in a Novotel near Lille during the 2014 Tour, a 'hurty' beer. I remember meeting a guy called Wilf, who had long-ish Bohemian hair and smoked with more assiduity than he breathed. I also remember a student bar called the Fac Bar, which appeared to have no actual bar and yet somehow facilitated an endless supply of little bottles of Duvel. And, if I am honest, I remember little else.

But that night laid the foundations (albeit slightly askew) to a deep affection for this nation of revellers, and for their determination to welcome and to share in their pleasures. A couple of years later, I landed up in Leuven again. This time I had turned up by train, accompanied by my Brel-loving friend, who by now was studying at the Sorbonne in Paris. I was working in Hamburg. We'd both run out of money in France, where I'd been to visit him, and made a mad, hitch-hiking, ticketless train-hopping dash for Saarbrücken, the nearest town in Germany with a bank that could forward me the meagre month's stipend that had just been paid to me. Once armed with the Deutschmarks (this was still before the euro), we changed them into Belgian francs and headed for Leuven, for want of anything better to do.

Wilf was there, Duvel was there, a better life was there, or so it seemed to us both as we worked our way through my salary in a few days in a blur of pinball-machines, aimless strolling around the Oude Markt and frequent steaming bowls of *spaghetti bolognese*. If my first visit had opened the door to Belgium, this one saw me falling over the threshold, and the next time I appeared in Leuven (on *another* theatre tour, this time as an appalling King Lear), I had picked myself up off the floor and shut the door behind me. After three intoxicating spells in Belgium, I wanted never to leave its warm embrace and a little bit of me never did.

* * *

So, all of this, while it has nothing much to do with cycling, is import-ant when I recall the time that David Millar and I went to the Ronde van Vlaanderen in 2024, not as commentators but as cycling fans. It was a trip that meant the world to me, connected loose ends of my life and hit home with the kind of profound resonance that is only really possible if you've already lived quite a long life. When the trip was over, I composed a message to David, which I sent him via WhatsApp the following day:

I love Belgians. Many are infernally rude, fiery, unpredictable, ruthless drunks who know exactly what they want from life, enjoy it and make me laugh. Most are deeply hospitable. They seem to celebrate much that is a bit shit. They have cycling teams sponsored by garden centres, kitchen utensil manufacturers and pornographers. Belgium is my favourite country in Europe, one which has made a point of harvesting the very worst of its three neighbours, France, Germany and the Netherlands, coupling it all with ponderous, if not downright terrible British weather and making it all gigantic fun. They have produced Tintin, Jacques Brel and Eddy Merckx. They have given rise to Wout van Aert. Belgians teach the world how to live. They belong to a mighty land, at whose very heart sits the sport of road racing – one which makes no sense on almost any level. Like Belgium itself.

It had come from the heart, and I had blurted it out in a couple of minutes, summing up as it did 35 years of affection for the little nation over the water.

David then replied, 'That's bang on. Love it. Don't forget to mention about their excellent suburban architecture.'

He agreed with me, it seemed, and had developed the theme to encompass the uniquely Belgian tradition of building no two houses in exactly the same style. Go to any terraced Belgian street and you will note that each neighbouring house has been constructed differently to every other house around it, often with hilarious results. It is an expression of total individuality, set within a context of tight communal regulation. It is a wild contradiction, that continues to produce wild architecture, as the social media account (one of the very best there is) 'Ugly Belgian Houses' will attest.

'King Charles would hate it,' David signed off.

Once I had worked out who on earth he was talking about (I couldn't figure out why the long-haired royal chap who fought Oliver Cromwell would be bothered), I realised that David had hit upon a deep truth. Belgium is counterculture. They love to do things entirely as they wish, like building hilarious houses, and designing ridiculous bicycle races. And that is why they understand road racing like no one else does. Not only do they *see* the absurdity, they *design* it into the sport.

* * *

The 2024 Ronde started in Antwerp, as it sometimes does. This meant, however, that to get to the heartland of Flemish *bergs, hellingen* and *muurs* (exactly how many words do they need for short, sharp climbs?) the race first had to roll along some main roads, wide enough for its normal purpose of allowing the free flow of a few lanes of commuter traffic, possibly containing lone sales reps for those garden centres, kitchen utensil manufacturers or even pornographers heading from Antwerp to Brussels for work. The real race wouldn't begin until the peloton had passed by the capital city and entered the Flemish Ardennes. But on Easter Sunday the roads were closed for the annual, quasi-religious ritual of the Tour of Flanders (it sounds better in Dutch, so I think I'll stick with Ronde).

The whole Holy Week branding that cycling has purloined from the Bible needed some explanation, not least to David Millar, who I had dragged away from our city centre hotel in Ghent to admire the baroque heft of St Peter's Abbey.

'Why are we here, exactly?' he asked, as we stepped back out of the church, after a cursory few minutes skulking in the transepts while an Easter service prayer-mumbled and organ-piped its way to its inevitable resurrection. It was the morning of the race, Easter Sunday.

'Only because I wanted you to know that the London Borough of Lewisham, where I have lived for nearly 20 years, used to belong to this abbey, for over 450 years,' I explained.

David looked blankly at me. It had been quite a long walk from our hotel and I could see by the subtle, but increasingly accentuated, lines on his forehead that he was questioning its worth. Indeed, he might now have been questioning our entire decision to experience the Ronde as a pair of bona fide, side-of-the-road, flag-waving cycling fans. I changed the subject. 'Anyway, Happy Easter, David.'

'Oh, is *that* why this week is called Holy Week?' At some point in the last 10 or 20 years, the cycling world had started to brand the week that begins with the Ronde and ends with Paris–Roubaix as 'Holy Week'.

'What do you mean?' I asked.

'Because it's always Easter?' I looked at him like he was daft, which he really, really isn't.

'Well, yes...' I replied, by now unsettled by this display of ignorance. 'Either at the beginning or the end of the week.'

'I thought it was just because cycling fans think that these races are holy.' He looked flabbergasted. It was as if someone had just told him that Christmas was also something to do with Christ. I decided to abort the conversation.

Walking back into Ghent and preparing for our day chasing after the race, we both reflected on the ecclesiastical subject matter that our passion for cycling had led us into. David had taken a picture to send home to his wife of a somewhat overly literal Christ having been taken down from the cross. 'Rather impressive propaganda,' he'd commented. I replied that I wasn't sure propaganda was quite the right word. Then, unsure of our ground, we both agreed that the Church had wonderful branding, a great logo and an almost limitless number of hashtags; invaluable assets in an age of social media. By which time we had made it back to our hotel and could abandon theology for the remainder of the day. We were ready to drive off in pursuit of the Ronde van Vlaanderen.

Not knowing where to position ourselves along the madly convoluted final 150 kilometres of the race, we headed with child-like obviousness to the first cobbled sector of the race. We parked up in a tiny farming hamlet near a railway line. This, in itself, is not a particularly revealing observation, since in Flanders you are never more than a metre away from a farming hamlet and a railway, like London and sewer rats.

Waiting with David for the Ronde van Vlaanderen to pass.

We then realised that we had at least an hour to kill before the race was due to come through. Indeed, far from jostling with a writhing mass of other cycling fans, we were pretty much the first people there, save for the occasional locals coming and going along their stretch of rural road which had for one day become the centre of the sporting world (if you can put to one side all the football that was being played).

A lady politely rang her bell at us, thanked us as we stood to one side, and then rode her bright yellow shopping bike past us on the cobbles, promptly turning right and through the gates of her court-yard. I imagined, not for the first time, but for the hundredth, what it must be like to *live* on the route of the Ronde van Vlaanderen or indeed any other landmark race. For 364 days of the year, it is a colos-sal irrelevance. And then for one day, it is either a mad delight or a massive inconvenience, depending on where you place yourself on the scale of cycling enthusiasm. I found this lady's possible fandom hard to gauge on our first, briefest of meetings. But I was heartened to note, when eventually we'd seen the peloton through and were heading back to our car, that she had made it out of her front door, to stand on the very slender patch of front garden, inches away from the riders, and had clearly been celebrating with her neighbours, given the density of human beings assembled on her property, the sudden appearance of flags, and the litter from half a dozen empty prosecco bottles lined up on her doorstep. It was clear that she embraced the annual street party foisted on her by the organisation of the Ronde van Vlaanderen, bringing along with it a polychromatic and unlikely selection of the international cycling curious to stand on her street and holler incoherent encouragement/abuse into the ears of strangers on bikes who took not a blind bit of notice.

As we waited for the race to arrive, we passed the time of day with an assortment of similarly minded folk who had chosen this anonymous point on the map to start their worship at the altar of Holy Week. They came from real but distant places like Buckinghamshire, Asturias, Brøndby and beyond. Some had arrived on bikes, others bearing provisions. The cleverest of these had even packed sandwiches, which David and I were eyeing with something approaching open envy.

The event was also being exploited by a political grouping, as we slowly began to understand. At first we were delighted to be handed a clutch of small 'Lion of Flanders' flags, as well as a giant one to hold aloft and flap in the faces of the riders as they passed. Reading the small print on the flag as we waited with our booty by the side of the road, I noticed that it had been produced and distributed by a grouping from the Vlaamse Beweging, who call for Flemish independence. It was, on further inspection, what is known as a *strijdvlag* or battle flag: the tell-tale detail being the absence of the colour red from the talons and tongue of the Flemish lion. In short, David Millar, former *maillot jaune* of the Tour de France, was about to be seen on TV vigorously waving a banner in support of Flemish separatism.

'Ah well,' he reckoned. That was his nuanced approach to wading into such a contentious area in the politics of the host nation. 'Who cares?'

David's big lion of Flanders flag.

Other roadside opportunists had invested preparatory time in painting home-made signs which only tangentially related to cycling or indeed did not have any relevance at all. A posse of young Flemish lads arrived on the scene carrying a beer-stacked cool box which they opened immediately upon settling into their spot a few metres to our left. They unfurled their signs, suspending the biggest of them, with some difficulty, from the spindly branches of a tree that was ignorant of its role in the unfolding pageant. 'LUKAKU' it declared in giant orange capital letters.

Each red, black and gold wig-wearing member of this ragged band also held aloft smaller signs, as if to augment their message, on which were written the single word 'LUKAKU', in homage to Romelu Lukaku, the Belgian footballer currently playing for AS Roma. It was only after the race had passed by, as we were all heading off to jump in our various cars and continue sector-hopping, that I exchanged a quick word with them.

'Lukaku,' I said, and pointed at their signs which said 'LUKAKU'. It was a fairly straightforward exchange, if I am honest.

'Yeah,' one of them replied, took a swig from his beer bottle and resettled his wig on his head. 'We didn't even see him in the peloton.' He marched off, looking disconsolate, to catch up with his Lukaku-loving friends.

It had been a few years since I'd had the pleasure of standing road-side, anticipating the arrival of a bicycle race. Normally, of course, the actual experience is denied to me, despite my physical presence at the race, since I am locked away in a commentary booth. And so I was once more surprised by the immensity of the forward convoy. In a race like the Ronde the stickered cars start to pass almost an hour before the peloton. These are the vehicles driven by the teams' *soigneurs*, who are tasked with getting ahead of their riders at half a dozen different pre-determined points on the map, to stand at the side of the road and hand out bottles, feed bags or even spare wheels. Then come the endless variety of motorbikes ridden by the press, the regulators, the marshals and the police. Then, finally, the lead cars announce with a blast of the sirens and flashing lights the imminence of the breakaway, which hones into view, led through the cobbles by TV's 'Moto 1', the cameraman sitting on the bike facing backwards. After that, and in the case of the Ronde in 2024 three and a half minutes later, the same series of lead vehicles brings the peloton through.

They passed in perhaps 20 seconds; a violence of colour and noise, filling every limited centimetre of cobbled road and spreading beyond it on to the pavement, forcing us all to jump backwards. I did so in the nick of time, my peripheral vision suddenly filled with the huge multicolour sight of Tim Declercq's Lidl-Trek jersey bearing down on me with uncompromising intent and at 45 kmh. To have ended my day in Flanders in a bone-crunching collision with Declercq's immense Flandrien torso would have not only been painful, but also ignominious. A sudden gust of air whipped across my retreating figure from the hole being punched into the earth's atmosphere by this behemoth of the bike. I had dodged that particular fate by not much more than the width of a Lycra seam on his XXL jersey.

* * *

Off we went to the excellently named Zottegem, by accident. We hadn't intended to go there, but were drawn instinctually and wordlessly to the little town by dint of sausages being griddled. The main square, through which the race had already passed, had been taken over by a fan park with a big screen showing the race and bad food concessions showing the worst of Belgian cuisine. Nonetheless we passed a happy half hour there, wolfing down fried food and drinking beer from plastic cups. Having eaten a hot dog and complained vociferously about the lack of *frituur* chip shops, the former prologue specialist David Millar spotted a branch of Domino's Pizza and vanished into the gathering crowd, only to reappear with a medium pepperoni that he single-handedly demolished, while watching Lidl-Trek work on the front with 89 kilometres remaining. With a lick of his fingers, he muttered, 'Van der Poel's going to destroy this race.' I didn't try to contradict his analysis, partly because I was more concerned with removing a ketchup blob I'd spilled down the front of the new puffer jacket that I was particularly proud of.

We decamped and relocated for a final time, this time pitching up at the Kruisberg, a little hillside on the outskirts of Ronse, over which the race passed twice, but via different approaches. On the way there, David told me all about his only proper attempt to win the Ronde during his long racing career, which was annually centred around the Tour de France to the exclusion of the Classics (a shame since he could have been really good at them).

'It was as if I'd been in a washing machine spin cycle for a few hours. I had no idea where I was, but I kept moving up and passing people. Then I got to a little group with Juan Antonio Flecha in it. "Oy, Flecha!" I shouted. "Where are we?"

"This is the front!" he said.

"You're kidding!" I was at the front of the Tour of Flanders – by mistake.'

'So, what did you do?'

'I attacked.'

'And then what happened?'

'I blew up.'

I enjoy it greatly when David describes getting things horribly wrong in bike races. He manifests a touching, humorous pride in his failures, which I find deeply human. It makes his successes even more meaningful. 'Lol' I told him – and then I lolled.

The first ascent of the climb, the Nieuwe Kruisberg, went up a long, straight, wide road. We stood and bellowed from the margins as Mads Pedersen powered his way up the drag. But the Dane was fading and, disappointingly, seemed unable or unwilling to react to our joint insistence that he should 'Allez!' Then we had another 50 minutes before they would magically reappear on the other side of the hill. Just enough time to negotiate the complex system of tokens which one had to purchase from one stand in order to buy a beer from another stand. It started to spot with cold Belgian rain, as I stood seven swaying bodies from the front of the queue, propped up on either side by beery Belgians shouting unflattering and unmannered stuff about the non-Belgian Belgian resident van der Poel.

Beer in hand, I pushed and barged my way jovially through to join David who was standing in front of another giant TV screen, erected this time in a clearing on the wooded hilltop, watching the exact moment that Iván García Cortina slipped his chain on the insanely difficult, and now made even more difficult by the rain, cobbled Paterberg climb. That was the moment Mathieu van der Poel chose to attack. A couple of beers into the afternoon and short of the commensurate level of inhibitions, I defaulted to the familiar practice of commentating. In fact I started to roar my makeshift commentary as if actually at work, while, in fact, standing in a muddy field, beer in hand with hundreds of total strangers, who were all pretty much doing the same.

And as I stood there in wonder and in Belgium, a voice within me, struggling to make itself heard above the voice without me, recognised that I had never seen anything like a Mathieu van der Poel attack before the Dutchman came along. There is a Tysonesque violence to it, which almost removes it from the sport of cycling entirely. He is a disconcertingly feral presence at the front of a race, effectively winning the contest before his disheartened and disorderly opponents have realised what is happening; an animal pouncing, both savage and sudden.

The obscenity of this attack on the Paterberg was another of those archetypal moments in van der Poel's career that will live in cycling consciousness long after he has stopped racing. It contained everything that David admired about him: a total belief, a willingness to gamble, a complete contempt for the qualities of his rivals.

There have been times when van der Poel has been surprisingly and roundly beaten; when he has shown a sudden explosion of weakness, to be oxymoronic about it. There are races that have seemingly suited him to perfection, in which he has somehow contrived to fail. But this was not one of them. David had simply gone quiet again. Of all the many enthusiasms he has for the current crop of cycling stars, he reserves a special respect and awe for van der Poel. I think, deep down he wishes he had been van der Poel. Or maybe not, I'm not sure.

'Let's get a place on the next climb,' David suggested, noting that, one by one, people were drifting away from the big screen and heading for the scrubby woods at the side of the clearing. He was excited and I was caught up with his enthusiasm, marvelling at how genuinely thrilled he was to be this close to cycling history being made. The fan in David Millar was iridescent in his day-glo winter sports jacket, which was flecked with rain and chilli oil from the pizza. I followed him as he made his way into the undergrowth, still clutching his politically questionable Flanders flag and following the herd of drunks.

Soon we were losing our footing as the banking dropped away to reveal the Oude Kruisberg. Scrabbling and sliding past brambles, nettles and the occasional wet, gnarly branch on to which we latched to break our descent towards the cobbled road, we became aware that the many spectators who'd taken up a spot on the other side of the road, the easier one to access, had a prime view of our undignified progress. I doubt any of them knew that the tall elegant guy, dressed impeccably, if flecked with chilli oil from head to toe, clutching a yellow flag with a lion on and trying his hardest to maintain a mystique, while on the brink of sliding the remaining 3 metres on his arse through the mud, had once duelled with Philippe Gilbert, Fabian Cancellara and Tom Boonen for victory at the Ronde van Vlaanderen.

Once installed at the side of the road, and having escaped the worst of the sarcastic whoops and cries from across the way, we didn't have to wait long. David was poised with his camera: for there came van der Poel, hunched over the bars, in a frenzy of controlled self-destruction, expressionless, impervious to the outside world, implacable in his intent. Seldom, perhaps never, have I witnessed such a cold-blooded rider. Winning the race without even making it look hard, and close enough for us to reach out and touch him. Flesh and blood, and not, for once, locked away behind the reflective screen of a TV monitor that can be turned off with the flick of a switch. Belgium does this.

We missed the end of the race. But that was OK. We knew the outcome from having witnessed what we could by the side of the road. Instead, as we drove back to our hotel in Ghent, already thinking about an early dinner, our chatter meandered away from the matter in hand. The day had unbottled a feeling of tremendous liberation in us both; the strong feeling of kinship that Belgium elicits in me and, not just me, in most. There is something about this country that places no demands on you other than to be human.

That's what I thought of later that night, when I closed my eyes. It was the last thing I would consider before sleep took me away from Flanders and away from Belgium. Please, this liminal hard-pressed country suggests, be a human with a bit of a heart.

Hollering support from the side of the road.

12

SOUP TO CRY FOR

Food fires emotional triggers in me when I am far from home. This is a discovery I have made on a few occasions. When I was in China in 2015, covering the unlovely and mostly unwatchable Tour of Taihu Lake, I would go for long solo runs through grey, muddy, brown-field, industrial-belt China, dodging electric scooters and trying not to breathe as I passed zinc smelting plants. But once back at the hotel, each one like the previous day's, I grew used to helping myself to hot restorative bowls of broth, to which I would add beansprouts, noodles, spring onions, tiny delicate mushrooms and a dash of chilli paste. The daily morning goodness of this simple soup made me want to cry.

Another time I ordered a risotto from a tiny bar near Palermo, just before a shift of commentary on the Giro di Sicilia. It was so simple and nourishing that it actually *did* made me cry. Without any warn-ing, the rice-based lunch suddenly transported me to a place of great emotional cossetting, like the experience of the ghoulish food critic in *Ratatouille*, who, in a Scrooge-like epiphany, is reminded of his mother's cooking in the eponymous cartoon. Matt Stephens looked up from his pasta at me as I snivelled. 'You OK? Is the risotto no good?' I'd been unable to answer him, so moved was I by the risotto. So, I just shook my head.

But it was in Malaysia in 2020, after a week or so spending many hours on my own every day, that a soup in Langkawi would make me openly weep. There were a number of reasons why, and very few of them had anything to do with the general classification of a race won by Team Sapura's Danilo Celano. The tears came because my senses had filled up to capacity. There was no more spare room left. And so they came out of my eyes.

* * *

Kota Kinabalu was the last place I'd imagined I'd find myself, partly because, prior to the moment that a WhatsApp message from an unknown Malaysian number made my phone ping sometime in the autumn of 2019, I'd never heard of it. It's very hard to conjure up an accurate image of a place you've never heard of, unless you have the imaginative powers of a science fiction writer, which I don't. I'm a cycling commentator and the two crafts are very different. I normally deal in solid, reassuringly familiar places like Nice and Turin. Or in the case of the Tour of Britain, Peebles.

My work as a commentator has taken me far and wide. From my first forays into the deserts of the Arabian peninsula, I have also followed bike races through an enormous range of different countries, from the heartlands of Spain, Italy, France and Belgium, to the islands of Corsica and Sicily, to the ports of Hamburg, Antwerp and Rotterdam, to Copenhagen, and the emptiness of Norway's endless north in the company of the recently retired Thor Hushovd. I have visited Ireland to make a documentary about the extraordinary successes of Irish riders, Portugal to watch Pete Kennaugh become a *directeur sportif* amid the cork tree groves and rolling interior, Andorra for tax reasons and likewise Switzerland.

I've been to Austria, Luxembourg and Germany, where I spent a blissful few days in Thuringia, re-establishing a long held but neglected love for a country I had taken to heart. I have circled Britain many times, from Aberdeen to Exeter. That week I spent in the People's Republic of China watching the most singularly unedifying bike race I have had the paid duty to observe taught me much: about systemic corruption, political coercion, chicken broth for breakfast, permanent smog, frighteningly polluted rivers and a young Italian sprinter of partially Polish descent. Of the nine stages, seven were won by Jakub Mareczko. This, too, is bike racing.

But Borneo? Even at the moment I was thrown forwards in my seat by the wheels of a jet hitting a hot-looking runway, I was not certain where I was nor how, quite, I had arrived there. Dizzily disconcerted, I pressed my nose to the cool plastic of the window. Borneo revealed itself to me for the first time in my life.

A tarmac strip, a tall, barbed-wire fence beyond and in the distance a dark green forest rising up the slopes of the Crocker Mountains, capped off by the mighty Mount Kinabalu, above which thick white clouds hung in slowly swelling clumps. Their white mass was sharply outlined against a sky of such a blue that suggested thumping heat. It seemed clear to me now, through a fug of jet-lagged wonder, that I was a very long way from the Lewisham home that I had left in the drizzle of a February morning an indeterminate amount of time ago.

Borneo was one of those words that took me straight back to the classroom, to geography lessons and the age-old, probably now rightfully neglected, habit instilled in British schoolkids of tracing the outline of continents and islands and then shading the coasts with a blue pencil. Borneo, with its bulk, sitting just off a shattered tangle of peninsulas and archipelagos impossibly far from home, was a name that conjured a recent post-Empire era of charts and flags, of clipped, black-and-white British accents, rifles, ancient prejudice, pressed shorts and imperial knees. Caught in the haze of my confused memory, this huge hot island with its manifest riches, both human and natural, was a territory so unknown to me that I approached it with trepidation and deep, almost insatiable, curiosity. Also, I was here for a bike race, which I was looking forward to seeing. That much goes without saying.

* * *

I had flown to the island's distant north-eastern province of Sabah, connecting from London via Kuala Lumpur. The mystery WhatsApp number had belonged to a contact from the Tour de Langkawi who had somehow been given my details. It hadn't taken me long to accept the invitation to join the race as the on-site 'world feed' commentator on its 2020 edition.

The phrase 'world feed' is one of those insider terms which the small number of English language cycling commentators take for granted. I suppose it sounds terribly grand, and certainly implies status and glamour. The reality is often very different. Outside of my work with ITV, which once accounted for two grand tours and a smattering of other stage races, but has now dwindled to just three events per year (very soon to be none), I often work as a 'world feed' commentator for a range of different races.

It works like this: when organisers of races try to market the broadcast rights to channels across the globe, they have also to cater for those territories in which audiences are so small that there is no way the local network could afford to pay for their own team of commentators. Think South Africa, perhaps. Or New Zealand. How many kiwi cycling fans are so dedicated to the sport that they will still be watching Milan–Sanremo at 4 a.m., when there are still 60 kilometres to go before the peloton hits the Poggio and the actual race can begin? Perhaps a dozen hardy souls, sleep-deprived and sunken-eyed in Auckland? Three drunken students returning from a night out in Christchurch, flicking through the channels looking for the rugby? It is simply a matter of cost then, as most things are in the perma-cash-strapped, financially illiterate world of professional road racing. This imaginary New Zealand sports network, by shelling out a few extra NZ$, buys the licence for the English-language 'world feed' commentary alongside the live pictures, which saves them the expense and hassle of adding it themselves.

Perhaps you are, sacrilegiously in my opinion, wondering why they bother with commentators at all. If so, then may I recommend that you try watching a race without any voice to meander along and guide you. It's a curiously unanchored, unengaging experience, unless all you are actually interested in is an afternoon nap, in which case it is an entirely legitimate approach. David Millar is very fond of pointing out to viewers that he and I have to watch races by definition entirely *without* commentary and are struck by just how disorientating an experience this is, to the extent that we find ourselves bounced into talking to cover for everyone's embarrassment.

Granted, it is possible to mute the annoying voices, though in the interests of my future and current livelihood this is not a trend which should be encouraged. It's true that I once watched an edition of the aforementioned Milan–Sanremo on a projector at home with all the colour drained from the image, the commentary on silent and instead Philip Glass's *Koyaanisqatsi* soundtrack playing loudly through some loudspeakers. It was a mildly diverting experience for about 15 minutes in an arthouse cinema, beard-scratching way. But I don't think that Eurosport will be offering it as a red-button option to enhance their Tour de France coverage any time soon.

World feed commentators (I can drop the inverted commas now since you are fully apprised as to their function) are almost always asked to be physically present at the race, to be on site at the finish line. For various boring technical reasons involving the expense of satellite links, it is actually cheaper for the organisers to have us travel around with the race than sit in a remote studio in London. Even during the Covid pandemic of 2020, this cost-saving principle held, which is why I found myself that benighted summer at an almost completely deserted Heathrow airport, boarding a mostly empty flight to Florence, so that I could commentate on the delayed 2020 edition of Strade Bianche.

* * *

My trip to Borneo came about in early February 2020, just about sneaking under the wire before the pandemic shut down the world. Although 'coronavirus' was a term I had already heard mention of, and Wuhan was the name of a city with which I had suddenly become familiar, the word 'Covid' was still alien to me, as was the practice of wearing face masks and having my temperature measured at the entrance to shops and hotels by people pointing white plastic toy guns at my forehead. This was to be my final prelapsarian race, the last guttering of innocence before the hitherto simple pursuit of travelling around watching bike races became an impossible-seeming thing, an act of wild and terrible irresponsibility. Allied with the growing sense of guilt that goes along with my commensurately growing carbon footprint, I am not sure my job has ever been the same since.

The Tour de Langkawi can probably lay claim to being the most prestigious of Asia's series of stage races, despite the fact that China hosts the final world tour races of the year in Guangxi. These Chinese races suffer by dint of their bovine pointlessness (the lack of crowds at the side of the road is matched only by the desert races of Saudi Arabia, Oman and the UAE), as well as the fact that their stupefying procession along arterial dual carriageways takes place deep in October, after Il Lombardia has effectively brought the curtain down on the calendar against the rather more beguiling backdrop of Lake Como. Plus, there is European elitism, too. There is that.

In 2020, Langkawi still had the advantage of being an early season race, when form was just starting to build and the season lay ahead for the European peloton at least; an as yet unwritten story that would take a dramatically different twist that year. Post-pandemic and in order to attract a still greater European presence, Langkawi has switched to an autumn berth and perhaps lost a bit of its purpose as a result.

The race is the personal obsession of one of Malaysia's most significant figures. It was called into existence in 1996 with the backing of Petronas, the Malaysian petrochemical giant, and at the personal behest of the longest serving prime minister in the country's history, the totemic Mahathir Mohamad, a controversial autocrat and nationalist who last served as Malaysia's leader in 2020 at the age of 94. On the final stage into Kuah on his home island of Langkawi, close to the border with Thailand, the PM made another much-heralded appearance at the race. He'd already dropped in on stage three in Kuala Lumpur, processing down the finish line in a huge cavalcade of official vehicles, one of which he was actually driving. Mohamad was not the kind of 94-year-old you easily took the car keys off.

In Kuah, where the surrounding colonial-era buildings were often decorated with huge images of Mohamad's likeness, he actually popped into the TV truck we were operating in to check we were all doing our jobs properly. My hard working, and even harder smoking, Malaysian colleagues had been in a state of nervous tension all day, fractious, bickering and raising their voices at one another seemingly at random as they stomped in and out of the truck trailing cables and power leads.

I only began to understand this high state of alert when, minutes after we had come off air, the crazily sprightly almost hundred-year-old prime minister appeared suddenly in our cramped working confines, wearing a neatly pressed white shirt covered in sponsors logos and a Petronas baseball cap, flanked by half a dozen security operatives who seemed to encircle him entirely in a ring of mildly twitchy human steel.

A close brush with Mahathir Mohamad.

I do remember how I thought Mohamad had glanced briefly in my direction and I flattered myself to think I detected the faintest nod of recognition, until I realised that he'd just caught a glimpse of his own reflection in the polished glass partition wall behind me. It was all very surreal and the relief when he had left the truck was unconfined.

In a curious footnote to the 25th edition of his own national race, 10 days later Mahathir Mohamad was forced to resign from office, having been brought down by scandal. So perhaps, with hindsight, it was unlikely that his mind was entirely on the big German Max Walscheid's victory ahead of Luca Pacioni in the bunch sprint, which, in only my opinion, I had so expertly called on the world feed. 'Walscheid!' I'd screamed. To no one in particular.

* * *

Langkawi was a very long way from Borneo, where the race had started. Staggering around as if I were Alec Guinness released from the iron hut in *The Bridge Over The River Kwai* after a night of overwhelming disorientation and almost complete lack of sleep, I was absorbing my first experience of real tropical heat, idly watching the little wooden fishing boats that bobbed and strained at their leashes in the tidy, intensely fishy smelling harbour of Kota Kinabalu. I was in a state of wonder at pretty much everything I saw, however mundane.

A few hours earlier, at dawn, having given up on finding anything that resembled night-time rest, I had set off for a run, away from the fascinatingly run-down hotel we had all been billeted in and up into the hills which flanked the little town. In doing so, I surprised a community of residents sleeping entirely outdoors. I don't know which of us were more taken aback at the encounter, the disturbed families or me in my baggy nylon shorts from which two white and undistinguished Anglo-Saxon legs protruded. I sent cats and small children scurrying, and was seen on my way by some watchful adults whose ad hoc homestead I had stumbled into.

On I ran, around a quiet mosque, its golden minarets suddenly lit by the rising sun's appearance from the wide Pacific behind my back, and past an adventurously modernist art gallery, which I later visited to inspect a terribly sad exhibition about the destruction of the natural habitat of the orangutan in the very hills behind it. Then, drenched entirely by middle-aged sweat although the sun was only just above the horizon, I returned at a desultory pace to our hotel to find my new colleagues in the Malaysian TV crew all at breakfast, animatedly smoking, shouting and spooning out rice, hard boiled eggs and tiny fried fish on to their plates. I sat in the corner, savouring the scene and happily crunching the bones of the tiny fish. Then, having rinsed my mouth and my running kit in the sink, showered and dressed in as little as I could justifiably wear within the strictures of an at least partially observant Moslem land, it was off to the opening day of racing; an 88-kilometre criterium race around an 8k circuit that ducked and dived its way in and out of town, avoiding or not avoiding potholes as it went.

* * *

Once at the finish line of the race and presented with the familiar last-minute mayhem that usually accompanies a live bike race transmission – increasingly panicked wiring, cabling running from truck to truck, tripods and microphone stands – I eventually located the tiny quarter-sized portacabin that (it now became clear) was to be my commentary position.

It was only marginally different to Alec Guinness's accommodation. It had a window that faced on to a concrete wall, with no other view. It had also been dropped partly on to a pavement, with one corner falling off the high kerb, with the result that the tiny little plastic studio from which I would theoretically be broadcasting to the world sat jauntily half on, half off the pavement. As a result of the slope, nothing would stay on the tiny desk I'd been given without rolling off, along the floor and out of the door that wouldn't close.

I looked at the tiny monitor wedged against the side of the cabin, so that it would at least stay put. It was still resolutely blank and baking in the mounting heat as the midday sun hammered down on the roof. I tested the microphone and heard nothing back. I stepped out of the booth and, not knowing what next to do, laid my damp, clean running kit out on the tarmac to dry, which I figured would take about one and a half minutes. Then I went off to hesitantly, and politely, request a start list.

I did not know which of my many new colleagues might be able to help me with this. Everyone seemed to agree, once I'd managed to make myself understood, that it was of course extremely import-ant that I had one, so that I could know who was in the race. Then, having agreed with me on the extreme importance of such information, one by one they all seemed to vanish, with no start list appearing and the start time of the race rapidly approaching. Not only that, but, disconcertingly, when I returned to my wobbly little super-heated place of work, my entire running kit had been removed. I later discovered that one of the wonderful young volun-teers had gathered it up and disposed of it, thinking that a vagrant had set out their stall outside the office of the Tour de Langkawi's official world feed commentator.

Later that evening I would spend a long time, before we had a flight out of Kota Kinabalu, strolling through its streets, festooned with glowing red lanterns, taking in the slightly more bearable evening air, watching games of open-air snooker on full-size tables and picking my way through acres of almost identical shops selling an exciting array, bordering on the infinite, of fake sportswear, all for sale at embarrassingly low prices, the kind of economics which suggest the world is indeed emphatically on a course of ruin, both industrially and ecologically. Part of the problem, I settled eventually on a navy blue, knock-off Nike shirt and a pair of Supreme socks, both of which I still admire every time I pull them on and think of Kota Kinabalu, with its hot wind, strong spice, blue seas and green forest. And its bike race, too.

Sunset in Borneo.

Though I cannot be totally certain, I think that the criterium race of early February 2020 marked the first time a professional bike peloton had ever visited the old trading post on the north-eastern coast of Borneo, Kota Kinabalu. The race made a tremendous racket, as such events tend to do. The excessive-seeming fleet of police outriders, sirens ablaze, announced its passage past open shops and cafés, sweeping within arms-outstretched reach of enthusiastic, if baffled, residents spilling on to the streets to whoop and holler as the riders came past. And that was only for their recon laps. The riders from across Asia, and from every corner of the world, were getting their first taste of Borneo's heat and Borneo's roads, both of which needed to be treated with respect.

Back in my melting booth, with the temperature approaching the point at which my buttocks would actually fuse with the plastic seat into which they were gradually sinking, I had finally got hold of a start sheet from the race director, an old Tour de France rider and acquaintance from the UK, who had found himself working in the Far East. There were teams from South Africa, Italy, France, Australia,

Indonesia, Japan, Kazakhstan, South Korea, Hong Kong and the USA. There were former Tour de France stage winners (well, there was Pierre Rolland). There were Colombians, Canadians, Irish. And there was the 30-year-old Thai track specialist Turakit Boonratanathanakorn.

In the very few minutes that I had to skim the list of starters for names I knew of among the many that I did not, my attention kept snagging on the name of Turakit Boonratanathanakorn. Working alone, without a co-commentator to share the load, I found myself repeating out loud various different and evolving versions of Turakit Boonratanathanakorn's lengthy name as the seconds counted down to the start of the transmission. I wondered how it would be if he made it into a breakaway.

* * *

As it turned out, I didn't have to wonder for too long. On stage one proper the following day, on a long race out of Kuching and back to Kuching, Turakit Boonratanathanakorn was indeed part of a two-rider breakaway which made it to the line ahead of the bunch sprint. He didn't win, which was unfortunate for a man who's only victory on the road was a stage of the Princess Maha Chakri Sirindhorn's Cup Tour of Thailand into Ranong in 2013. But, equally, it was fortunate for me in that I wasn't required in the end to shout the name 'Boonratanathanakorn!' very loudly into a microphone as he crossed the line, as I sat in my plastic box, all alone.

A teenage Kazakh won the stage instead, with a bold solo attack. The TV pictures were so incoherent that I was only really able to follow what was going on courtesy of a series of helpful Whatsapp messages from a friend in the convoy.

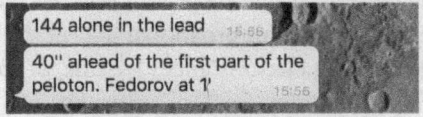

Without these messages, I might as well have had my eyes closed.

One of the treasures of being at races such as the Tour de Langkawi is that I am able to ferret away impressions of seminal moments in the developing careers of young riders who one day will make it to the very top. This has happened to Yevgeniy Fedorov, who was a valuable part of Mark Cavendish's final two Tour de France squads in 2023 and 2024. Watching him work on the front in the closing kilometres of a sprint in France I was transported back to the sweltering humidity, the grand colonial square in which the finish line had been set up and the passing rain bursts of Kuching on Borneo's northern coast. I was glad I'd seen that.

* * *

Though a great deal of effort went into it, a lack of resources and a certain need for experienced producers meant that the coverage of the race was necessarily patchy. I am being kind. If I were to be less kind, I'd have to say that it was mostly so incoherent as to be completely unwatchable: intermediate sprints missed entirely, shots so distant that nothing was recognisable, oddly positioned fixed cameras, an almost total lack of graphics, no distance to go information, etc. etc. etc. I feel bad recalling this and I think that it has now greatly improved (it was a new team taking over the TV coverage in 2020). But the lonely hours of broadcasting all on my own were not made easier by the pictures' total lack of narrative sense. We take for granted the way that conventional coverage of bike races conforms to a certain TV grammar (breakaway from behind, front of peloton, breakaway from alongside, front of peloton, helicopter, peloton from the side, repeat and fade). This gives order to what is often a disorderly affair. The race coverage was so sub-standard that my colleagues back in the UK who were trying to commentate for GCN Eurosport were stood down after just one stage. The way the race was covered was deemed simply too bad for broadcast.

There were mitigating circumstances for this, of course. Malaysia is a very developed country for the large part, but with a multitude of issues to overcome nonetheless, like most places around the world. One of them is corruption. The race had effectively been held to ransom for the two days of its stay on the island of Borneo by the contractor who had agreed to supply the statutory kilometres of barriers required by the UCI. The day before they were due to arrive, they simply doubled the price. Because they could and because no one else on the island could supply them.

But regardless of how it was being received across the world, the race rumbled on, talking mostly to a domestic audience, I suspect (and of course those three inebriated Christchurch rugby-playing students who I always imagine are watching). We flew back to the Malaysian mainland and restarted the race on the eastern coast of the peninsular, along which I ran for a few blissful kilometres very early the next morning, dropping my barefoot step into pristine white sand, and completely alone.

Early morning, looking out to sea in Malaysia.

At the end of my run, improbably hot and sweaty, I ventured into the inviting azure waves which had been crashing into the beach. I got no further than ankle-deep into the water before I lost confidence and turned around, sensing a vicious undertow that swept away the sand like a magician removing a tablecloth as each wave passed. Only just able to scrape a pass in my swimming competency badge at Robinson

Pools in Bedford in 1983, I decided against trying to outwit a vast and deeply unknowable ocean whose shores I had never before seen or felt beneath my feet. I trudged off instead for another bowl of rice, boiled eggs and small crunchy fish, washed down with black tea and accompanied by animated Malay chatter and the overbearing sweet perfume of Marlboro.

The race crashed in and out of Kuala Lumpur, for a start and finish beneath the preternaturally ugly Petronas towers, for reasons of naked petrochemical greenwashing. A start and finish in the same place once again allowed me to engage in one of my favourite pastimes at a bike race: introducing myself to people getting ready to race and pestering them with inane questioning which I could then turn to my advantage in the hours of commentary to come. I have done this often, sometimes extremely badly. I recall with a shiver the moment in Brussels that I decided to ask the young Belgian star Jasper Philipsen, making his debut at the 2019 Tour, which part of Denmark he came from.

'I'm Belgian,' he'd replied, accurately.

'Are you sure?' I wasn't about to go down without a fight.

So it was that in the shadow of the Malaysian capital's skyscrapers, I decided to bother the young Aussie sprinter Taj Jones, all bleach-blond and full of the usual Antipodean bonhomie. Jones was one of a fairly large contingent of Australians who rode in 2019 for continental (third level) teams who mostly race in Asia. All this heat and light and wonder was quite familiar to him, therefore, but would become less so when eventually he signed for Israel-Premier Tech and would perform his duties on mostly European soil. For only the second time in my life I tried – and failed – to get the South African climber Louis Meintjes into conversation. The first occasion had ended abruptly, after I'd asked him how he pronounced his name. 'Meintjes,' he'd answered me (a joke that will perhaps work better in the audiobook version of this chapter). The second time was in Kuala Lumpur.

'Hi Louis,' I said.

'Hi,' he said back, then rode off.

I chatted to the cerebral and very talented Metkel Eyob, an Eritrean rider whose career had washed up in Malaysia, riding for arguably Asia's biggest team, Terengganu Inc TSG, managed by former Team Sky rider, Jez Hunt.

Jez and I reminisced briefly about the time at the 2012 Tour of Britain when he and Bernie Eisel had decided to spend all night at a hotel bar near Crewe, and had found the next day's racing rather problematic. It got harder still when newly crowned Tour de France champion Bradley Wiggins took it upon himself to hit the front and explode the race as it wound up in the Peak District. Instantly Hunt, Eisel, and the race leader and World Champion Mark Cavendish, were shelled out of the back. Derbyshire seemed a very long way from Kuala Lumpur and, briefly, I fell into a reverie of wonder at how far the bicycle had taken us both, and couldn't really understand how or why any of it had happened. Then I spotted Cyril Gautier and his old mate Pierre Rolland, and left Jez for dead.

Rolland has always fascinated me, for reasons I can't explain. A brilliant double stage winner at the Tour in the early 2010s, he was never quite able to fulfil the unrealistic weight of expectation placed on him by elements within the French media. Then he made the fateful mistake of over-embracing the polka dots, when he led the king of the mountains competition, and his fate was sealed. He became something of a sidenote in the peloton thereafter, and the hubristic and oft-heard 'Attaque de Pierre Rolland!' settled into Tour folklore as a standard bearer for a probably ill-timed, almost totally pointless attack. It was unfair.

On only one other occasion had I had the chance to talk to Rolland. That had been after a stage of the 2017 Tour de France in the Alps when David Millar and I had ridden our Bromptons to the front of an almighty traffic jam, only to find the EF Education First team bus at the front of the queue. David, only a couple of years retired back then, decided to knock on the door and hitch a lift for us both. And so it was that I found myself sitting, ridiculous in my difference, at the front of the actual EF bus, alongside all their Tour de France riders, including Pierre Rolland, who was FaceTiming his family, debriefing after his modestly unspectacular 35th place on the finish line at Finhaut-Emosson. That had seemed the wrong moment to introduce myself.

My timing in Kuala Lumpur was once again inopportune. I strode boldly up to Gautier and Rolland, hand outstretched in greeting, and launched into my spiel. It was only then that I noticed both men were naked from the waist down and were trying hurriedly to get dressed with their modesty intact. Rolland looked pained and asked me to go away. Which I did. Perhaps he made the connection between the grinning fool in Malaysia and his sudden, and unwanted, bus companion of three years previous.

* * *

The next day's stage was the centrepiece of the race, the queen stage and the most important of them all for one of the pre-race favourites, Pierre Rolland (perhaps that explained the lack of a warm welcome from him the day before. Perhaps). The finish line, an annual occurrence at the Tour de Langkawi, was at a place called Genting Highlands, to the north-east of the capital, on the top of a steep, 21-kilometre climb into the Titiwangsa mountains.

Genting Highlands has nothing to do with Rob Roy, but everything to do with gambling. In fact, it is a simply colossal hotel complex built on the top of Mount Ulu Kali for one purpose alone: to lure Chinese tourists. Among the casinos, theme parks and shopping malls, there are seven hotels up there in the permanent clouds which shroud the top of the mountain all year long, including the First World Hotel (in which we had been billeted). This is the biggest hotel in the world with over 7000 rooms. The consequences, as I was to discover, of setting out from reception without asking for specific directions, are severe. I walked for what seemed like kilometres (because it actually was kilometres) down artificially lit corridors with lino on the floor and the walls, past gaily coloured doors all of which opened into identically designed micro-pens for people. It was one of the strangest places I have ever stayed the night and that includes the hotel in the Auvergne which was run by an over-productive taxidermist. To add to the David Lynch-ness of the experience, this was February 2020. Covid had already started to sweep across China. There *were* no tourists. As a consequence, the corridors were all empty. Outside a storm raged, black clouds whipping around the huge dystopia of Genting Highlands. The view from the concrete shaft outside my single cell, peering up through the weird light and cascading rainwater, was straight out of *Blade Runner*.

Genting Highlands looking dystopic.

The next day, having endured a terrifying, wet and frigid run along a new access road that was literally being hacked from the side of Ulu Kali by giant machines, I went to work in all the clothes I had with me, quite unprepared in my packing for the temperature, which had dropped by around 40 degrees. It began to sleet. The Costa Rican climber Kevin Rivera, in the logo minefield kit of Gianni Savio's Team Androni Giocattoli, emerged from the gloom to take the win. I had to wait nine minutes and 42 seconds (by which time I had stopped commentating and had started to jog back to the hotel) before I saw two figures complete their ascent of the final climb on the stage. Cyril Gautier and Pierre Rolland failed to acknowledge me again as they rolled over the line, largely ignoring not just me, but each other too. I raised an unreciprocated hand in greeting as I passed them, scampering to the warmth in the opposite direction.

Pierre Rolland coasting to the finish line, followed by Cyril Gautier.

The Tour de Langkawi came to an end after we had hopped our way up the western coast, via George Town on Penang, to the island which gives the race its name. The final stage saw repeated ascents of a very small climb on a finishing circuit, enough for the race to split, but not quite hard enough to drop Max Walscheid from the final selection. The German won the sprint, the Italian Danilo Celano won the overall, and the Tour de Langkawi came to a happy conclusion, at least as happy as it could be for me, given the fact that I was still dealing with the side effects of a frankly dangerous tom yum soup I had consumed all alone for lunch.

That soup was the single most violent food I have ever encountered. Whenever I feel a chill in my bones, I need only to cast my mind back to the agonising half hour of vicious sweating I endured, sitting in baking sunshine on the unshaded terrace of a restaurant in Kuah, feeding infinitesimally small amounts (in each spoonful enough liquid, perhaps, to nurse back to life an ailing elephant) of the fearsome soup into my commentator's mouth, which intermittently uttered the words 'I'm fine, thanks' when the waiter emerged once more to ask if everything was OK.

It was not OK, but on the other hand it was also OK, which is the way it goes on a lot of these trips.

So I left Malaysia, extremely hot, a little bothered, but deeply happy that I went. In my life, only bike racing offers this kind of crazy dive, deep into another land, from which you surface a week later sputtering, near drowned, but a far richer soul for it. And crying about soup.

13

FROM OUNDLE TO THE ALPE

In October of 2024 I travelled on my own to the World Championships in Zürich to watch both the women's and the men's elite road races. The first of those two, a race won with great panache by the astonishing Lotte Kopecky, was a brutal affair, conducted in freezing cold rain over a long and attritional course.

At the start just outside Zürich it was hammering with rain. The Swiss national team were called to the front of the bunch to stand still in the deluge and remember the extremely recent death of their young colleague, Muriel Furrer, who had lost her life in the Junior World Championship race. At the side of the road, hundreds of supporters, including a clutch of Eritreans, there to support their country's sole representative, bowed their heads. It was the hardest of days to win a race. It was beyond sombre.

Kopecky is, at the time of writing, a back-to-back World Champion, her career rapidly evolving as if in a test tube, acquiring all the different DNA required to thrive on the track, in bunch sprints, in the Classics and maybe in the future in the high mountains of the Tour de France, the Vuelta and the Giro. She is a complete rider and a remarkable human, who has proven impossible to crack, physically and psychologically. I will never forget watching her use the famous one-day race Nokere Koerse to push back against the pain she was enduring after losing her brother, Seppe. A promising young rider in his younger years, Seppe had died by suicide scarcely a week before the race. There should be more written about her. There should be a bloody statue to Lotte Kopecky, if there aren't already multiple monuments to her in cycling-crazed Belgium.

Back in Zürich, she had to overcome hellish conditions on the climbs and descents, and the combined might of a Dutch team which had perhaps four viable World Champion contenders in their ranks, one of whom was Kopecky's still-just-about-teammate Demi Vollering, with whom she had most profoundly fallen out. I remember speaking to the two of them at the glitzy Vélo d'Or ceremony in Paris in the autumn of 2023. I had no idea how little time they had for one another. They had masked their differences with dazzling aplomb.

At one point I found myself by the side of the road in a thick clump of spectators hard up against the barriers just outside the elegant brickwork and towering spire of the Frauenkirche. I fell into conversation with half a dozen semi-inebriated Dutch men, there to cheer on their national team, who had all the best cards to play in the race and yet still managed to make a complete arse of things. Each time the race came past us, they roared beerily at the bunch, trying to pick out the flashes of orange jerseys, whose bright shade had been dulled by the endless rain and grit of this greyest of days.

'Hop, hop, Marianne!'

'Allez, Demi!'

Round they went! To see Niewiadoma, Moolman-Pasio, Vos, Vollering, Longo-Borghini, Kopecky, Faulkner that close... it was every bit as thrilling for the crowd as the following day would prove to be when Pogačar battled Evenepoel and van der Poel for victory on the very same roads. And all around them supporters, mostly men, from across the continent and beyond were leaning across the barriers and bellowing. I don't know why, but that women's race, more than any other I had been present at, felt to me like the culmination of a process. It felt like it had no further point to prove, like the argument had been won.

* * *

Of course, one of the most profound changes in road racing since I was first exposed to it in 2003 is that women are now allowed to talk about it. Because they pretty much weren't back then. There were almost no female reporters when I started out, with the exception of Italy's national cycling treasure, the mighty Alessandra De Stefano, and certainly no female commentators. That started slowly to change. I think that Eurosport's multi-lingual reporter Laura Meseguer might have been among the first female reporters. Then, in her wake, the American networks, the Danes and even BskyB (when they'd bought a team) sent women to cover races. Since then, they have even started to write about cycling, too! And, in perhaps the most surprising move of all, women get to race some of the same races as the men.

This so-called 'equality' trend was *so* far from showing up as a blip on my radar screen back when I was first grappling with the sport that it might as well have been totally absent. Shamefully, I think there are a total of two female characters who make an appearance in *How I Won The Yellow Jumper*. No more than two in a cast of hundreds. One of these female walk-on parts in this phallogocentric paradigm is my partner, Kath, who appears at my side in Lewisham hospital after I have come off my bike and banged my head. She picks some gravel from my heroic elbow wound and suggests to the doctor that asking me which member of the royal family got married most recently is not a fit and proper concussion test. 'Ask him who won the Tour de France,' she had suggested instead. To which I had ventured, 'Was it me?'

The other lucky woman to make an appearance in what is otherwise a desert of white European men going about their arid business is Odette. Fittingly, Odette did the catering. Both of these cameo appearances by women are in 'nurturing' roles. Perhaps now you can see the length of the journey that I had to embark on.

It is, in microcosm, the same journey that the sport I cover has been on as well. The changes over the last 15 years have been extraordinary. It is fair to say, I think, that when I was first introduced to the sport, women's racing, whilst nominally a thing, was scarcely functional and by no means professional. A lot has changed, even if there remains much to do.

* * *

That pivotal year in the development and subsequent collapse of the UK cycling scene – 2014 – was the first time I was sent to cover women's racing. It was to present TV coverage of the inaugural Women's Tour. The word 'Britain' was omitted from the title of the race, incidentally, so that the race organiser, a company called Sweetspot, could avoid having to pay a six-figure annual licence to British Cycling. Yes, the sport really is that mad. Whatever it was called, the week-long stage race had the stated aim of becoming the most important date in a racing calendar that was even more patched together than the men's and significantly more threadbare. The Women's Tour hasn't yet achieved that stated aim and will now almost certainly never rise to be the biggest race in the world, given that ASO have resuscitated the long-dormant Tour de France Femmes. But the race played a big part in the growth of women's racing. I loved it straight away.

For a start, it fiddled around places of no distinct attributes, like Oundle, Northampton, Hinckley and Bedford, which I was allowed to be affectionately dismissive of since these are the places where I grew up. The race got off to a low-key start, in some ways, but in other ways the opposite was true. It had an immediate impact and not least on the women on the start list. They were instantly impressed.

I remember Marianne Vos turning up to a press conference at a venue in Bury St Edmunds and being overwhelmed by the turn-out. Unused to the sight of journalists actually bothering to cover women's racing, she had not anticipated the demand for her time that was evident in a packed conference room. Perhaps it was a function of Britain's Olympic fixation and Vos's still recent victory ahead of Lizzie Armitstead (as was) in the pouring rain on the Mall in 2012, but the buzz caused by her appearance certainly took her by surprise.

Even more surprising, perhaps, was when one of the journalists from a local newspaper asked her for her opinion on the state of Suffolk's roads and the number of potholes. Without so much as breaking stride, the 2012 Road Race Champion of the London games dealt deftly with the questioner and politely side-stepped the debate to a quick round of applause from the other members of the press with slightly better questions up their sleeves. Slightly.

'Is this a bit like the Tour de France, would you say?' the next one piped up, notebook in hand.

* * *

The race went about its business with all the usual eccentricities you would normally associate with road racing. In Felixstowe, during a torrential downpour ahead of the race, the riders tried to keep dry by warming up in the doorway of a branch of Clinton's Cards. The shop, I remember, was open for business. Behind the display window with its mugs, calendars and fluffy red love hearts, I could just about make out the shop's staff gazing back at the sight of four athletes blocking out the light as they balanced their bikes on rollers and started spinning their legs out. This was not a common sight in those parts.

That day the race finished in Clacton-on-Sea. In the final couple of kilometres, just as the race route swung the peloton into town for another bunch sprint (every day was a bunch sprint), a resident on a mobility scooter, presumably infuriated by not being able to cross the road, spotted the slightest of gaps in the peloton, stuck the vehicle into gear and just went for it. How he managed to avoid unseating himself and a hundred riders travelling at 60 kph it is impossible to say. But the margin for error was slight. Given that somehow nothing bad came of a potential calamity, and once we knew that disaster had been averted, it was OK to laugh. Nothing, but nothing, said 'bike race in Clacton' more than a mobility scooter darting through the middle of a leadout.

That said, the first year of the Women's Tour was, from a competitive sporting perspective, a humdrum affair. Back then, and it is only just over a decade ago, the women's peloton was far thinner than it is now in terms of top talent. Lotte Kopecky was only just starting out as a teenager, Demi Vollering was still five years away from her professional debut, and Annemiek van Vleuten had not yet begun her extraordinary rise to the very top. It was, in fact, the Marianne Vos show. After Vos, there was something of a gulf to the rest. As a result, at the Women's Tour there were very few breakaways to speak of. The peloton simply rolled through, each and every day, towards the inevitable finale.

Notwithstanding all that, Vos was somehow beaten by Emma Johanssen on stage one and her team allowed two Italians to escape on stage two to Bedford, on another day of horrible rain. But after that she won everything, including the next three stages, the GC and the points classification. At the final podium back in Bury St Edmunds, she seemed thrilled with the outcome. And not just because of her results. The race had been a triumph, enjoying the kind of support women's racing almost never got back then, outside of an Olympic Games.

* * *

The following year, when Marianne Vos was injured, she was somehow persuaded to work for TV instead, joining me as a pundit for the week of the race. On her very first day in the role, she and I witnessed a freak accident that has entered cycling history. It was a completely unprecedented incident and remains to this day a historical curiosity.

Sprinting to victory on stage one in Aldeburgh, Lizzie Armitstead put her arms in the air to celebrate, only to find a gust of wind catching her wheel. She briefly lost control and, though she somehow managed to plant her hands back on the bar, she flew towards the line of photographers fanning out into the road to catch the winning shot. She clattered straight into the hi-viz-wearing marshal trying to push the snappers out of the way, who also just happened to be the race director, Mick Bennett. The impact nearly broke his arm and, more importantly, she nearly broke herself. For a long, long time, paramedics stayed at her side as she lay prone on the tarmac. The crowd was asked to retreat to give them space to work. After what seemed like an age, they then placed her on to a stretcher and heli-coptered her off the race.

Marianne and I had to record the closing chat of the TV show without the faintest idea how bad Lizzie's injuries were, but at the time it seemed to us that they might genuinely be career-ending, if not life-threatening. It was the Dutch champion's first day at work doing TV and straight away, in a second language, she had to deal with something like that.

Astonishingly, Lizzie walked out of hospital later that evening, declaring that she quite wanted to carry on (she was talked out of it). But to this day, she is the only rider in the history of the sport ever to have won the first stage, taken the leader's jersey and never pulled it on. She never made it to the podium; a unique achievement and one that I would often remind her of when we started to work together many years later.

Travelling around East Anglia in a small hire car with Marianne Vos was a fine privilege, replete with surprises, as I got to know the idiosyncrasies of this phenomenal athlete. In the mornings we would call in on her mum and dad, Henk and Connie. They were in the habit (and as far as I am aware, they still are) of following the Women's Tour in their camper van, which was all the more remark-able given that their star daughter wasn't even in the race. They had a cat too, which would slink around East Anglian car parks on a lead. It went by the excellent name of 'Sjekkie', which translates as 'Rollie', a tribute to Connie's devoted habit of smoking endless loose-tobacco roll-your-own ciggies. This Vos family context was not what I had imagined it to be.

But Marianne was great company; faultlessly patient with the public, gently amused and amusing on the journey. She would contrive to ride all the way to the stage finish as soon as we had done the opening to the show in the morning and, once she had figured out that she would only be seen from the waist up, was often ready to go riding the moment the cameras stopped rolling.

Marianne Vos wasted no time getting changed.

I remember turning up at the stiflingly twee stage start in Henley with her and pausing at the statue to Sir Steve Redgrave. 'Who's he?' she asked. And when I explained, she looked thoroughly underwhelmed, as if to suggest that she was confident of winning far more gold medals than he ever did.

But rowing wasn't the only other sport we discussed. She was intrigued by my association with darts, having met the Dutch superstar of the sport, Michael van Gerwen, at some TV awards event in the Netherlands.

'He's the guy who looks like a giant baby, right?'

'He does, Marianne.' I nodded. 'He does indeed look a bit like a giant baby.' Then I asked her if she had ever thrown a dart, slightly surprised to be having this conversation at all with the former World and reigning Olympic Champion.

'Never,' she answered.

I told her I thought she'd probably be brilliant at it. Then, at the end of the week, and after our work together was complete, I had some special MV-initialled rainbow-band dart flights made for her. Then I bought her a set of darts to match, which I intended on posting off to her house in the Netherlands. It was only as I was packaging it up that I realised they would be completely useless without a dart board to throw them at. So I had to buy one of those as well. The whole thing cost me a fortune to post. And to this day, I wonder what she did with it. My best bet is that it's half-unwrapped and up in her loft, gathering dust. I like to think it was the thought that counts, but perhaps some thoughts are better off being jettisoned rather than unnecessarily enacted. Sending a dart board to Marianne Vos might be just such an idea.

Marianne and me, somewhere in East Anglia, 2015.

Bit by bit, after that shaky introduction to women's racing, my involvement grew; admittedly from non-existent to something-almost-existent, rather than an avalanche of races coming my way.

At one surreal point in 2015 I even found myself almost brokering the first ever foreign *Grand Départ* for a British stage race, when I suggested to the CEO of the port of Rotterdam that he brought the Women's Tour to the Netherlands. He seemed genuinely enthused by the prospect, discussed over a fairly boozy dinner in Utrecht on the eve of the men's Tour de France. Along with one of the senior race organisers of the Women's Tour, we even named him a price (made up, I suspect, on the fly), to which he seemed readily to agree. I became giddy at the completely illusory influence I misguidedly believed myself to wield. And although the idea never came to fruition, I didn't hesitate to claim credit when eventually the Tour de France Femmes came to the Netherlands in 2024 and spent time in Rotterdam.

* * *

For the next few years I was sporadically involved in commentating on women's races, but far fewer than I would have wanted. There was the now defunct Tour de Yorkshire, with its women's version that made history for offering parity in prize money. This, while being a good thing, papered over the very obvious fact that for most men the prize money on offer is of little consequence, but for the women it is sometimes pretty much everything, even for the stars. Proper salaries in the women's peloton were mostly wishful thinking.

I was fortunate to have worked on a couple of editions of Strade Bianche, too. And for a clutch of years we showed La Course during the men's Tour de France on ITV. In the course of those duties, and by working with colleagues like Dani Rowe, Lizzie Deignan, Sarah Storey, Joanna Rowsell, Lucy Martin and Hayley Simmonds I learned to understand that the women's peloton operated according to a very different style of racing.

During those years, with Marianne Vos no longer 'The Unbeatable' that she had been pre-injury troubles, especially at world tour races, the same group of riders seemed to contest every finale, whether it was a hilly Classic, a flat sprint or something in between. As a result, it was fun to follow. Viewers got to know the protagonists, to know their strengths and weaknesses. It introduced a welcome sense of soap opera into the racing, as viewers warmed to the various characters, and it was all the better for it.

And almost routinely, the racing seemed to offer up unexpected plot twists and drama with a frequency that left men's racing looking stolid and predictable. Lizzie's victory at the 2020 edition of La Course, outsprinting her old rival Marianne, was a good example, but so too were the previous years of that stepping stone of a one-day race, the precursor to the re-launch of the Tour de France Femmes. The previous summer, Marianne Vos had claimed the victory with a vicious attack up the steep final ramp before the finishing straight in Pau. It was a perfectly calibrated effort that looked unlikely to succeed, but with hindsight was absolutely irresistible. And prior to that even, in 2018, the way that Annemiek van Vleuten caught Anna van der Breggen *just* before the line in Le Grand Bornand was one of the most extraordinary finales to any race I had ever seen. Yes, this was good stuff. It was, in fact, fantastic.

* * *

It would be a few years until Lizzie (by now) Deignan came to work with us on ITV's coverage of the men's Tour de France. This coincided with her second pregnancy, with baby Shea.

Lizzie at the Tour for ITV in 2022.

She dropped into our team during the first rest day of the 2022 Tour de France, by which time we had reached the poshest part of the Alps, which automatically triggered my usual diatribe about this over-populated, over-rated mountain range which seems to act as a magnet for the most tiresome people on the planet. This is an unreasonable position, of course, but it's one that I have built over many, many summers and after witnessing annually how these great mountains are overrun by humanity. But not just humanity: humanity with a free polka dot Carrefour hat on, a half-empty bottle of rosé in one hand and a selfie-stick in the other.

We were in Megève. It was my birthday. David and Pete decided that they would buy me dinner, an act of generosity that greatly amused Lizzie as it became apparent just how much each item in the restaurant's ridiculous menu cost. A vegetarian like Pete, Lizzie ordered the only thing she could eat from the list of options, which turned out to be a €40 artichoke. Her bafflement at the extravagantly leafy vegetable, smothered in olive oil, was matched only by her mirth at how much it was costing Pete and David. This amused her enormously. It was over the course of that long summer evening in July 2022, over unnecessary desserts and digestifs (not for Lizzie, of course, but she egged us on), that I started to discover for the first time what an excellent person Lizzie Deignan is: how wicked, how grounded, how bright and how, simply, excellent.

She is also a bona fide pioneer. That much goes without saying. Along with a number of other riders of her generation, she bridged the divide between a sport that few paid attention to and the juggernaut that women's racing is now threatening to become. I remembered years ago hosting an event that we both attended in London, shortly after her World Championship win in 2015, in which, bereft of a proper line of questioning, I asked her the slightly lazy journalistic cliché, 'Do you ever find yourself watching back some of your victories on TV?'

She wrinkled her nose dismissively and shook her head. 'No, never.' I asked her why.

'Almost none of them were on TV,' was her honest reply. 'Those tapes don't exist.' It was a fact I had never considered before. Only the very biggest races in the women's calendar had any kind of TV coverage and it was almost never live. More often than not she had pursued her career in a vacuum.

Over the course of those three weeks of her late pregnancy in 2022 (ahead of her second comeback from maternity leave, the first of which had instantly resulted in her winning the inaugural Paris–Roubaix for women), I got to understand just how deceptive the appearance of women's racing had been for so long. Though it appeared to look like a professional sport, the women were treated with contempt by a system that had not even started to monetise and professionalise, let alone distribute the spoils to the riders. When

Lizzie told us what she had been offered by her long-time team Boels Dolmans, for whom she had won a hatful of races, we all assumed that she was joking. She, a former World Champion, and one of the biggest names in the peloton, could have earned more in six months stacking supermarket shelves part-time than racing for the biggest team in the peloton.

It has only really been the last few years of her career which have seen her rewarded with anything like an appropriate salary for an athlete of her stature, something which goes some way to explaining why she has continued to race perhaps a little longer than many people were expecting. After all, after a decade and more of dedication to the sport, for precious little in return, she was just beginning to be rewarded and why on earth would she walk away from that? Not that there is any bitterness in her attitude. Regret that things have been slow to change, perhaps. But pride also that they have finally changed and that her young teammates (she is particularly fond, it strikes me, of Gaia Realini) can look forward to a long and productive career; proud of her part in the revolution.

Preparing to descend Alpe d'Huez on folding bikes.

My memories of descending Alpe d'Huez on folding bikes with a heavily pregnant Lizzie Deignan after commentating on Tom Pidcock's win there in 2022 are among the fondest of my many years of the Tour. Baking heat had by late afternoon given way to a luxurious warmth that tumbled off the mountainside, and down towards the thousands of immobile vehicles and tens of thousands of people inching their way through Bourg d'Oisans. Pete and David, Lizzie and I all left at the same time, faced with the same descent off Alpe d'Huez to rejoin the car, which David and I had driven down to the bottom and left there earlier on that morning. Years of hard-won experience at the Tour invariably results in a military-style battle plan being drawn up before work to best facilitate the most painless exit available; something that is not always possible.

But this seemed like a good plan, at least once we had broken free from the various arbitrary police cordons detaining everyone from progressing down the mountain: car drivers, pedestrians and the many, many thousands of cyclists. In such potentially fraught situations, and with a natural and inbuilt fear of authority and uniforms, I have learned simply to follow pro riders. Deignan, Kennaugh and Millar, armed with decades of racing years behind them, a lanyard with some form of legitimacy dangling around their necks and a fairly ingrained if subconscious sense of entitlement, were simply not going to be delayed for the simple reason that an officer of the law was in the way.

From my place at the back of our quartet of Bromptons, I could best observe the tiny signs from any one of them that signalled they were about to attack: a twitch, a duck of the shoulder under police tape, a rolling back of the pedals in anticipation of an imminent sprint. And with the curious sight of the three pros (two ex-, one very pregnant) trying to get all aero on a bike with, to put it bluntly, clown's wheels, we were gone again, followed down the Alp by nothing more effective than the increasingly distant shouts from the gendarmes and whistle blasts that had faded into the background noise of a summery afternoon at the Tour by the time we had reached the next hairpin.

And it was there that we caught up with the publicity caravan; all its constituent parts still doing battle with the 21 switchbacks of Alpe d'Huez and the tens of thousands of inebriates on the road. The road was blocked, as far as the eye could see. To most people, this would have been seen as something of a setback, but to David Millar and Pete Kennaugh it was simply the unspoken flag drop on a new kind of race; the first time that they had duelled with one another for any kind of major honour since battling out the British National Championships in Glasgow 2013. In an instant they were gone, threading impossible-seeming lines between trucks with massive carbon fibre cheeses on the back and still bigger vehicles built to resemble bottles of washing up liquid from which students in brightly coloured clothing were being suspended upside down.

Letting David and Pete indulge their irresistible urge to race one another, Lizzie and I took our time descending the 13 kilometres of hairpins, weaving our way through the crowds flowing off the mountain and threading a path through a slow-moving armada of brightly coloured floats from the publicity caravan. Lizzie took it rather easier than the retired show-off men. By the time she and I had crawled through the traffic and made it to the car at the bottom, Pete and David had been sitting in wait for us for quarter of an hour.

'At least Ned stayed back and made sure I was all right on the descent,' Lizzie said, berating Pete and David. 'He was a gentleman.' I beamed at the other two blokes, not wanting to admit to the fact that I couldn't actually have gone any faster on the descent and there was no 'staying back' involved. But I let Lizzie carry on her assault unabated on my two male colleagues and close friends.

'Fragile masculinity,' she concluded. I couldn't have agreed more. David and Pete offered nothing by way of defence. Because there was no defending the fact that, with a combined age of 80 or thereabouts, the pair of them had just behaved like a couple of 11-year-olds. To this day, however, I suspect they are secretly proud of themselves.

And then, instead of sitting in a traffic jam, we all went to a very modest bistro for an even more modest dinner, in which we all laughed about the glorious absurdity of it all: France, summer and the madness of a sport which defies logic, challenges everything and might finally be dragging itself into the 21st century, where men and women share equally not just in its dark privations, but in their mirror opposite: the glittering prizes for which successive generations have been quietly fighting.

* * *

I have been fortunate to have witnessed these years, and experienced my occasional forays into the pelotons of the women's World Tour, in the company of two such outstanding humans, racers and rivals as Marianne Vos and Lizzie Deignan.

One day I will ask Marianne about the dart board and, who knows, perhaps I might get to play a leg of 501 against her. Or Round the Clock. Come to think of it, that might be less ambitious.

In the spring of 2023, the day after I had commentated at Milan–Sanremo, I called in on the Deignan family at the compact flat that they used to rent in Monaco. With their newest addition, Shea, still very much a babe-in-arms, Lizzie had tentatively resumed her training regime. Not one member of her team's medical or physio staff had offered her any support or advice on how to approach the considerable complications and potential pitfalls of training after a second birth and while breastfeeding. So Lizzie, resourceful as ever, was simply getting on with it herself, devising her own methodology. Let's face it, she knew more than anyone else about how to go about it. There wasn't much they could tell her that she didn't know anyway.

I spent a few hours in their company, with little Orla repeatedly offering me toys from her collection of fairies and mermaids, before Phil (Lizzie's ex-Team Sky rider husband) took the kids out for a walk. Then I left them to it, feeling nothing but respect for this family that has determinedly done things their own way, subverting established gender roles and pushing for equality in a sport that has started, belatedly, to move in the right direction.

The advent of the Tour de France Femmes has moved the sport to a position it could scarcely have dreamed of occupying 10 years ago, when such progress still seemed fanciful and drunken talk of bringing the women to Rotterdam was just that: drunken talk. But there it was. The women's road race at the Paris Olympics produced one of the most fascinating final five kilometres of any race that year and, in Kristen Faulkner, a worthy champion. The American was rewarded in extravagant fashion for an intuitive move which was nothing short of tactical genius when she attacked the trio of riders that included Vos and Lotte Kopecky.

However, I would argue that the duel just a few weeks later between Kasia Niewiadoma and Demi Vollering for the overall victory at the Tour de France on the slopes of Alpe d'Huez was the single day of racing which sealed the deal in the public's mind. Unable to be there in person, I was glued instead to the live stream on a laptop at my desk in London, gripped to the last exhausted gasp of a race that had held us in a four-second suspense to the final finishing line on the most famous mountain of them all. I just wish the mountain had been as crowded for Kasia and Demi on the way up as it had been for David, Pete, Lizzie and me on the way down. One day it will be and I suspect that day will come sooner than expected.

14

GIROSCOPE

I can't be sure, but I think I may have had a spiritual awakening on one of the many, many long drives at the Giro d'Italia. It might be the first time that this has happened to anyone while at the wheel of a hired Fiat, speed-eating Haribos simply to stay awake. But awakenings come in all shapes and sizes, and I guess some are possible while listening to the Bee Gees and scratching the side of one's nose.

The drive to the hotel, 'transfers' as we like to call them, coining pseudo-military terminology to give our journey more drama, are often three hours long and come at the end of a six-hour commentary shift. They follow the route of Italy's endless, winding network of *autostrade*, which narrow with terrifying suddenness as they cut through rearing Apennine massifs. The geometric perfection of the bewildering thousands of mighty tunnels drilled through the country's rock draws you on towards the vanishing point of electric lights and kerbside paint until, in a flash of white-yellow light, you are propelled into a valley on the other side of the mountain. That's when the awakening happened.

Out into the light Italy reveals itself to you once again, for the hundredth time, slightly changed; her features re-assembled, the scale either shrunk or expanded, the play of shadow and green re-shuffled to give the land a fresh, surprising countenance. In the distance, still-snowy peaks, mute and unforgiving behind huge plains set at angles into the horizon. There are dots of humanity, salmon-roofed Tuscan farmhouses, Abruzzo's grey-slated villages and those hilltop towns, tokens of corralled nature which people have shored up against the infinity of the scene; cypress trees pointing to a painter's sky indifferent in its immensity to the world it drifts past at its uncontained azure depth.

I was watching all this through a moving windscreen during my fifth lap of Italy when I fleetingly caught a complete but intangible sense of the purpose of the Giro; its conception and meaning. I had a vision of all of Italy and the terrifying tininess of a single human life; an individual placed in the land, unwillingly perhaps, not out of choice. Asking themselves, with a sweeping gesture, 'Now here I am, what am I to do with all this?' The answer to this enormous question, or at least one possible answer of many, is: 'I will do the Giro!' I will make up a profoundly beautiful procession through Italy's manifest wonders. A ridiculous undertaking; a pilgrimage of the mind and a calvary of the body. A poetic screed written in asphalt and in seconds. A homage to being in a specific place at a certain time.

There are, of course, three grand tours in the calendar. Much of my attention and my focus, over many years, has been centred around July and France. But there is something more untamed and intimidating about the Giro d'Italia's capricious weather and nervous, twitchy nature. It's like the charismatic but slightly untrustworthy kid you knew at school who slid between friendship groups with ease, found respect wherever they ended up, but would drop you as a friend without so much as a flicker of regret. Friends like that are capable of great charm. But they can inflict the gravest harm with a look or a cutting comment.

I have grown to love the Giro, but it has taken time, more time than I needed to grow to love the Tour. And the process has been entirely on its terms and not mine.

* * *

I could have picked out any edition of the Giro d'Italia, pulling its bundle of wrinkles from the suitcase into which it had been packed away, unpacked and then packed away once again, every day for the last 21. Then I could have smoothed out its crumpled contours, ignored its pinkish wine-stains and coffee-cup marks, and noted down all the many visible traces of another journey round Italy, the dried liquid reminders of a race that does what it does. This three-week trip in May consistently leaves me with memories of the greatest intensity that the world of cycling has to offer. And each time I go back, rather than growing accustomed to it, the impressions seem grander, more colourful, more full of life with everything that entails; sensory pleasure, great serenity, foreboding and awe. Lots of awe.

I could have told you about the year that the valiant, broad-shouldered Steven Kruijswijk came to within a day or two of victory, only to find himself spooked by the light blue, spectral presence of Vincenzo Nibali. In 2016 I watched that all unfolding on a tiny monitor, freezing cold in a commentary truck whose heating had failed, not for the first time, and clutched my pen that bit harder as the likeable Dutchman, unable to live with the pressure of the moment, catapulted himself into a snow-bank in the thin mountain air and relinquished his challenge. Or, five years later, when the race re-booted back to May, post-Covid, watching again in bobble hat and puffer jacket, as Egan Bernal hung on to victory three weeks later in the face of a titanic collapse of morale. The Colombian was rescued only by his compatriot and teammate Dani Martínez turning around in his saddle to roar at his leader, berating him for succumbing to defeat. That is a picture from the Giro that I will never forget.

The next year it began in Budapest, intriguing in its meat-based cuisine, its Austro-Hungarian elegance and uncomfortable present-day politics. Matt Stephens and I spent those few sunny days before the opening time trial enjoying this great city, with its ancient metro line and views across the broad sweep of the Danube, in the occasional and cheerful company of the great (former Giro winner) Stephen Roche who had temporarily taken up residence there. Stephen's life has always been an adventure; one which shows no sign of slowing up.

With Matt Stephens and Stephen Roche in Hungary in 2022.

That year the story of the race centred on how Jai Hindley broke the spirit of Richard Carapaz, leaving his defining attack until the very last kilometres of the very last climb of a mighty race, high, high up in the jagged peaks of the Dolomites. And how Geraint Thomas was similarly put to the sword by Primož Roglič in 2023, again at the very last opportunity on a day when Slovenians poured across the border into Italy and annexed the freakishly steep Monte Lussari for their homeland. Tears flowed that day and the next. Mark Cavendish, who won the final sprint in Rome, thanks in no small part to a spontaneous leadout by Thomas, told me later in great detail about how he and the Welshman had both started to cry uncontrollably as they waited to sign on for the last stage. It's what the race does.

I could have written about the wild dogs, openly corrupt police (we once paid a traffic fine by swiping a contactless card at a reader behind a bar and left without any kind of receipt) and the broken roads of Sicily, with its olives and lemons, its empty interior and sultry coast. We could have spent time in this chapter in a sudden downpour along the Amalfi coast; wondering at the shepherds' cottages high up in the Campania Apennines; standing at the top of Gran Sasso as snowflakes settled on my nose; staring at the edifice of the fascist-designed hotel building from which Mussolini had been freed by the SS after his removal from office.

And all this before even talking about the race, with its pretty hilltop finishes, its annual riders' strikes and its carnival of suffering. The book would run to a thousand pages and we might not have got past stage three.

* * *

But then, in 2024, Tadej Pogačar decided to race the Giro for the first time. And everything changed again.

It wasn't the first time that he'd been to the Giro, of course. As a child he used to be driven across the Slovenian border to follow the race in the Dolomites. But now he was at the race. He decided to turn up with a number on his back for the first time and won it by a recent record margin. And in doing so, he helped me understand the race in an even more complete sense.

It was as if something about his ridiculous mastery of the Giro stripped away those residual feelings of uncertainty with which I'd always approached the Italian grand tour. Just as Pogačar had never before raced the Santuario di Oropa, the Prati di Tivo or the Sappada climbs, the weight of all that accrued history at the Giro, most of which centred on Fausto Coppi, Gino Bartali and Marco Pantani, had intimidated me for years. I had long been grappling with unfamiliar terms that I knew were ingrained into the soul of Italian cycling, and the old imposter syndrome with which I had begun my career in cycling returned once more to plague me. But Pogačar's insouciance swept away my tired preoccupations with feelings of inadequacy. He simply turned up and won. He made it look simple. He tamed the Giro. Its mythology didn't need to be as frightening as I had always assumed.

* * *

My plane dropped into Lombardy, losing altitude just as the Alps gained theirs. Slowly, I was being inserted into another edition of the Giro d'Italia. I knew already that the next three weeks would pass in a succession of late-night arrivals at hotels, dumping luggage damp with rain in foyers that smelled of roasted meat and melting cheese, being handed a key attached to a wooden fob. *La camera* 201, 312, 208, 15, 420, 128, 307, *la terzo piano*. Brightly lit breakfast rooms with insipid fruit salads, incredibly dry toast in plastic sachets, dull pastries, perversely red orange squash. Finish lines debasing the splendour of Renaissance piazzas, tiny hilltop villages, fog-bound peaks, beachside boulevards with shops selling sunglasses, beach balls, and aprons and mugs with Mussolini's or even Hitler's face on them. Days passing through violently bright sunshine to hailstorms and every shade of weather in between. A din of hyperbole, language stretched beyond its meaning, snow-banked mountain passes, baroque gilt skies, sweet cakes on the tongue and bitter coffee at the back of the throat, pink balloons that stay with you when you close your eyes and the thud of rotor blades as the backdrop to all of life.

From time to time, as I pressed my nose against the vibrating, scratched Perspex, I caught sight of the Po river, switching, bifurcating, passing through little towns with a campanile still proudly at their heart. It was an unseasonably chilly late spring, 1 May to be precise. Different layers of cloud were stacked up at dizzying altitudes; clumped in waves, piling up ever greyer into the heights or stretched like fine dough above, suspended in the ever-reaching nowhere of a grey sky. The plane's wing dipped smoothly but briskly to reveal an orderly town beneath, laid out in the circularity of the passing centuries, like the bark on a tree. And beyond, I could see the brown/silver waters of the rice fields catch the late afternoon sun as, for the umpteenth time, I approached Malpensa's long slab of a runway from the air.

An hour or two later, standing in the shuttered gloom of a tiled Italian hotel room, patting down all the pockets in my clothing (and there were many), I realised with a sense of predictable malaise bordering on something Jean-Paul Sartre would have had a specific term for, that I had lost my passport. It had dropped out of my pocket somewhere in the terminal. Here I was, days away from the start of the Giro, without any means of identifying myself: stateless, in effect. Yet somehow, I didn't really mind. That, if nothing else, speaks to the heart of the Giro's power to strip all before it of importance. I hadn't, in fact, lost my passport. It had slipped down into that gap between car seat and door; a typically treacherous Giro-style move.

In Turin it poured with cold rain, the last grip that winter exerted on Piedmont that year, one which had loosened by the time the race got underway a couple of days later. Matt Stephens and I just about made it to a pizza place near the Valentina gardens before the deluge began. But by the time we had hungrily sliced and swallowed our dinners, and Matt had seen off a half litre of wine in a glass carafe ('It's only the team presentation'), a serious storm had set in, battering the elegant streets that lead down to the river with a consistent, vertical onslaught of rainwater that did not let up until every rider had got a soaking. Matt and I had to run to the neo-classical elegance of Castello del Valentino, avoiding as many puddles as possible. He had a silly little fold-away brolly, far too small to share, but big enough just about to keep him dry, if not entirely sober. His opening line of commentary, as the presentation got underway, had us both reaching for the mute buttons to allow for the first spontaneous fit of laughter which we would suffer. The first of many.

'The veteran of the 2000 Giro and two-time British national champion Matt Stephens, alongside me for the next three weeks ...' I introduced my colleague for the first time. 'What are you expecting from the race?'

Matt had pressed the red 'on-air' button and before he knew it, had blurted out, 'Well, I think we're going to see the most open race in years...'

It was of course, the opposite of what he meant – and entirely wrong. He switched off his mic and, doubled up with laughter, mouthed at me, 'It's the first thing that came out of my mouth!'

Tadej Pogačar was an unprecedentedly certain favourite to win the race, something of which everyone with even a cursory under-standing of the Giro was all too aware. Wine had intervened in Matt's thinking, rendering his words instantly wrong, but no less funny for being blissfully stupid. He looked once again at me, this time in blind panic, turned the mic back on and tried to wrench his sentence through a handbrake turn, hoping that no one would notice, '...open in as much as we are going into a race in which it could be that one rider is dominant.'

Pogačar was the last of 176 riders to be introduced. It was almost 9 p.m. before he sauntered up the ramp and on to the massive stage, purpose built for the occasion. Ignoring the ponderous question put to him by one of the three co-hosts of this wonderfully sentimental and overstated event (the dance troupe from Kyiv had no idea why they were there, but had themed their performance along the eter-nal lines of dreams and journeys, and something to do with pink), he grabbed the microphone and saluted the audience, turning away from his interviewer. 'It's actually amazing that you have waited here in this terrible weather.'

* * *

The next evening, Matt and I suggested the crew ate at the Taverna dell'Oca, an unremarkable-looking *ristorante* in the Via dei Mille, which we had discovered a year or two previously when, together with my partner, Kath, we had gone on a brief holiday after Milan–Sanremo, ending up in Munich, but stopping for a couple of nights in Turin. I have been there many times since. It is quite simply the best place I've ever eaten in, not just because of the food (simple, a bit unusual, and made with such care and pride), but mainly because the lady who runs the front of house is just the right mix of rude and charming. She also looks like a cross between Ruth Madoc from *Hi-de-Hi!* and Sinead O'Connor, if you can imagine such a person serving perfect raviolis and pouring Nebbiolo into massive wine glasses. It takes a certain amount of Nebbiolo to achieve such a heightened state of awareness.

One of our crew was actually from Turin, born and bred, so to invite him to a restaurant he didn't even know existed had been a substantial act of faith. The responsibility of introducing an Italian to an Italian place in Italy had left me reeling, but when, at the end of the evening, as we posed for photos with 'Ruth O'Connor' and the rest of the team, he turned to me with Nebbiolo-fuelled sentimentality and declared that this was the 'finest restaurant in all of Torino', I almost kissed him. This was a young Italian's way of proclaiming that I was his best mate. For the next three weeks at work we pretended nothing had happened.

Posing with the chef and waiters at the Taverna dell'Oca, Turin.

The next day, the sun shone brightly. I made my way up the Superga climb overlooking Turin, making sure to call in once again at the memorial around the back of the hillside to the victims of the Grande Torino air disaster of 1949, which claimed 37 lives. By a rather extraordinary quirk of fate, the race was due to start in Turin on the exact day of the 75th anniversary of the tragedy. The synchronicity of the timing, for a race which celebrates culture and nods to the wider context like few others, carried with it enormous significance in the Italian psyche. It was to be a very moving occasion, when eventually the riders (Pogačar already marauding) made their way through thick crowds of cycling/football fans, all wearing the dark blood-red of Grande Torino.

Most of the dead on the terrible night were members of that great Torino football team, returning from a testimonial match in Lisbon. Their plane had crashed into the back of the Superga hill, behind the famous domed Madonna delle Grazie basilica. One of the dead was an Englishman, Leslie Lievesley, who was a coach at Torino.

I made my way to the other side of the church and looked north towards Turin, laid out in its entirety at the foot of the climb. Antonelli's famous tower twinkled in the sun. The river Po flowed swiftly across the city and Turin's succession of broad avenues led dead straight towards a horizon which ended abruptly with the start of the Alps, still snow topped and unimaginably high. It was there that I was contacted by someone travelling to Turin with Bill Lievesley, Leslie's son.

The following morning, before the race started, I spent a sun-blessed hour in the company of Bill, drinking a cappuccino and watching him slowly consuming a croissant (confusingly referred to as a *brioche* in Italian) outside the elegant Caffè Elena on the Piazza Vittorio Veneto. Bill, as frank and funny a Yorkshireman as you could ever wish to meet, was back as a guest of honour for the commemoration. Bill was just days short of his 11th birthday and had been looking forward to his dad's return from another overseas work trip when his mother called him. He had been playing on the streets of Turin outside the apartment that the club had hired for their family. 'Something's happened,' she said. With those words a blissful life in Italy came to an abrupt end and the family returned to Grassington ('What a dump' as Bill would describe it 75 years later).

Bill's life forged a tangible connection between the two events: the 2024 Giro and the 1949 Grande Torino disaster. Sitting opposite me, smiling at a lifetime of recollections, Bill joined the dots of the story. Settled now in England, Bill went on to discover cycling through his workplace in a metal workshop. He even raced two editions of the Tour of Britain in a peloton that featured Jimmy Savile, but that's another story. He knew Tom Simpson, who sold him his Great Britain kit from the World Championships as he was skint at the time. His late father's football career gave way in Bill's life to a passion for cycling, which endures to this day.

Listening to his extraordinary testimony, sitting in the sudden warmth of another 1 May, 75 years on from his terrible bereavement, it would have been tempting to conclude that the race I was about to commentate on had suddenly become trivial, an irrelevance. But that would have been fundamentally to misunderstand Bill's understated message of a life well-lived. His was a tale of pleasure and forbearance among the pain. Frankly, never had the race which was about to start seemed more relevant.

'I've got used to it now. It's OK,' he told me, searching for and then finding the exact words. 'My father's dead unfortunately. But life goes on, dunnit?'

I could only nod.

With Bill Lievesley at the Caffé Elena, Turin.

'I've always followed the Giro d'Italia,' he said, with a sharp look to the light cloud above, which had temporarily cast a shade over our table.

'Who's going to win?' I asked with a stupidity even I was surprised at.

'Well, I've no idea,' he said, quite honestly. 'My real interest came in the days of Coppi and Bartali.'

* * *

We had no Coppi or Bartali to observe. But, as I made my way to the commentary booth for stage one, clutching my handwritten notes and still with Bill's words resonating, I had an unspoken suspicion that we were about to watch a rider of equal historical significance, at the absolute height of his commanding power.

It started with an attack on the second ascent of the Bivio di San Vito, 2.9 kilometres from the finish line of stage one on the southern embankment of the River Po. Unable to shake off the limpet-like Jhonatan Narváez, and ultimately outsprinted by him at the finish line, Tadej Pogačar banged his fists in frustration. Only much later did it become clear that he had intended on taking the *maglia rosa* on stage one and holding it for the entire race. Pogačar is absolutely undaunted by inconceivable targets no one else would even for a second consider.

The usual grand tour amnesia started to set in after a few days on the road. Impressions stacked up so high that, Jenga-style, the artifice started to fall apart. I remember walking on the city wall of Lucca, learning about how Chet Baker had spent months in prison there after being arrested shooting up in the toilets of a petrol station. I can recall having breakfast at an *agriturismo* set in perfect Tuscan countryside, watching swallows dart about in the eaves of a barn, listening to the proprietor tell me about her gap year teaching English in Welling. I remember very, very nearly treading on a dead cat in Naples and then being chased by three tiny, murderous dogs.

One afternoon Matt and I, preparing to go on air, spotted an elegant man at the window of an ancient town house in the heart of medieval Perugia, looking haughtily out at the gawdy chaos beneath. He sported a lemon-coloured silk shirt, open to midway down his smooth chest, his head was shaved and he wore a cravat at a rakish angle. Behind him, we could just about discern aesthetic-looking folk drifting around the airy apartment, whose whitewashed walls were studded with expensive-looking art.

'I wonder what his day rate is?' I asked Matt. I obviously had no idea what his profession was, but felt certain that it must be well rewarded.

'€4000,' he replied without hesitating.

I agreed entirely with Matt's assessment. You weren't going to be able to get him to come round for less, we both agreed. And even then, I reckoned it'd be six months before he'd be available. At no point did we ever discuss what service he provided. But we knew he wasn't cheap.

The story of the Giro d'Italia wound around such moments, occupying with vivid intensity the long afternoons at the microphone and then melting away in the evenings. For three weeks we followed Tadej Pogačar's fortunes (there really was only one type of fortune and it was good) as closely as anyone else on Planet Earth, locked into a commentary booth at the finishing line, which we shared with the crew from Italian TV. We gazed on from the gloom of our truck, as Pogačar struck again and again.

All day, every day, we remained glued to our screens as the *maglia rosa* accrued lines on his Wikipedia page with indecent haste, justifying on a daily basis the brave souls who had started to whisper in 2020 about another *new Merckx*. By the early summer of 2024 they didn't just have a point, they had a complete set of them, sharp-tipped evidence that Pogačar might perhaps be the greatest there'd ever been.

He'd casually destroyed all hope as early as stage two. That was the first summit finish. Intimately bound up in the saccharine pseudo-religion of the Pantani fetish, the race finished at the site of one of the Italian's greatest victories: at the vast sanctuary built to house the cedar wood 'black' Madonna visited by millions of pilgrims every year.

If those pilgrims had directed their attention away from the questionably sourced wooden statuette that is said to get impossibly heavy if anyone attempts to remove it, they might have witnessed something just as astounding, but actually real: Pogačar effectively winning the Giro (while not really trying that hard) after just 24 hours of a three-week race.

That day on which Pogačar would later pull on the first of his 20 *maglie rose*, I strolled down the hillside at the Santuario di Oropa towards the finish line, passing through the quadrants built in the shadow of a crazily oversized basilica. On my way to work I bought a little Jesus for €3. Perhaps caught up in the heady air of Catholicism which seemed to swirl around the mountaintop, mingling with the almost invisibly fine drizzle suspended in the still-wintry air, I had stopped off at the window of a tiny shop that stocked nothing but Jesuses. There he was, robed in white with a blue trim, with a sacred heart beating rudely from his chest, standing on a porcelain plinth, gazing skywards with eyes rolled back. And again, rendered in wood, but this time in surprising serenity, despite the obvious agony of his crucifixion, lovingly recorded by the sculptor, with a slightly worrying delight in detail. I opened the door and went in.

My request for the smallest little Jesus of all, a tiny plastic figurine standing no taller than a Bic cigarette lighter and bearing the legend 'Made in China' on the base, met with a good deal of consternation. It had clearly been a long time since anyone had walked into their premises and asked to purchase the smallest, cheapest depiction of the Messiah. The elderly lady behind the counter went through a 10-minute regime of dipping arthritically down to access long printer's tray drawers at ground level, before pulling upright and muttering to herself, then swiftly and deftly sliding a climbing stool into place so that she might reach the tallest of the shelves. Eventually, triumphantly, she retrieved the little chap, popped him in the tiniest paper bag and took my €3 with barely the outline of good grace. I took my leave with a perhaps overly cheerful *Ciao*.

'Look, Matt,' I said to my co-commentator on my arrival at the commentary position.

'Ah, lovely,' he said. 'A little Jesus.'

The tiny figure who watched over our Giro d'Italia in 2024.

And so it was that for the opening half of the Giro d'Italia, we were watched over by his presence. From time to time, when approaching an intermediate sprint or a minor king of the mountains finish line, I would pick him up by his head and, unconscious of what my hands were doing, start to 'worry' him with my thumb and forefinger, as Edward Theuns and Simone Consonni started their leadout for Jonathan Milan to increase his total in the *maglia ciclamino* (points classification) competition. It was a ritual that, once established, was hard to shake. Which I guess is the point.

And our little Jesus watched on again from his lofty perch as Pogačar attacked on stage three (a sprint he very nearly upset), took the Perugia time trial on stage six, then won again on stage seven, picked up two more stages, including the queen stage, before thundering to victory into Bassano del Grappa, with an almost 10-minute winning margin. Along the way he picked up two other second places, one third place and a wholly unnecessary king of the mountains jersey which he didn't really need or want, but won nonetheless. By the end of that Giro he had broken all the rules, starting 31 races and winning 14 of them in a 2024 season that was barely halfway through.

* * *

We left our commentary position only rarely; perhaps to rush to the plastic construction-site toilet outside the double-decker truck, or at best to grab a takeaway espresso to bring back to our colleague, carrying on the stream of cycling consciousness alone. What fresh air we could enjoy from 11.45 a.m. until we came off air at around 6 p.m. every day was impaired by one Italian commentator's habit of standing in the only doorway of the commentary unit, still with his headphones on, but at the fullest extent of their lead, chuffing away on his 12th fag of the afternoon, allowing the smoke to drift across all our positions. He shall remain nameless unless Franceso Pancani rings a bell with any of you. Primly, Matt and I expressed our discomfort by petulantly wafting copies of the Giro road book in his general direction rather than confronting him. Best to keep our resentments unspoken, we thought, with our confident British cowardice.

At some point, after a crazy drive into Napoli at night, following a diversion out of the Apennines along a terrifying road, we reached the most southerly point of the race. From the baroque weirdness of Naples we started off again after the race, this time heading back North. The haphazard vagaries of our accommodation, booked entirely by a third-party agency, could often leave us feeling disappointed or even bereft. But on this occasion they had booked us into a special little *albergo*. We spent the rest day in a Campanian village, surrounded by vineyards, orchards and meadows bursting with birdsong, languid dogs, wandering chickens and a bar with a penchant for heavy metal. And then set off on our journey back up the peninsula along the Adriatic.

Just south of Fano, we stayed in the extraordinary Hotel Biancaneve, owned by a Canadian-Italian whose parents bought the place in 1975 with the cash they'd made overseas. When they died, he committed to renovating the place at vast expense and had themed the entire establishment with images from *Snow White*, but strictly the Disney version. We all had rooms named after different dwarfs. I was Happy, which, by and large, I was.

I was also fascinated by the depths of our host's satisfaction with his lot, his sense of enormous wellbeing. Nothing could disturb his Pogačar-like equilibrium (although he was, physically, very far removed from the Slovenian cyclist). Not even the extremely tiresome fact that, just as we did, every single arriving guest takes the wrong turn down the side of his hotel and parks in his private space. Every time this happens, he gets up from his *Snow White* seat in the *Snow White* lobby and walks slowly down the drive to ask them to reverse back out. A simple sign might have prevented this from happening, but that didn't seem to occur to him.

After dinner, I fetched something from our re-parked car on the other side of the road and returned to the hotel, only to see him standing in the middle of the street gazing up at the strangely lit side of his establishment in quiet pride.

'How many times a day do you have to tell the guests to come back out of the drive?'

'All the time. That's life.' Perfectly content. I left him admiring his hotel.

And a few days later, on the Saturday of the second week, we were already bracing ourselves for the high mountains on the shores of Lake Garda. Sitting at a café with a red checked tablecloth in summery weather, looking out over the choppy waters towards the mountains in the North, I marvelled at the immensity of our daily jumps from Abruzzo to Marche, Emilia Romagna to Lombardy, butting up against Italy's natural border to the north. A staggering endeavour, somehow, the Giro. Even in 2024, in the age of the motorway and hire car, it still seemed improbable.

The next day we headed into the Alps to Livigno, as the weather changed. Suddenly Italy went ink black, with a moon emerging from behind a sheet of cloud. I wound down the window to feel the blast of chill, thin air – and shouted into the unimaginable void between two mountain passes. All those Apennine ranges, which had seemed so huge at the time, were suddenly put into perspective by the Alps. All around me was geometry and distance, laid out in snow, rock and unthinkably black sky.

The conventional cliché we would normally have applied in our commentary was: 'This was where the race will be won.' But in truth, that had already happened a long, long way back.

* * *

But of course, it is a forlorn hope that one can adequately put into words in one short chapter what could barely be contained in three weeks of racing. Do the maths. Each of the 176 riders had entirely different experiences. Multiply those 176 by the millions at the side of the road and the many millions more watching TV screens across the world, and you'll get a sense of how uncontainable the experience is.

Matt and I ran out of hyperbole towards the end of the first week, started recycling adjectives by the second week and then needed our vocabulary completely transplanted by means of a thesaurus during the third week, all in time for me to say the following as he crossed the line on stage 20 to win the race with the biggest margin of anyone since 1965's Vittorio Adorni's 11 minutes and 26 seconds, some 33 years before Tadej Pogačar was born.

'Ruthlessness with a light touch. Greatness with a smile. A 21st-century marvel: the incomparable Tadej Pogačar.'

* * *

And yet, at its heart, the Giro is tiny when set against the landscape on which it plays out. Like any and every bike race, it is also a tiny affair and a human tale. Three times I saw Pogačar in the flesh, excluding those daily flashes of pink past the window of our commentary booth, when he was the public property of RCS and the Giro d'Italia. But those three occasions were so absurdly small, backdoor, unobserved, almost private, that at times I found it hard to reconcile the different faces of this sport, which goes from red giant to white dwarf and back again with every passing minute of each expanding and contracting day.

On one occasion, hurrying away from the finish line in the quite fantastical Prato della Valle in Padua, trying to dodge the heavy sequence of thundery rain showers that had scattered the crowds, but had held off until the end of the race on a day of sweltering heat, I ran into him. Or at least I very nearly did. Sprinting for a gap in the fence which had suddenly appeared, presenting me with a short cut to my parked car, I was suddenly stopped in my tracks by a moving cortege of black-clad security guards, jogging alongside a boy in a pink Lycra onesie on a bike. Passing within a couple of feet of where I had come to an abrupt halt, the *maglia rosa*, acknowledging that I had been minutely inconvenienced by his escorted passage from podium to transport, smiled faintly at me, as if to offer a fleeting apology.

Another time, stuck in an almighty traffic jam coming away from Sappada on stage 19, Matt and I ended up behind the blacked-out UAE Team Emirates minivan in which, every day, after the podium protocol, he was chauffeured to his next hotel. At one point, when we had ground to a total standstill once again, his *soigneur* got out of the passenger seat, came around the side of the stationary vehicle and lifted the tailgate to retrieve something. There on the backseat, clearly silhouetted against the brightness of the windscreen ahead, was Tadej Pogačar, turning to ask him something, no doubt as bored as we were in the endless-seeming traffic jam.

Suddenly, a few places ahead in the line of cars, a similar van in the colours of Bora-Hansgrohe sprang out on to the other side of the road, accelerated and then vanished down a left-turn ahead. Though I had no evidence for the claim, I decided that it must contain Dani Martínez, their Colombian climber. After 21 years of traffic jams at grand tours my instincts are finely tuned and I realised in a split second that I had to get on his wheel. Their driver had clearly spotted a shortcut and was committing to it. I followed, with a screech of the wheels and a hail of expletives not only from Matt, but from me too. We roared past Pogačar and straight on to the wheel of Martínez. It was the only time in the Giro that he was caught napping. I had 'flicked' him at a crucial moment in the race and now had to put up with the presence of the race leader's car right on my bumper as we three hurtled down a series of switchbacks on an even smaller back-road in the Dolomites.

And a few days and a thousand kilometres later, Matt and I walked alongside Pogačar, lolloping along in the early evening sunshine of Rome, towards a caravan parked up outside the Colosseum. Having won the Giro an hour previously, he was being escorted to the anti-doping area to submit his daily tests. As he walked, he exchanged a very brief word with us, but mostly just smiled the smile of a Lycra-wearing deity who had accomplished a very great task, saw that it was good, knew that it was good, if not perfect, and was about to rest; mentally and physically shut down. He was, in two words, tremendously happy. I can think of no other word to describe him on that particular occasion.

Another journey around Italy had come to its completion. Dozing off the following day as our EasyJet flight was stranded in the baking sun of Fiumicino Airport for an hour, I relived the vibrancy of the experience in episodic impressions that flickered through my fading consciousness.

Each one on its own was a meaningless fragment, but together they built up to form a collage that would, viewed from a distance, constitute the image of a country which, more than anything else, is founded on nothing greater in ambition, nor lesser in scope, than a super-abundance of life. Just that. Life.

Distant snow-topped peaks somewhere in Abruzzo.

15

A FIVE-STAR REVIEW

I was mid-theatre tour when I received a series of quite urgent-sounding messages from Italy. This was not in itself especially unusual, because ever since I'd first started to commentate at the Giro d'Italia I'd communicated more and more frequently with a network of friends and acquaintances from Italy. Over time, a WhatsApp group had established itself, splintered into various different time-specific subgroups that came and went, lay dormant for months at a time and then suddenly sprung into life for no particular reason.

But this was a bit different; it was the cycling off-season and I was out for an early-morning run along a canal tow-path on the outskirts of Swindon. My contact was messaging me from Milan. The connection between the two locations was fragile, I felt, especially in November.

'Ned, are you free to interview Tadej Pogačar in about an hour?'

I stopped in my tracks, trying to work out how on earth this might have come about and what it might involve. But, as a place-holder reply, I said, 'Yes, I think so...' Then I turned on my heels and started jogging with a sense of renewed purpose back to the Premier Inn. It was Tadej Pogačar, after all.

* * *

I was already deeply into 'veteran' status at the Tour by the time this smiling lunatic of a rider started to emerge from the celestial cloud of possible stars and set about writing the story that he has been busily, hurriedly, churning out ever since. What's more, he's not the only rider to come along over the last five or six years with the innocent ambition of destroying preconceived wisdoms. Nothing is truly certain any longer: no one can definitively say what is, nor what is not, considered doable or impossible. Since that final stage of the Tour de France in 2020, when Tadej Pogačar wrecked Primož Roglič's aspirations (terminally, as it turned out, at the Tour de France), it has been unwise to assume anything.

Throughout the early years of my understanding of the Tour, although I almost need to measure this in decades instead, and prior to the Pogačar generation, I had only really known methodical winners. Such a comparison, of course, is normally strenuously avoided and for good reason. But the Sky/Ineos years did play out in a similar rhythm to the Armstrong years, to the extent that the outcomes of each edition of the race seemed like foregone conclusions. There was no room for an upset from 1999 to 2005, nor from 2012 to 2018, except for that one year when Froome crashed out early. Along with so much else, Armstrong was just incredibly lucky.

The Texan had normally sewn up the GC race by the opening week's team time trial and Froome had often put it to bed by the time that his black and blue army had delivered him to the pre-determined point of attack on the first mountain-top finish of the Tour. Even those one-time winners of the Tour in the aftermath of the Armstrong years, from Contador to Cadel Evans and Carlos Sastre, did so with a certain understanding of when to play their cards and when to hold back; a certain tactical reserve. That obviously excludes Floyd Landis in 2006, whose dope-fuelled rampage has no parallel, although even that also conformed to a method of sorts. And the same went for stage hunters, who would pick their moment to strike and otherwise lay low, conserving their resources.

Not so the uninhibited lunatics of the here and now.

Maybe it was Thomas de Gendt who started to effect the change, with his crazed assault on the 2012 Giro, in which he conquered the Stelvio Pass en route to a podium finish. But with due respect to his complete lack of respect for the rules, I think he was too peripheral a figure to have been the principal dynamo of change. He was more of an attendant lord in the peloton, useful in a breakaway to swell a progress of a stage or two in the king of the mountains.

More likely it was the gnomic muscle-man Peter Sagan with the constantly evolving haircuts and facial hair who changed everything. Certainly, by the time that he'd finished blazing his rainbow-banded trail across the cycling world, a fair amount of the conventions that had kept cyclists locked into certain patterns of behaviour and isolated in their silos had been dismantled, brick for brick, or simply bulldozed by Sagan's lack of compliance.

In the autumn of 2014, when I wrote my account of that year's Tour, *101 Damnations*, I could think of no other way to describe his sheer presence at the race other than to invent the word 'Saganian', which had no clear definition attached to it other than to 'display the unique personality traits of Peter Sagan.' These mostly consisted of an oddly carefree playfulness, a casual, unwitting violence on a bike, a plaintive sense of melancholy and injustice when denied his rightful victory, and an almost child-like nasal laugh which he emitted at a pitch and frequency, and with a spontaneity, that never ceased to delight me. When I stood in front of him trying to figure out what I could possibly ask him next, I could not quite believe that he was real. He seemed... too unlikely.

'Is today a day for Peter Sagan?' I'd routinely ask, knowing that Peter Sagan quite enjoyed talking about Peter Sagan in the third person.

'Every day is a Peter Sagan day.' And then the high-pitched whinny of a giggle, emanating from somewhere inside his head cavity, but whether it was his mouth, nose or ears I had no idea.

He had entered David Millar's life on stage three of the 2010 Paris Nice, a race that David was invariably ill-prepared for, having gambled his entire off-season on being naturally extremely fit and able to get fast quickly when he needed to. He has often told me his first glimpse of Sagan was that year when, still a teenager, the Slovakian had blasted his way to the front, a smudge of green Liquigas jersey in rapid motion, and taken his first professional win. David had finished in a group at six seconds to Sagan and had turned to his teammates, Dan Martin among them, and simply asked, 'What the fuck was that?' followed quickly by, 'Who the fuck is that?' Two days later, they stopped asking, as Sagan took the second race win of a career which ended in 122 victories.

What none of us knew was what would happen next, as Sagan drifted away from his best years into his TotalEnergies pre-retirement home in which he suddenly found himself sliding down the far end of a surprisingly steep bell curve. Sailing along in his wake, half a generation younger, came a cohort of young riders who had absorbed the wider philosophy of Saganianism and were about to explode road racing from the inside, but this time en masse, as a collective of highly distinct individuals.

Together they remind me of a kind of new breed of Marvel super-heroes appearing over the horizon, competing for the lead story line: first came Julian Alaphilippe, then Mathieu van der Poel and Tadej Pogačar, followed by Wout van Aert, with Remco Evenepoel taking a few diversions along the way, but gaining momentum all the while. Each one of these five was like the best Top Trump in a very select pack of cards, but for very different reasons.

* * *

It was no coincidence that in the early 2020s Netflix turned up at the margins of the Tour de France and started to turn the race into a nail-biting, cliff-hanging psychodrama spread out over eight episodes, completely ignoring the significant flip side of consuming road racing: that boredom makes the highs so irresistible. Delayed gratification is kryptonite to Netflix.

But it was this golden generation, only now coming of age, that had attracted them to the Tour de France. After Alaphilippe's star had started to wane he was readily, greedily replaced by the two 'vans', Aert and der Poel, Pog and Remco. That's before we have even brought into the discussion the implausibly brilliant Jonas Vingegaard, perhaps the best Tour de France rider of them all. But, and it's a truly significant 'but', he was not like the rest, and as a result is unfairly overlooked, even in this paragraph, in which he only gets referenced in the penultimate sentence and only in passing. He is also the only one of them to have worked in a fish-processing plant and I cannot help feeling the two are somehow related.

The fascination lies when their race programmes pit them against one another and certain race situations see them unexpectedly align on the road at the same time. Their presence in the racing calendar year after year feels like watching the gently spinning parts of a mobile collide with one another. Each one of them acts like a separate ring of a multi-layered gyroscope, rotating on every axis and sometimes falling into random alignment with one another, which causes the whole mechanism of the season to lurch again in another direction, with another impulse.

Most of these interlocking Venn diagram subsets come about because of Pogačar's irresistible force of attraction. He is raw physics. His own gravity draws races and racers together, confusing everyone and perhaps even himself in the process. He is the commonality which connects the muscular Mathieu van der Poel, against whom he races in the Classics, with the ballerina-like Jonas Vingegaard, the anti-van-der-Poel. The Dane has gone out of his way to pretend that Belgium doesn't exist, a bit like King Willem Frederik I of the Netherlands did until he was forced to concede it was a thing. As I write these words, Vingegaard has only raced there six times, didn't finish two of the those and finished in an average 66th place on the other four occasions. You suspect a bottle of Duvel would completely wipe him out, while van der Poel would be on to his seventh. Pogačar is the bit in between these two poles, a couple of bottles down and still smiling winningly, while van der Poel has started to scowl and

Jonas is unconscious. Sorry, come to think of it, this may have been a dream I had.

* * *

But Jonas's great Tour de France rival, the man he has twice routinely and clearly beaten, Tadej Pogačar, likes to try and take on all-comers over all terrain. The last few years have seen him arm-wrestling Mathieu van der Poel and Wout van Aert on the Poggio at Milan–Sanremo and the Koppenberg in the Ronde van Vlaanderen. Sometimes he wins and sometimes he loses. What is remarkable is the fact that he's even there. Not since Bernard Hinault in the 1980s has a Tour winner also attacked the Classics campaigns. Pogačar takes on Remco Evenepoel in the Ardennes Classics and again at Lombardia. He normally wins. In fact, at Lombardia he literally always wins: he has a 100% record.

But then Remco and Wout decide, in their own ways, to battle Pogačar in the grand tours, riding GC in the case of Remco and winning individual time trials in the case of both men. And in Wout van Aert, Pogačar has a rival working in support of his Tour nemesis. That, again, makes no conventional sense. According to the unwritten rules of the game, Wout van Aert should not be a thing. But he is.

* * *

Wout Van Aert is definitely a thing, even though he has yet to win a World Championship on the road and may not ever do so; has 'only' one Monument victory to his name (at the time of writing); and will forever unfairly be measured against his childhood rival Mathieu van der Poel, I have a place in my cycling heart that is purely dedicated to Wout van Aert. I have a brass plaque on the entrance to my cycling soul that bears his name. And almost all my hagiography is based on what he completed in the summer of 2022.

Van Aert is one of those riders whose ascendancy post-dates my disappearance into the commentary box, hence my enforced distance from him, and perhaps that helps with the deification. I have interviewed him over the phone and sometimes have caught a glimpse of him from afar, on those odd occasions when I have been able to jump out of the booth in time to catch the back end of the podium presentation for the green jersey, when he has finished perhaps in the grupetto on a mountain stage with a significant delay. And once I was able to pop open the window of our commentary truck on the Via Roma in Sanremo and watch him just across the road, popping off the cork of a sweet, fizzy Italian wine. His smile is one of the broadest in the peloton when he wins, just as his frown can be among the most deeply furrowed when he loses.

I ended up, accidentally, worming my way into the cultural forest that has grown up around this brightest of Belgium's national heroes. My TV commentaries of his 2020 victories at Strade Bianche and Milan–Sanremo (the boy had a GOOD pandemic) were lifted from the internet, sampled and ended up as the refrain in a stickily catchy Belgian pop song performed by two chaps from the Flemish podcast *Achter de Schermen* from West Flanders. The video features rudimentary green screen footage of two Belgians in stripey shirts jigging about and miming the song over shots of their hero winning Milan–Sanremo. I am heard periodically to chime in with 'Van Aert with his arms in the air!' before the lads join back in with '*Wouteke, Wouteke, wat doe je nu?*' ('Woutekin, Woutekin, what will you do next?')

The 'Wout Van Aert Sing-Along' was a surprising hit, gaining a certain viral enthusiasm in cycling circles and, in my mind at least, grafting my fate on to that of Wout, as if our destinies were now aligned. I suspect that this would be news to Mr Van Aert. But it was his mind-bending ride two years later, at the 2022 Tour de France, that cemented my view of Van Aert's unique place in cycling history.

There have been green jerseys of note in the distant and recent past. Those won by Sean Kelly, Erik Zabel and Peter Sagan stand out for obvious record-breaking reasons. Most recent in my memory as I write these words in the winter is Biniam Girmay's ground-breaking ascendancy in 2024, taking home to Asmara in Eritrea the first ever Tour de France jersey to be won by an African. That was glorious, a little unexpected, but then again entirely consistent with the career trajectory of a hugely versatile rider who has been threatening to kick down the door of this whitest, most European of sports for some time. Girmay did it, at least to a great extent, *with* the support of his team. Granted, he had first to prove that he was the fastest of the two sprinters which Intermarché-Wanty had brought to the Tour. But once he'd incontestably made that point, and banished the potential internal threat of Gerben Thijssen, the team was at his disposal.

That was the difference between Van Aert's 2022 green jersey and all the others in the history of the sport. He won it almost single-handedly, though Christophe Laporte played a role. Not only did he accomplish this mostly solo feat with rude ease and in almost record time, but he also picked up three stage wins on three very different kinds of terrain. He won a sprint, a time trial and a puncheur's stage with a long-range solo attack.

The first of those three victories had happened on stage four of the Tour, after we had all relocated to north-eastern France. The day before the race, Pete Kennaugh and I had ridden out on our Bromptons to the final climb outside Calais. Pete had dismounted, citing fatigue, but also he couldn't be arsed. It was blazing hot. I had ridden on, fuelled by false pride, to the top of the Cap Blanc-Nez, down the other side and back up again, while Pete waited patiently, trying not to fall asleep. Then we had both ridden slowly, via a pizza shack that sold us life-saving cold Oranginas, back to the hotel where we spent the afternoon playing snooker on a full-sized table, managing only two frames in three hours (one each, if you're interested).

The next day was Wout's day. Having taken the yellow jersey on the final day in Denmark, he attacked on the final climb, passed the monument to a fallen airman of the pioneering years and came over the line on his own into Calais, making a giant swooping motion with his arms, like some oversized Belgian Lycra gull that someone had sprayed yellow. This was a moment that in some way sums it all up: the present calling out to the future with a shrill bird's call.

He would soon relinquish yellow at the services of his leader, canter into green and also very nearly win the polka dot jersey on the Hautacam, the final mountain test of the race that year. He didn't quite manage that feat, which would have been truly absurd. But instead he did something even more remarkable: he intervened in the race for the yellow jersey, delivering his team leader Jonas Vingegaard to land his decisive blow against Tadej Pogačar, with a climb that defied description and put the defending champion in real difficulty.

Never before had a champion, a rider of his winning pedigree, also gone to the Tour de France with such extensive and critical domestique duties. There were a handful of occasions, notably on the cobbles of stage five, when you could easily construct a compelling case that without Van Aert's interventions Vingegaard would not have won the 2022 Tour. Netflix's interpretation of their relationship, when it eventually emerged in the first of their Tour de France docudramas, tried to insinuate an antagonism between the two men, which I am not convinced was really there; and if it was, then not to anything like as dramatic an extent as they tried to suggest with artful editing.

* * *

David Millar and I have a long-standing game we play about our own personal fandoms. In the past I have developed strong and not always directly explicable affections for riders as diverse as the New Zealander Paddy Bevin, who had the misfortune of being interviewed by my slightly star-struck self at the Tour of Britain shortly before he retired. Perhaps that was why he hastened his retirement announcement. I also very much admire the Italian breakaway specialist Davide Gabburo, who I once helped to operate a coffee machine at a breakfast buffet towards the end of the 2023 Giro. Come to think of it, he too has announced his retirement.

David, similarly, has pronounced soft spots and blind spots for certain riders, but he is more fickle. I recently discovered a film I shot on my phone of him glimpsing Sepp Kuss from the window of our commentary booth at the Tour and literally squealing his name.

David peering excitedly at riders passing our little window.

He has traditionally reserved his greatest fandom for both Remco Evenepoel and Mathieu van der Poel, both of whom he gets extremely excited about. I have always been more inclined to the side of Wout Van Aert, and this schism in our differing affections is the source of endless and pointless debate.

There was a moment during the 2023 Tour when Wout temporarily won David over. Having ridden the first few kilometres of the mighty Joux Plane pass and having set up his climbing colleagues to take over, Van Aert pulled off the front of the bunch and, in time-honoured fashion, came to an almost complete standstill. A moto camera noted this moment, as Van Aert slowed to instant walking pace, and then it sped off, leaving the dropped rider to make his way incognito up the rest of the climb. But about 500 metres further on, watching live pictures of the remains of the bunch being led now by Rafał Majka of UAE Team Emirates, we suddenly both noticed a figure moving up at speed on the left side of the remaining climbers.

'Hang on, is that…?' I think I asked in commentary.

'It is,' David answered, before adding, 'That. Is. Insane.' Or words to that effect. It was a Superman script moment.

Rafał Majka, one of the greatest climbers in the world, spotted Van Aert, who had by now ghosted up all the way to the front. Majka immediately pulled away and dropped like a stone, effectively just giving up under the pressure that Van Aert was exerting at the front. This second turn by the Belgian might have been brief, but it was devastating and it broke the laws of racing. It was, as David correctly described it, an act of insanity. And again, as so often before, one of those moments which not one of us had ever witnessed before or since, nor ever expected to see. It simply didn't make sense.

* * *

However, no sooner have I written that definitive statement, than I am put in mind of another occasion, two years previously. It was the famous Mûr-de-Bretagne stage in 2021, the year of van der Poel's debut at the race and only eight months after his dearly loved grandfather Raymond Poulidor's death. There was a heap of pressure on the Dutchman's shoulders and at times it showed.

Riders like van der Poel have limited opportunities to take the yellow jersey at the Tour. If they haven't done it early in the first week, it will be too late. On stage one, a rolling race through Brittany, looping around the sharply hilly farmland to the east of Brest, van der Poel had found the finish too hard and had lost time to the stage winner and first *maillot jaune* of that year's race, Julian Alaphilippe.

He started the next day 18 seconds down. That meant that if he wanted to take the jersey from Alaphilippe, he would need to take the time bonuses on each of the two ascents of the Mûr and win with a big enough gap to ensure he took the race lead. He did just that, attacking solo on the first ascent, then sitting back up, recovering and doing it all over again almost immediately afterwards. He won the stage and put eight seconds into the Frenchman, more than enough to fulfil his dream of wearing the yellow jersey that had forever been denied his dearly admired and greatly missed grandfather.

Emotion ran high at the finish line in Brittany and almost as high in the car park in Maidstone, where for the second year running we were confined to barracks by Covid, but that didn't stop the immediacy of the moment from transmitting itself to our commentary booth.

David was stunned. Even when the red light went off and he was no longer commentating, he continued to be stunned. Long after we were done for the day, and were settling down to a glass of something cold and a bag of fish and chips outside Pete's ground floor hotel room overlooking the golf course of the Marriott Hotel, he still hadn't stopped being stunned. Again, that refrain; a precursor to his assessment of Wout Van Aert's ride some two years later, 'That. Was. Insane.'

Pete agreed, 'It was bonkers.'

And then, 'Are you going to finish those chips?'

Ever since he so absurdly stormed to victory at the Amstel Gold Race in 2019, chasing down Alaphilippe and Jakob Fuglsang, towing home the remainder of a shattered peloton for kilometre after kilometre and without assistance, catching the leaders in the final few metres and then launching an unanswerable sprint (this was his first act of insanity), van der Poel has exhibited a targeted violence in his approach to racing that is unmatched. When he rises, alien-like, from his saddle, his head bowed low to reveal a neck and shoulders more befitting a hundred metres sprinter, he has a terrifying intensity about him. I have never seen a rider so completely concentrated in the moment of destruction. He is a hammer.

* * *

Once, in conversation, we were idly comparing riders to herbs and spices. It was in the car at the Tour (it was a long drive, so please bear with us). Pete, David and I were trying to agree on which characteristics riders shared with garnishes. Remco Evenepoel bore great similarities with mint, we decided. Van der Poel, incidentally, was chilli (explosive and sometimes too much), Vingegaard was basil (admirable, but not versatile) and Pogačar was coriander (utterly unique), a comparison made even more remarkable by the statistically unlikely fact that all three of us agreed that we absolutely loved coriander. Van Aert was salt (indispensable, ubiquitous). But Remco was mint; cool, smooth and fresh. By the way, I find it almost impossible not to reduce him to his outstandingly well-suited first name only – Remco sounds less like a name, and more like a brand, a philosophy and an entire way of life.

I remember my excitement when Remco checked into the same hotel in Pescara that I was staying in ahead of the 2023 Giro, a race he was hotly tipped to win. His Soudal Quick-Step teammates had already retired to their rooms when Remco breezed into reception wearing a blue tracksuit and carrying nothing more than a white leather rucksack. He then took a seat in the restaurant, whose chef suddenly sprang back into action to ensure that some fresh linguine was rustled up for the star of the Giro peloton.

Finding it hard to concentrate on the conversation at my table, I found myself watching this supernaturally self-possessed young rider holding court at a table at which the old warhorse *directeur sportif* Davide Bramati and long-standing head of PR Alessandro Tegner sat, hanging on his every word. Once he had eaten his pasta, he waited for the ice cream to arrive, which he duly ate in two or three hungry spoonfuls, before pushing his chair back and raising a folded leg to the side of the table, a picture of relaxation and ease. Faintly awestruck (this is how seldom I meet the riders these days!), I sent David a message telling him who I was sharing a dining room with.

'David, Remco is literally in my hotel. He's having dinner at the next table.'

'Holy shitballs! Get me his autograph!' came his instant reply.

Eventually, I walked to my room, passing close to the Quick-Step table, and greeting Alessandro with a handshake and brief exchange of pleasantries. I nodded a greeting at Bramati and then, slightly more purposefully at Remco, who smiled back. Later on that evening, I sent one of Quick-Step's other press officers a message about David's need for an autograph. He found this very funny and promised me to get him a signed bidon, as if he were a 10-year-old. Sadly the bidon never materialised and David's wait goes on. And Remco's hugely promising Giro came apart at the seams when he narrowly won the second of three time trials and then climbed off, chock full of Covid.

In the summer of 2024 Remco planted his bike with pre-planned pomp in front of the Eiffel Tower, prompting all the photographers present to zoom out to the very widest extent of their lenses in the hope that they could incorporate the whole scene or risk losing the shot to grab for another, more suitable camera at their side. He had just won the Olympic double, something no other male rider had done before him, and he could now add these to his World Championships in both the time trial and the road race, his multiple one-day victories, his GC successes across the calendar, his Tour de France podium on debut and his victory at the Vuelta. With everything that all the other members of this crazily gifted cartel of talents were winning, it was a wonder there was anything left for the others to pick up. But Remco was hoovering up an incredible collection of extremely prodigious scraps.

A few weeks later, in the autumn of 2024, and equipped with a golden bike and gold helmet, he returned to Il Lombardia, the most mountainous of the one-day Classics and the final race of note on the European calendar. It was the first time that Remco had been back to Lombardia since the time he'd almost lost his life when he sailed over the parapet of an old stone bridge and dropped many metres into some rough undergrowth. That had been 2020. He had been only 20.

The day before the race, we drove up and over the quite staggeringly beautiful Colma di Sormano mountain pass, with its tiny little observatory pointing to the distant galaxies. After a stop at a café with a terrace for a macchiato with a view served by the Rudest Man In Italy, we set off on the helter-skelter descent, stopping impulsively when we all recognised the very spot where Remco had come to grief. It only became apparent, stepping out of the car and walking towards the bridge, just how far Remco had fallen that day, to lie immobile at the bottom. Sometimes only by seeing these places which shape races and careers can we get a sense of how terrible the ordeal is, how steep the roads, precipitous the drops, how much personal danger these riders place themselves in.

After the 2024 race, in which Remco finished a more than valiant second to the unfathomably superior Pogačar, he spoke movingly about his encounter with his past, as he rode past the bridge on the Sormano climb which nearly ended his career or indeed his life. The location has become a part of his narrative, the chapter he would have liked never to have written, just as Jonas Vingegaard will forever be haunted by the memory of the crash in April 2024 that left him in hospital for weeks and quite possibly cost him a third Tour de France win. These riders, Pogačar, Van Aert, van der Poel, Evenepoel, Vingegaard: they all carry the scars of their trade. They all race with their own histories of battles won and very occasionally lost.

* * *

Back in Swindon, I carefully followed the instructions that I had been sent and logged into the online meeting. Instantly an image of an artfully if dimly lit chair in an expensive-looking empty room opened on my laptop screen. Voices from off camera were audible. One of them was Tadej Pogačar's.

'But I thought you told me it would just be a simple message!' He was complaining to his press officer, sounding aggrieved that his time was once again being stolen from him at the expense of yet more simpleton requests. I found myself thinking, for the hundredth time over the course of my career, how little patience most athletes have. I glanced at the reasonably long list of strangely-translated questions that my Italian clients wanted me to run through with Pogačar, who by now was sitting down in the chair, avoiding eye contact either with those people in the room with him, or me on whatever computer screen he had in front of him, beaming my awkwardly smiling bespectacled presence from my standard Premier Inn room into his exclusive Abu Dhabi suite. It was a mismatch, for sure.

On a Zoom meeting with Pogačar between Swindon and Abu Dhabi.

Pogačar, however, to his great credit and because I suspect he is the kind of human who can't stay grumpy for long, changed from night to day as soon as we started the interview. Engaging, supplying more detail than he really needed to, expressing himself in honest, simple terms, he spoke enthusiastically of how he remembers going to the Giro d'Italia as a child with some other cycling-mad teenagers and collecting as many bidons from as many teams as he could.

As he disappeared down what passed for a nostalgia rabbit hole (if such a thing can really be deemed to exist in the life of a 26-year-old), I found myself trying to imagine what year this might have been, when Pogačar went off to collect souvenirs. I remembered the first edition of the Giro I went to in 2016, when I spent the best part of a month on the road unsuccessfully badgering the *soigneurs* at the iconic, now defunct Androni Giocattoli team (run by the recently deceased Gianni Savio) for a musette or a cloth cycling cap. I came away with neither. If it was that year Pogačar was gathering bidons in Italy, then he would have been 16 and I was 47. Both of us, though, were doing the same things; we were two cycling fans, although with rather different futures ahead of us and only one us already forced to wear glasses.

Setbacks, from minor inconveniences to major disruption, seem not to leave Tadej Pogačar shaken for long. I remember how his former coach and DS Allan Peiper told me how, on the morning of the famous time trial at La Planche des Belles Filles in 2020, which won him the Tour and secured his place in history at the age of just 21, the youngster had a difficult moment just before the race. He had to overcome the doubts of others, in order to maintain his own extraordinary belief that he could turn around a mighty 57-second time deficit to Primož Roglič.

'They don't believe I can do it, Allan,' he told the Australian.

'Then go out and show them.' So he did.

And when things end badly (and let's not forget how often in 2022 and 2023 Jonas Vingegaard made him suffer), he seems supernaturally able to let his disappointment melt away within minutes.

The very worst day of his Tour de France career came on stage 17 in 2023, when he conceded the race over the radio, extinguishing all remaining hope that he might be able to take time back on Vingegaard. 'I'm gone. I'm dead,' he said. It was the first time in Tour history that we had heard the words of a rider at such a moment in the middle of the race. By the time he laboured to the finish line in Courchevel, he'd shipped almost six minutes.

Later that evening, and to add to Tadej Pogačar's woes, the entire Tour de France got caught up in a gigantic Alpine traffic jam once again, composed of that toxic mix of publicity caravan, mobile homes and actual team buses. There was not a gendarme in sight. The view from the side windows of our stationary vehicles was great: a honeyed sun setting slowly over the valley below and Mont Blanc in the east. But ahead, and behind every car, there was the bumper of another, going nowhere. Pete and I unfolded our bikes and told David we'd ride ahead to the next town and bring back some takeaway pizzas, which was easier said than done on Bromptons.

Just as were returning through the motionless traffic, balancing on our handlebars boxes with molten cheese and tomato sauce slopping around inside, we almost rode into Tadej Pogačar and his partner Urška Žigart. They had clearly abandoned the stranded UAE Team

Emirates bus, jumped on two extremely expensive Colnago racing bikes and, without wearing helmets (shock!), were weaving slowly through the traffic in the opposite direction, grinning broadly and waving at the many people shouting out of car windows in surprise.

I remember thinking at the time, as they passed me, that there could scarcely be a more archetypal Tour memory than nearly colliding with perhaps the greatest rider who has ever lived as he made his way through a traffic jam one way, as I passed in the other, bringing pizzas to our car. But that is the truth of it.

This sport may have just thrown up the greatest generation of champions in its entire, rich history, but that doesn't stop it being wildly, charmingly homespun. I hope that never changes.

16

IS HE BEING A TWAT?

It was because of Chris Froome that I ended up on stage. Not just once, but (so far) 138 times and counting. I am sure, as the four-time Tour de France winner finally winds down his extremely lucrative and yet painfully disappointing final professional contract, he will have no idea that it was his aborted involvement in a joint venture which led, via a circuitous route, to me dressing up and messing around in theatres up and down the land.

It was because of Chris Froome that I ended up touring places like Bury St Edmunds and Exeter, telling stories, putting on awful accents (Peter Sagan), and generally pretending to be other people like Eddy Merckx, Phil Liggett, Mark Cavendish, Wout van Aert playing the saxophone solo from 'Careless Whisper', Jonas Vingegaard and Jonas Vingegaard's colleague, who he left behind him in the fish-processing factory in Jutland, where the two-time Tour de France champion plied his trade before becoming one of the greatest riders of his exceptional generation. If you've ever bought a ticket to one of my shows and have hated it, then it's not on me. It was all Froome's fault, you see.

It was in the winter of 2015 that the initial idea was hatched. Along with my long-standing friend and representative, Jay Marks, and in consultation not just with Chris himself, but with his wife Michelle, it was decided that he wasn't getting the respect and recognition from the British sporting public that his already significant achievements merited. Already a two-time Tour winner (twice a Wiggins, in other words), he was still largely an anonymous presence in the British sporting consciousness.

I remember the late journalist Richard Moore telling me that he'd once seen Froome walking down a London street pushing his bike alongside him, dressed in a Team Sky tracksuit, being totally ignored by every single passer-by. And this was after Froome had won four Tours; a quatro-Wiggins. Richard had been amazed to see he had moved through the crowds without a single head turning. He was, as I was, used to the sight of Froome in the yellow jersey at the Tour, being besieged by interest and surrounded by microphones wherever he went. We had both fallen into the occasional trap of forgetting what a marginal pursuit cycling is in the UK.

'It's almost as if no one cares in this country, Ned,' Richard had said, in a surprised fashion. Having grown up in the world of football reporting, in which players are locked away in gilded palaces and kept at arm's length from the great unwashed for fear of being mobbed, I had to agree with Richard.

'It is,' I'd said. 'Never underestimate how tiny a sport it really is.' I still don't know if I quite believe that take, given everything I feel and know about the Tour de France, but the lack of impact it has on these shores never fails to surprise me.

So, swimming perhaps against the tide, Jay and I had devised a plan to elevate Froome's standing in the eyes of the public; to give them a chance to get to know him, and for Froome himself to feel a bit of the residual but genuine warmth that existed towards him. It *was* there, we assured him. You just had to seek it out. We suggested to Froome that he and I went on a week-long tour of big theatres across the land, and put on *An Evening With Chris Froome*, in which I would interview and try to tease out from his normal guarded self the kernel of what is a genuinely engaging story. And Chris could be funny, too. I wanted people to see that.

Jay, together with theatrical promoters, found a sponsor, provisionally booked some venues and waited for Froome's commitment. We were just about to confirm the tour and put the tickets on sale, when the Froomes went collectively quiet. As the weeks ticked by our worries grew. Eventually, word came back that Froome was no longer quite as willing as he had been to tour the UK. Instead he embarked on a programme of post-Tour criterium races; those baffling local show affairs in which unaccountably huge appearance fees encourage the stars of the Tour de France to turn up and compete in a rigged charade. Normally, this involves Froome outsprinting Sagan to 'take the win', for example. Anyway, at the last possible minute, he withdrew his consent and the project collapsed.

* * *

But that wasn't quite the end of the story. The promoters had, in preparing the mini-tour, established that there seemed to be an appetite for some sort of communal show about cycling. And so, after the dust had settled, they came back to me. The thrust of their argument was this: sooner or later someone will come along and tour a theatrical evening about cycling, and it might as well be you.

I thought about it for a few days and then decided to take the plunge. At no point did anyone, including me, stop and wonder whether or not I was remotely capable of doing such a thing. Not them, not me. We just blindly sailed off into the project, without so much as a second thought. And before I knew it I had a list of 14 venues, a terrible show title (*Bikeology*) and a poster which featured me comedically pointing at the camera, wearing a bike helmet with a Go-Pro sticking out of the top of it. The only thing we didn't have was a show, but that seemed less important somehow; a detail that could be filled in later. Anyway, the tickets had gone on sale and were already selling fast. So, there it was.

* * *

My first tour was in 2016 and it passed by in a flash of chaos, from the moment that I walked on stage in a try-out theatre hidden away in the

Cotswolds to the first sold-out show of my tour, at the legendary City Varieties in Leeds, erstwhile home to the iconic show *The Good Old Days*, which graced the TV screens of my, and many in my audience's, youth. My hour and a half on stage consisted of extended diatribes on the evils of Lycra, the horrors of cycling forums, a garbled history of the first bicycle, in as much as it related to the explosion of Mount Tambora in 1815, and the ongoing culture wars between cyclists and motorists, specifically the London Taxi Drivers' Association. The whole evening ended in a riot of bicycle-related fun as some poor contestant from the audience volunteered to change an inner tube against the clock, live on stage. It sounds like hell when I write it all down like that.

With this particular form of purgatory I went to Yeovil and to Whitley Bay, too. I played Northampton and Melton Mowbray, Blackburn and Portsmouth, a growing list of towns that wouldn't have looked out of place on the race route of the 1954 Daily Express Tour of Britain. I travelled around with a tour manager whose arduous task it was to run all the cues from the wings and make sure we got from A to B on time. A wry Kiwi called James, he had come to the UK a while ago having worked with the stratospherically successful and talented duo, Flight of the Conchords, who were taking the comedy world by storm. Now he found himself driving a hired van through the pouring rain en route to Eastbourne with a cycling commentator. A few shows into the tour, he offered up his first evaluation of the experience as we stopped for a wee in a motorway service station. On our way back to the van, he addressed an issue that had clearly been bothering him.

'Your audience,' he said, with an intent look in his eye and leaving a substantial pause, 'it's like a bloody *Star Trek* conference.' I think he meant we collectively bore all the hallmarks of a cult. I think, too, that he might have been right.

It certainly felt that way one night in Liverpool, at the famous Epstein Theatre. It was, I recall, the day after Donald Trump had been elected President of the USA for the first time, with access to the nuclear codes. That had emboldened me to steal one of Billy

Connolly's jokes about Ronald Reagan being older than his father 'and we don't give him the controls to the telly!'

At the end of the second half, and on the advice of one of my producers, Emma Brunjie, who had long experience in theatrical promotion, I read out written questions from the audience, which had been placed in an upturned cycling helmet on the stage during the interval. For the umpteenth time on that tour, and following a tradition that is still repeated at almost every venue almost a decade later when I tour, I was asked, 'What does Gary Imlach do for the other 49 weeks of the year?'

It is a question of perennial fascination to our audience and one which I have no good answer to, since Gary and I only ever see each other for the Tour de France, plus the other bike races we have covered together. Even the act of simply reading the question out gets a laugh, which I have never understood, but I suppose it stems from the fact that everyone in the audience must have wondered the same thing from time to time. I was just about to launch into an answer, when I heard a rather gruff isolated voice pipe up from the dark rows of seats in the auditorium.

'He does the hoovering.' It was Boardman. He stole the show, which was rather annoying.

* * *

Actually, it's not quite true that Gary and I never see one another outside of working at bike races for ITV. But it's very nearly true. We once attended the BAFTA TV awards together, in the aftermath of the 2014 Tour de France, which had started in Yorkshire. Amusingly, the ITV Tour coverage had been nominated for an award and we had been sent thick cards with gold embossed invitations to the event at the Theatre Royal Drury Lane. The invitations were accompanied by screeds of detailed information concerning protocol at the awards ceremony, most of which related to where our chauffeurs should drop us off. Half-jokingly, I suggested Chris, Gary and I cycle up the red carpet, not expecting a reply from our WhatsApp group.

Boardman loved the idea and, much to my surprise, so too did Gary. The only person who was less enamoured with the idea of making a spectacle of ourselves on the telly was me – and it had been my idea. And so began an epic exchange of emails between Boardman and BAFTA, which really should be archived for posterity in the British Library. Tense negotiations were finally resolved and, at the allotted hour, we all met in St Martins Lane; all of us in dinner jackets, Chris and I with our bikes, and Gary without one, due to the fact that he doesn't own one. This slight stumbling block to our plan was overcome when I produced my little blue plastic Barclays bike key and unlocked one of the big blue hire bikes for Gary. We duly rode sheepishly up the red carpet, and round the corner where Chris and I locked our bikes to the theatre railings. Gary just left his hire bike propped up, not particularly bothered that the meter was running for the entire three hours of the BAFTAs and that it was my account.

On the red carpet at the BAFTAs.

To add to the disappointment of the evening, we were roundly beaten in our category of 'best live event' by *Monty Python Reunited*. It would be two years before I set foot in a theatre, but never again in a dinner jacket.

* * *

Thinking back to the gargantuan act of hubris that went by the name of *Bikeology*, it was extraordinary that I wasn't lynched by the audience. The hour and a half of half-arsed performance was mostly an opportunity for me to get off my chest a succession of petty grudges and grievances that I had been harbouring about the behaviour of people within the cycling world. Without stopping to think whether or not this was a good idea, I launched into a string of diatribes against people who use Strava, people who wear Rapha, people who over-use hand signals and vocal warnings when out on rides, people who have bike-fittings, people who conduct bike-fittings, people who are interested in bike technology, people who are interested in bikes... and so forth. It was the work of a madman. I was not so much biting the hand that fed me as chewing it off. How I thought I could get away with it, I'll never know.

But the theatres filled and the audiences chuckled along, and somehow I came back in 2017 and did it all over again, only enlarging the show's scattergun mauling of the cycling world to include people who watch the Tour de France by the side of the road or even on the telly: by now I was reaching out from the stage to directly lampoon my core audience.

That year, to my astonishment, I sold out the huge Lyric Theatre on Shaftsbury Avenue, normally home to Michael Jackson's *Thriller*; a show, so the stage hands informed me, that was so bad it was about to fold and was only saved by the artist's premature death, after which it was consistently sold out. Being able to use their stage on the only night of the week when the musical wasn't scheduled (a

Monday night), these grizzled lighting techs and carpenters watched on from the wings in amazement as their theatre filled up with the very particular demographic of viewer who is minded not only to watch the Tour de France on ITV during the summer months, but then, still more hearteningly, buy a ticket in November to go and see the commentator prancing around on stage being chased by a giant jiffy bag (literally, as I recall). I also remember how my tiny dressing room in the cramped Edwardian space behind the stage was stuffed to bursting with seventies afro-wigs and sequinned dresses, normally pulled on by the room's week-to-week tenants, the backing singers from *Thriller*.

It was somehow the right setting for a mental stocktake of everything that had happened to me. An hour before the curtain went up, and amid the smell of stale hairspray and rising damp, I perplexedly tried to retrace the steps in my career which had taken me from a first encounter with Lance Armstrong in 2003 to the peeling paintwork and worn carpets of a West End musical theatre. I was about to step out on stage in front of 900 people and attempt to get them to focus on the specific nasal vowels of Peter Sagan as he is beaten in a sprint by Fernando Gaviria, a rider I pretended for the sake of comedy he had never before seen in his life.

'Hey, Blue Guy!' shouted my version of Peter Sagan, in a wild and whinnying Slovakian accent. 'Who're you?'

You had to be there.

* * *

With two theatre tours behind me, I had started to figure out what I was doing. But only just. What made the experience all the more surprising, as well as rewarding, was that I had also started to understand that audiences would return. I toured again in 2018, with a show specifically about the 2018 Tour de France. I did a try-out night in a small venue in south London in September that year, which David Millar came along to watch. I think most of the audience were more taken by the fact that he was there in the front row than with anything I did, as I fumbled around on stage pretending to be Peter Sagan (again) getting to grips with one of those French hotel showers that won't clip on to anywhere. I can't remember why I did this, but it made sense at the time. Also featured in the 2018 show was an almost fully sized caravan, from which I emerged to recreate a day in the life of a fan at the side of the road on the Tour de France; full of unexpected excitement, interminable boredom, merguez sausages, free tat from the publicity caravan, and ending in a puddle of ketchup after the race had flashed by in 20 seconds flat.

That 2018 show also contained a sequence in which I donned some thick, black-rimmed glasses and a bald wig in order to play Dave Brailsford, explaining some slightly murky stuff in a Dave Brailsford manager-speak kind of a way, with his extended hands arcing around all over the place and making no sense at all. One night in Edinburgh, as I was signing books after my show, I noticed that Dave's brother Andy, who I have got to know well over the years, was waiting to say hello. I had no idea he had been in the audience and was suddenly alarmed.

'Oh, bloody hell, Andy,' I said, shaking his hand, anxiously. 'I should have warned you about the, you know, the Dave bit.'

'I thought it was spot on, Ned!' he laughed. But then again, Andy's just a really nice man.

'No need to tell him about it, is there, though?' I suggested.

'Too late.' He'd already Whatsapped a picture to Dave from the front row, which he'd candidly taken while I was in flagrante. He showed me his phone, and sure enough I could see the whole exchange of messages. It went something like this:

Andy Brailsford: Ned is doing you on stage.

Dave Brailsford: Is he being a twat?

Andy Brailsford: A bit. But he's got you spot on.

Andy then insisted that I put the wig and glasses on and do it all over again.

My Dave Brailsford impression, with Andy Brailsford joining in.

Down the years, a surprising number of current and former pros have been hoodwinked into coming along to see my shows. The Barnes sisters came to my first show in Northampton, Hannah politely declining to take on the tyre challenge to prevent her ruining an expensive manicure. The Downing brothers, Russ and Dean, are regulars to the South Yorkshire venues. The late, and very great, Brian Robinson came to see me, too, and must have sat there mystified throughout. Steven Burke, Rob Hayles, Rod Ellingworth, Keith Lambert and Brian Cookson have all come along. Young Oscar Onley was dragged along by his mum to see me in Edinburgh just weeks after he had almost beaten Jonas Vingegaard twice at the Tour of Croatia. What a reward! And Phil Liggett was kind enough to be in the audience with his wife, Trish, when I last started touring, on the opening night in Hertford. Mind you, as he told me, he had almost no choice. He had just bought a house about 150 metres away and kept walking past my face.

* * *

The last show I performed was a bit different. After I had written *1923: The Mystery of Lot 212 and a Tour de France Obsession*, I often wondered whether I could distil the story down to an hour and a half on stage. It seemed an ambitious task, as anyone who has read the book will perhaps realise. There are a lot of strands in the book that loop around my discovery of an old reel of film from the 1923 Tour.

Working with one of my oldest friends from home, who has spent a long career in theatre as an actor, director and writer, we stripped back the tale to what mattered and managed somehow to tell the story in a whole different way, turning the stage into my spare room, an attic in Flanders, a restaurant and a bridge in Brittany. It was the most challenging thing I have ever tried, by far, and I spent much of 2024 working on it, but I deeply enjoyed the experience of touring it.

That profound pleasure was strengthened by two things, I now understand. Wherever I went on tour, I was met with an audience comprised of a vast majority of people who had already seen previous shows and were therefore predisposed to be on my side. Secondly, the news of ITV's imminent exit from the Tour broke just as my tour was getting going. In each and every subsequent venue there was a sense of community; of a kind of commonality of purpose. We were all there, in those lit theatres, as summer 2024 receded into memory, because of our inexplicable bond with those eternally replaying three weeks in July. What had brought us to that place was the same thing. And it seems we are people who don't want to let it go. We cling on.

17

THE EMPTY MARMITE JAR

I put the full stop to the end of a sentence and pause to look out on a uniformly grey November sky hanging sullenly over the flat roof of an industrial unit on the outskirts of Coventry. I am on my theatre tour and this is my everyday. It's early in the morning. I don't sleep well on tour. I can feel the strong pull of memory, the undertow of something which I thought would always be there. I wonder if this is the last time I will sit down at a desk to write about Mark Cavendish.

A thought occurred to me last night, when I was brushing my teeth, just after midnight. It wasn't a great observation, but it pleased me as I stared gummily at my ageing reflection in the mirror of another Premier Inn. 'What can you extract more out of, just when you think it's definitely empty: a toothpaste tube, a jar of Marmite or the career of a sprinter from the Isle of Man?'

I went to bed happy that I was a great satirical mind. Mark Cavendish was a Marmite jar. Instead of counting sheep I imagined repeatedly the sensation of scraping a knife into every corner of a Marmite jar. Then I stopped doing that and started trying to remember as many Cavendish wins as I could. Then I stopped doing that as well and fell asleep.

There is a knotty clump of time that has wound itself around a decade and a half of history at the Tour and it is to do with Cavendish; this most complex of humans, this compact presence at the heart of the race. God knows, I have written so much about him already: newspaper and magazine columns, whole chapters of books. I have filled hours of radio airwaves, dozens of podcast episodes and kilo-metres of live commentary discussing the man and the many, many observable and non-observable characteristics that make up his ridiculously driven, deeply unusual personality. But maybe this is the time to put it all behind me and to tie it up with a ribbon. I flick the kettle next to me on the hotel desk. Its slow groan gradually drowns out the constant rumble of traffic on the M42 outside my window. And I set out to consign Cavendish to the past.

* * *

Last night on the stage, in front of a packed Wednesday-night audi-ence, attentive and alert to the show, the Cavendish section had landed with a particular thump. There is a moment in my most recent show when I step away from my retelling of the story about the century-old Pathé film and reflect, very briefly, on the start and the finish of Cavendish's winning career at the Tour. I step into a spotlight and approach the microphone, and as soon as I drop his name into the darkness in front of me, I can tell by a sudden change in the mood in the room that the audience are bracing themselves. I start by simply uttering the word 'Brest' into the mic. That normally gets a titter, so to speak, because after all, it's a British audience.

But Brest is where it all began, back in 2008. That is where the Tour launched off in the year that he started winning. A few short minutes later I have shown the audience the footage of Cavendish's 35th stage win on the 2024 Tour and there is an ovation, which is as much collective relief as celebration. It is both of those things, I think. And the only response is to clap.

The early years, the peak Cavendish years in the blue and then the lemon yellow and white of HTC-Columbia, went by in a flash of winning. Each edition of the Tour characterised by a rash of victo-ries and unstoppable-seeming string of successes, which endured up to and then beyond his Milan–Sanremo win of 2009 and his World Championship in Copenhagen in 2011. I have written at length about these years, and, besides, they are part of our collective memory of the race and of the man: the sheer *reliability* of his career, the *dependability* of his delivery. This was one side of a character who was anything but predictable in his public-facing persona, where he could be dismissive, rude, intolerant, gracious, furious, poetic and extremely funny, all within the space of one sentence.

When I was still the guy doing the interviews for ITV, before switching to commentary, an impression grew up around our relationship that it was somehow difficult. To be honest, I never felt that particularly. Cavendish and I certainly never had a falling-out. Sure, there were a number of occasions when he was remarkably truculent and uncooperative, and for as long as I have known the man I also understand that there will be more to come. But those times were often counterbalanced by the more memorable interactions, when he would be fulsome, effusive and, frankly, incredibly interesting to listen to.

It's true, though, that the most compelling of the various Cavendish archetypes is the feisty one. There was his crushing retort to the reporter on the Mall in 2012 asking why the GB Team had failed to deliver him an Olympic gold medal. There was the stealing of the journalist's Dictaphone. There were as many withering stares and deathly pauses as there were stage wins. No journalist ever approached an interview with Cavendish with the same nonchalance that you might put a microphone under the nose of, say, Geraint Thomas. But those are the rules of engagement. You take them or leave them.

Yet there was a time, hard to pinpoint with any degree of precision, when the Cavendish certainties became fuzzy; when all that clarity and focus, and their attendant conversion into achievement, grew harder to define. At some hazy point, sport's most reliable winning machine started to silt up with doubt.

* * *

One early memory, perhaps one I have retrofitted to suit the subsequent sequence of events: it was the evening of stage 20 of the 2012 Tour de France. The race had been won by Bradley Wiggins in the final time trial. The team, as dysfunctional and factional as it was (and it *was*), was going through the motions of celebrating together in the separate dining area of the Chartres Nord Campanile. I'll never forget Bernie Eisel, part of the Cavendish contingent in the team, wearily walking across the car park, spotting me, and asking if 'the arsey one' had returned to the hotel yet. He meant Bradley Wiggins. The team was split three ways, with Chris Froome's presence also creating schisms and, to be fair to Wiggins, he had every reason to be 'arsey', if indeed he was. He had a Tour de France to win, I guess. But that remark of Eisel's stuck with me.

Barely able to raise a smile among them, the atmosphere was stilted to say the least. Dave Brailsford's rather performative speech (mostly for the benefit of the two or three documentary crews hovering around the scene) did little to allay the awkwardness, as perfunctory glasses of champagne were raised and sipped in minute measure by athletes with zero body fat and a race the following day. On which subject, Brailsford piped up.

'Don't forget, though, it's a big day tomorrow. The race isn't done yet. We've got Paris and Mark to look after. He's hardly ever lost on the Champs-Élysées.'

Across the table, I caught sight of Cavendish wrinkling his forehead. He glanced across at Dave Brailsford and snapped back at him.

'What do you mean "hardly ever"?' Cavendish looked genuinely appalled. 'I've *never* lost there.' And it was true. He never had.

Nor did he in 2012, though that was to be the last of his victories in Paris. It was the occasion when cycling Top Trumps played an unbeatable hand: two teammates and compatriots, one in the yellow jersey, the other in the rainbow bands, the Tour de France winner leading out the World Champion to victory for a record-breaking fourth win on the cobbles of the Champs-Élysées. Obviously, it was going to be downhill from there. There was no improvement possible.

Weeks after that, during the Olympics, and just as Cavendish was calling time on his one-year-only and not totally happy stay at Team Sky, I was talking to Dave Brailsford in a lift at a sponsor's event on the fringes of the games. When he'd finished cursing Shane Sutton for dragging him along and stopped complaining to me that he hadn't been home for three months, his chat turned to Mark Cavendish. He seemed convinced that Cavendish should try and develop his career elsewhere, by which he meant away from the Tour.

'I told him, how about the Classics? How about Flanders, I mean why not?' Brailsford remembered suggesting. 'Chasing Tour stage wins is just the law of diminishing returns. What's the difference between 20 and 25? No one is greatly impressed any longer.'

* * *

That was fully 12 years before the entire cycling world proved the exact opposite to be the case. One by one they lined up, the constituent parts of the 2024 peloton, like guests at the door of a church at a wedding, all wanting to shake the hand of the groom: in this case, Mark Cavendish, who moments before had ridden to victory for the 35th time at the Tour de France, prising from the reluctant hands of the great Eddy Merckx one of the few records he will ever relinquish (although Pogačar might yet make that prediction look premature).

All that was still to come, of course. Mark Cavendish never did drop his obsession with the Tour de France, almost to the exclusion of everything else, but for a few years the Brailsford prophesy, so casually articulated as the lift ascended to the fifth floor of some pristine new building in the Westfield Shopping Centre, looked pretty accurate. Though Cavendish won two stages at the Tour the following year, he crashed out on stage one in 2014 and only picked up a solitary victory in 2015.

His comeback, the first of at least three, came in 2016. It was, by pure chance, the day on which David Millar and I had been pitched headlong into commentating at the Tour for the first time, replacing, to the disgust and shock of many, the very well-loved and familiar tones of Paul Sherwen and Phil Liggett. To say that we were apprehensive would be an *hors catégorie* understatement. No one had warned the public. We were about to come as an almighty shock.

The finish line of stage one, weirdly, was at Utah beach. The whole lead-up to the *Grand Départ* had been strangely military, with the riders being driven up to the team presentation in the village of Sainte-Mère-Église by actors dressed as GIs behind the wheels of vintage

US army personnel carriers, in each of which eight bemused-looking riders looked sheepishly out at the largely unimpressed crowds of Normans at the side of the road. For the dozen German riders in the peloton, some of whom might well have grandfathers who had served in the war, it must have been a disconcerting experience; assuming that they even had the faintest idea what was being commemorated, which I suppose was not necessarily a given. Some bike riders tend to know a lot about bike riding and not a great deal else.

Having been driven close to Utah Beach, we decamped from the car, walked along the finish line and settled into our commentary position in the back of the ITV truck. Once I'd added the notes I needed for the day, and with half an hour to go until the start of the race, I went for one final breath of sea air, stretching my legs as far as a tourist cabin selling D-Day tat to cycling fans and assorted other bewildered tourists. I bought a little 'Voie de la Liberté' kilometre marker and went back to the truck, and set it up next to my notes and the monitor. It became the first totem in a tradition of buying something small and tacky at every *Grand Départ* I commentated on.

A commentary milestone from Utah Beach in 2016.

And it was an auspicious day. Cavendish beat Marcel Kittel to take stage one and, with that, for the first and only time in his career, the yellow jersey. This he promptly relinquished to Peter Sagan the following day, causing the great, odd Slovakian to tell a journalist that if he lost the yellow jersey, he'd still have the green jersey, and if he lost that, he'd only have to fall back on the rainbow bands. I have no idea what I yelled as Cavendish crossed the line, and have even less desire to go and look it up on YouTube as I rather suspect it was, at best, humdrum. It was my first day commentating at the Tour de France, after all.

As David and I embarked on the opening week of our commentating careers at the Tour, overwhelmed at times by the backlash that accompanied our having so suddenly replaced Phil and Paul, Mark Cavendish was suddenly in the thick of things once more. Clad in the all-white of Dimension Data, once he had given up his much yearned-for yellow jersey, he set about reminding the watching world of what he used to do in the yellow of HTC-Columbia. He won again on stage three and then once more on stage six. He got himself over the Pyrenees and up Mont Ventoux on the infamous day that saw Chris Froome running up the mountain without a bicycle. Then he struck again on stage 14.

It was his first four-stage haul since 2011 and it could have been more had he not decided to climb off before the Alps to focus on his unsuccessful bid for gold on the track at the Rio Olympics. This was the second time, after 2008, that Cavendish had voluntarily left the race in pursuit of that elusive medal. And when you also tally up those editions of the Tour when he either crashed out early (2014, 2017, 2023), was sick (2018) or was not selected (2019, 2020, 2022), you could argue that the Merckx record could have fallen a great deal sooner than it eventually did. He might have had 40. Maybe 50. Seriously.

The sometimes-fraught internal team politics at Team Sky, Dimension Data, Bahrain-McLaren and Deceuninck-Quick-Step were one thing. The injuries were a simply brutal, but perhaps inevitable, consequence of plying his trade where he did in the race. But his long-undiagnosed battle with the Epstein-Barr virus and the accompanying acute mental health crisis represented just as big a hurdle to overcome, as Cavendish resolutely refused to acknowledge what was universally held to be true for pretty much everyone watching his career slide away. He was not, contrary to all the abundant evidence, finished.

* * *

It had felt very different at times. Often, in fact. I remember how his 2018 season had started. I had been out in Abu Dhabi to commentate on the eponymous race at the beginning of February. Making my last commentary notes ahead of stage one of the race, alone in my crazily expensive hotel room, I hesitated over the number of professional victories Cavendish had to his name. Different versions of the total were in circulation and I didn't want to get it wrong should the need arise to call him home as the winner of another race.

So, perhaps against my better judgement, I sent Cavendish a direct message on social media. This was the only way I had of contacting him, since he had steadfastly refused to share his mobile number with me ever since I first asked him for it, disembarking from a little propellor plane on the tarmac at Brest airport ahead of the 2008 Tour de France. 'I don't give my number to journalists,' he had rather cuttingly replied. Trying not to appear snubbed, I had succeeded only in appearing snubbed. And I remained pretty much snubbed, despite frequent and often unpredictably warm face-to-face contact with Cavendish for the next decade. Which is why his almost instant reply to my DM was unexpected in a couple of ways.

'Hi mate' – firstly, he neither knew nor seemed to care what the correct number of wins was – 'I honestly don't know. It changes on what you count. Think 146 is about right as a pro. Did win more pro races as an amateur, but don't know if it counts. I honestly don't know though I'm afraid.'

I wasn't certain that he was actually as relaxed about it as this made him seem, but it was interesting to note that he didn't have a hard and fast interpretation of what constituted a win either. I had thought this number would have been seared into his every waking moment.

But, if that was something of a surprise, it was nothing compared to the message that followed: 'Thanks mate. If you need me, here's my number.' And he added his mobile phone number, the same one he still holds today.

The next day Cavendish crashed out of the first stage of the Abu Dhabi Tour before the flag had even dropped. He had been riding on the bumper of the race director's car, setting a steady pace during the neutralised roll-out. But this was Abu Dhabi and so the sponsored director's car was some fancy-pants brand with too much tech, including, it seemed, an automatic braking function if something appeared too close to the front of the car. Which is what happened when a TV moto crossed just ahead of it. The chain reaction was instantaneous. The car slammed on the brakes, Cavendish slammed into the car. Race over.

I was in Italy a few weeks later for the start of Tirreno Adriatico, as he attempted to re-launch his season. The race began with a team time trial. In the closing kilometre, having done his final pull on the front, Cavendish hit a pothole in the road and was violently unseated. He crossed the line outside the time delay, with blood streaming down his face and cuts all over his body. Much later, as Matt Stephens and I drove away from the finish line, we passed Cavendish being escorted by one of his *soigneurs* from a check-up at the hospital to the airport and off the race. Though we noted him in the passenger seat behind the glass of the car, we quickly looked away, not wanting to make eye contact, nor intrude on the quiet, private bleakness of the moment.

And then, the highest-profile crash of them all. Making his second season's comeback at Milan–Sanremo, nine years after having won the Monument, Cavendish rode straight into a road divider on the lightning-fast approach to the Cipressa. It was the kind of impact which finishes a career, or even worse. His three attempts to start the 2018 season in February through to the end of March now read: did not finish, outside the limit, did not finish. Remember, this was all *six years* before he broke the Merckx record.

* * *

The next time I saw Cavendish in person was at the Tour de France. It was the celebrated ride to the top of La Rosière in the same year, 2018. That day, two GB riders finished in first and last position. Geraint Thomas won to take the yellow jersey and stake a huge claim to the overall victory that would come his way. And well over half an hour later, Mark Cavendish would be the last rider home, knowing that, for the first time in his Tour de France career, he was going to be outside the limit, but wanting to complete the job anyway.

We had long since finished commentating over the podiums and the post-race chat. I was actually already heading away from the TV compound with David to find our parked car, when we stopped to watch him finish. Cheered home by hundreds of Tour fans from across the cycling world, who had delayed their departure to witness his arrival, this moment, at the top of an Alpine climb, in the warm late afternoon sun, felt profoundly significant. It did indeed seem like he was signing off. As the noise drifted up into the deep blue above the ski resort, and as we watched Cavendish round off the moment with a trademark minor altercation with a cameraman (what else did we really expect?), there seemed to be no way back from this glorious/inglorious exit.

David had rushed ahead to be directly at the finish line. He sat on the tarmac, watching the proceedings through the lens of a camera he had taken to the race that year. Cavendish would not have known for a second that one of his closest friends in the peloton, the road captain who had marshalled Team GB's resources to deliver him to the line in Copenhagen for his sole World Championship win, was also trying to process what he was witnessing. Later that week, David wrote a moving tribute to his relationship with Cavendish. The career obituaries were piling up.

And that sense of finality was only confirmed, for me, when I was at an event with Cavendish a few months later. Though we had an appointment to conduct a live interview on stage, it was the conversation which took place backstage that struck home. In a rather functional waiting room at Birmingham's brutalist NEC conference centre, surrounded by half-emptied polystyrene cups of tea, stacks of bike brand publicity leaflets and a mostly full packet of Hobnobs, Cavendish was telling us (the three or four people in the room) how he had finally had a diagnosis that explained why he had been feeling so empty for so long. Apparently it was Epstein-Barr virus he told us. The mere fact that he now had a tangible label for his physical malaise had given him a degree of comfort.

But another guest at the event, a recently retired female mountain bike racer, who was not directly part of our little group, had been listening from a seat at the other side of the room. 'I hope you don't mind me interjecting,' she said, 'but I couldn't help hearing what you said.' As Cavendish turned to face her, a trace of concern suddenly showing, she went on, 'I had that. What you've been diagnosed with. For a year, I could hardly get out of bed.' Cavendish was now looking intently at her. She continued, 'Just to say, please don't underestimate what you're faced with. It took three, maybe four years of my career from me, and even now I'm still not right.'

There was complete silence in the room. Cavendish, who is not averse to silences when you least expect them, but normally has a wisecrack or a response to any given situation, seemed utterly bereft. The moment passed and perhaps didn't last as long as I remember it. But it looked like someone had just punched the wind out of him. He fell instantly quiet and started twisting around a polystyrene cup of lukewarm tea, so that the grey, milky liquid lapped up the walls in an attempt to escape. A profound discomfort filled the space.

* * *

So continued the wilderness years, in which I was asked dozens of times in many different ways, at events, giving interviews, responding to viewers' questions, whether or not Mark Cavendish would ever win another stage of the Tour de France. 'Absolutely not,' I would reply, not wanting to gloss over a very obvious demise. 'Sadly, I can't see it,' I would add. And then, perhaps unnecessarily, I would expound further: 'It's not just that he's no longer winning sprints, he's not even getting to the finish at the front to be in a position to contest them.'

From time to time and out of the blue, Mark and I would exchange messages. This didn't happen often and when it did I was almost always caught out. During the pandemic, he checked in to see if things were OK, just as the first weeks of lockdown were starting to really bite. He was one of those people who was finding the experience strangely positive, spending a lengthy period of time at home with his young family for the first time. But he was also aware that not everyone felt that way and when he found out that Kath, my partner, was a nurse, he went out of his way to send a supportive message.

Many years later, once racing had resumed and we were all back on the road again, messages would land in the middle of the night, because he had been listening to whatever David, Pete and I had been fumbling around trying to understand on our *Never Strays Far* podcast. He was in the habit of listening and would sometimes pick up on the thread of a half-baked discussion about astrophysics or amateur psychology. He loved Pete's contributions, in particular, describing his old friend from the Isle of Man as being a bit like Ricky Gervais's sidekick Karl Pilkington. 'I love listening to you three,' he once told me. 'You're just all so different, but you seem to get on so well.' It was true. He was right. He has always tended to be annoyingly right about things.

Like so many others were, I was caught out entirely by his sudden resurgence. I do remember, during the spring of 2021, noting that he was suddenly appearing again towards the front of races, visibly in the mix. And there was a disbelieving exchange of messages between David, Pete and myself when Cavendish eventually started to win again, first in Turkey, then in Belgium. 'Bloody hell, Cav actually won another bicycle race!' As July approached, it seemed that Cavendish would be at the Tour de France once again, this time in the blue of Quick-Step.

Five years had gone by since the last time he'd won. Five years in which he'd crashed out, been eliminated and not been selected. But just in case I needed it, I had scribbled in my commentary notes (it was the second year of our Covid-enforced absence from France, the second of those Maidstone-bound exile tours) a few thoughts about what it might mean if he were to roll back the years and sprint to victory again. When it happened, it seemed the most natural thing in the world. 'Stop the clocks! Turn back time! History is not in charge here. Mark Cavendish is!' I somehow yelled, while an open-mouthed David Millar sat speechless (temporarily) alongside me.

Of course, that wasn't the end of the story at all. Out of nowhere he started to close in on Eddy Merckx's record of 34 stage wins at the Tour, a feat everyone (perhaps even, in his heart of hearts, Cavendish) had given up on. But he drew level with a few opportunities remaining and was even waved off at the start of stage 19 by the great Belgian himself. Merckx, however reluctantly, had dropped into the race to pose for a photo with Cavendish at the start line of a stage his team would go on to squander, when a breakaway made it to the line instead.

Cavendish won four stages and the green jersey (for the second time in his career) in 2021, in almost every case piloted to the line by his leadout man Michael Mørkøv, in whom he seemed to have developed an intuitive trust. The difficult-to-pronounce Dane (who I had once asked for help in pronouncing his name, only for him to answer, 'I don't really mind – Just don't make me sound Russian') was a masterful rider, smoothly guiding Cavendish through the chaos of the final kilometre before dropping him off with 200 metres to go. Cavendish's decision to leave his wheel on the final run to the line in Paris perhaps cost him the chance to win a 35th stage and to draw clear of Merckx. And if that had happened, we might have been spared the drama of the next three years. But this was Cavendish and drama is in the small print of his contract with the world.

* * *

Almost a year on from that warm Paris evening in 2021 when the record slipped through his fingers, I found myself standing in Castle Douglas in torrential rain. It battered down all morning and then began slowly to clear through the afternoon, as the British Road Race Championship peloton rode through the demure little town on half a dozen circuits, before heading out into the rolling fields of Dumfries and Galloway once again. Each time they came through I left the warm confines of Imperial Hotel on King Street, in whose carpeted lounge several trays of dainty sandwiches and hearty scones had been laid out in the tradition of a semi-amateur British sporting event. Heading to the side of the road, I watched the front group get smaller and smaller, whittled down by one rider, who seemed intent on attacking from the first to the very last of the day's attritional 201 kilometres. It was Mark Cavendish and he was making a point.

I had never seen him race like that before. He took it upon himself that day, personally, to shred the peloton. He, and he alone, destroyed the field, until there was no one left there to threaten him and he duly won. With his national champion's jersey on his shoulders once again and wearing the hilariously cheap medal that British Cycling hang around their winning riders' necks, Cavendish broke a silence that had endured for weeks about his presumed non-selection for the Tour.

'I've not heard a thing from the team,' he told me, with the camera rolling. 'But it'd be beautiful to take this jersey to the roads of France, don't you think, Ned?' I did think so. But, with far greater pertinence Patrick Lefevere, his boss at Quick-Step, didn't agree. Cavendish stayed at home, while his teammate Fabio Jakobsen took the sprinter's berth on the Tour de France team. And that was another year done.

In 2023 he had been picked up by Alexander Vinokourov's Astana at the very last minute – quite literally, as he had been spotted being met at Alicante airport by a liveried team car in the blue of the Kazakh team, ending months of speculation in which he had remained silent about his future. One more tilt at the Tour de France, it seemed.

That year, as the race rolled out of the Basque Country and into the flatter roads of the deep south-west of France, Pete Kennaugh, working with us again on ITV, had got into the habit of riding the last couple of kilometres of each 'sprintable' stage and sending Cavendish a little video recon via WhatsApp. For some reason, on the morning of the Bordeaux stage (one of the many towns and cities across

France where Cavendish had already won), towards the end of the opening week, Pete wasn't there to do his usual filming. I have no idea why he wasn't available that morning to help his old friend, but I can clearly remember him ringing me from a posh menswear shop in downtown Bordeaux asking what my shoe size was as he was about to buy me an expensive pair of socks, for no other reason than he is a lovely, genuinely mad man. He was shopping instead.

I don't quite know what possessed me, other than a feeling of goodwill towards the world in general, Bordeaux with its white stone and bright river, and Pete Kennaugh in particular, for the fresh pair of socks that cost 10 times more than I have ever spent on cloth for my feet, but I was in a tremendous mood. An hour or so before we went on the air, I walked along the river, pacing out the final couple of kilometres of the finish. Noticing that there were one or two complications, most notably a section of light cobblestones with 400 metres to go, and knowing that Pete wasn't able to offer his old mate Cavendish the usual reconnaissance, I stepped into the breach, sending the sprinter a series of WhatsApp messages, which ended with a picture of the cobbles.

My 'detailed' recon, as seen by Mark Cavendish.

I imagined him, phone in hand, sitting in the cool of the Astana team bus. At 9.57 a.m., around 45 minutes before the start of the stage, he replied in a series of messages which started with a trademark swear.

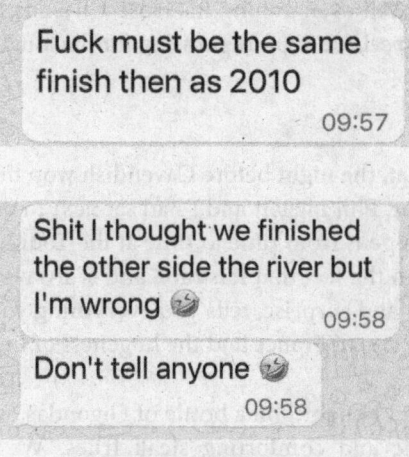

Fuck must be the same finish then as 2010

09:57

Shit I thought we finished the other side the river but I'm wrong 😂

09:58

Don't tell anyone 😂

09:58

Mark's reaction.

Little has ever spoken as clearly to me about the wonderful chaos at the amateur heart of road racing than reading this exchange from a rider who, later that day, came to within a hair's breadth of breaking an all-time record, unaware of where the race finished and relying on partial information generated by an enthusiast with a smartphone. I like to think it was a consequence of my brilliant recon work (it wasn't really, it was Cavendish reading the race perfectly and understanding that Mathieu van der Poel's leadout wasn't strong or long enough) and I often claim credit for that afternoon in Bordeaux in 2023 when Cavendish very nearly broke the Merckx record for the second time of asking, after that misjudged sprint in Paris in 2021.

He was agonisingly close to achieving what was obviously his last goal, though he steadfastly refused in public to acknowledge the notion that this was his objective. The next day he crashed out of the race and went home in his self-avowed 'final' Tour. It was nothing of the sort of course. He was always going to return to the race, having come that close to victory. David and I spent most of that winter annoying Pete by mining him for intel; the Isle of Man cycling community is small and there were days when Cavendish came round to the Kennaughs' and vice versa. But even among his closest friends he has a way of keeping his counsel. He kept us guessing for the longest time.

* * *

It was fitting that, the night before Cavendish won his 35th and final stage of the Tour, Phil Liggett and I had sat next to one another over dinner. This happens from time to time at the Tour, when itineraries collide, although the fact that it is rare, and is always celebrated with delight, hilarity and surprise, tells you everything you need to know about the sheer size of France and the hugeness of the race. It doesn't happen often.

That evening I bought Phil a bottle of Gigondas, which we shared over our classic and comforting steak frites. We swapped some memories of times when things had gone right and other moments when things had gone wrong, and we talked at length about talking about cycling. The evening passed in that familiar way at the Tour, a quiet, restrained sense of joy at being part of such a huge adventure. I realised, as I often do, how much I love the race. But neither he nor I was prepared for what happened the following day in the little town of Saint-Vulbas.

It was, appropriately, a faintly ridiculous hotel, almost a long stone's throw from the curiously underwhelming town which will forever be remembered as the place The Record was broken. It was themed in an American style and modelled on a motel. Bernard Hinault was also there, but we only saw him the following morning at breakfast, chatting intently with the lady who ran the place.

I got up early and went off for a run, heading towards the modest church spire in the distance and away from the cacophony of the barriers being clattered into place to form the final kilometres right outside our hotel. Galumphing my way into town, I got sidetracked by the temptation of a park through which a gravel pathway was threaded and ended up doing a few circuits there, before turning and heading home. Saint-Vulbas was, I concluded, one of the most humble host towns I could remember at the Tour; archetypically French, with very few of the Tour's international froth to suggest a sense of global significance. But then it was, after all, stage five and a weekday. Long enough, just about, into the race for people to have started to lose interest and forget that it was on. All around the park, rotund gentlemen were emerging from camper vans to wipe the dew from their plastic tables, plonk themselves down in a foldable chair, rub their eyes and blearily assess the scene, as they contemplated how to kill the hours before the race would shoot into town. It was the most ordinary of settings.

All the more remarkable then, that this was the chosen time and place for Mark Cavendish to round off his career, gift-wrap it for posterity and present it to the Tour de France; as if to say, 'Here you are. Thanks for having me.'

Neither David nor I had seen it coming. We had already spoken about the prospect of Cavendish battling his way through the first visit to the Alps (uniquely in 2024, the race called into the mountain range twice) and the Pyrenees, while other sprinters fell by the wayside, and then leaving it until the last possible opportunity in Nîmes to break the record. What we hadn't accounted for was the prospect of him doing it on stage five, in this most prosaic of locations.

They were all there, all the Cavendish attributes on display for one last time. His bravery, bordering on recklessness; his unreal mental agility; his astonishing lucidity in the moment as he flitted from wheel to wheel, making progress through the bunch until he found himself exactly where he needed to be and pulled the trigger, coming off Pascal Ackermann's fading sprint and launching for the line.

And in the end it was won in the blink of an eye. Just enough time, in fact, for David to slump in his seat, once again struck dumb, and for me, suddenly standing at his side, to yell into a microphone, 'It's done! It's done! The story is now complete!'

* * *

The sun is trying to break through a sheet of very slowly drifting cloud. I think I'm in Loughborough tonight, so not too far to drive. Around me in the hotel, doors are slamming and the high-pitched whinny of tiny suitcase wheels on hard-wearing carpet fills the corridors. Coventry is going to work and so must I. Besides, my tea went cold a long time ago.

I will save this file now, but in doing so I still can't be sure it's the last word I'll write about Cavendish. I think I have finally learned that much.

18

UNFOLDING STORIES

I don't know any way of accompanying the Tour de France other than on a bicycle which collapses around a central hinge and then folds in on itself like a puppy that has no idea how to walk.

To me and to David Millar alike, the lived experience of covering the Tour has become so intimately connected to the act of riding our Brompton bikes up and down dale, through storm and heatwave, past villages, churches and fields, through cities and finish lines, as to be unimaginable without the funny little contraptions. They get us to where we need to go, even if we don't always know we need to go there until we arrive, parched, happy and very often completely lost.

Stopping off in a little hilltop village somewhere near Brives.

This unexpected plot twist began in 2016. I don't remember any pre-amble, any discussions about what was about to happen. The bikes just suddenly appeared.

David has a habit of doing things like this – conjuring equipment from thin air. We'll check into a random hotel somewhere near Saint-Étienne or Blois and there'll be an enormous box of *stuff* at reception awaiting Monsieur Millar's arrival. On one occasion it was full of brand-new pairs of shoes, which he spent weeks handing out to every single ex-rider at the race, until even Laurent Jalabert was wearing them. Another time there was a massive consignment of T-shirts and then socks. He seemingly has a network of people moving *stuff* around Europe in boxes at his command. Anyway, on this occasion, the tall time triallist had arranged to have two Bromptons, liveried in his own branded design, delivered to our hotel on the Cherbourg peninsula on the evening of stage one of that year's Tour de France. It was the first time I had ever really seen one of these now ubiquitous bikes up close. Back then they still had 'mad Professor' vibes. But then, so, too, did David.

Having broken bread, or more likely begged the chef for a steak frites before he closed the kitchens at 8 p.m., with some colleagues from Eurosport who happened to have been put up in the same hotel, David got to very public work in the foyer with an Allen key. He assembled the bikes, tightening a bit here, loosening a bit there and generally making them look like they could be ridden. Then he removed the production line saddles that the two bikes had been delivered with and instead fixed two exquisite black leather Brooks seats into position; the 1940s types with brass rivets all along the side and one on the nose. Our new bikes looked odd with their retro saddles, granted. But they looked odd with a certain defiant distinction. Which I guess was the effect he was looking for. Anyway, who was I to argue?

As we all gazed on, David set about delivering a tutorial to me on how to fold and unfold the bike. How quickly his life had changed, I found myself thinking. Within two years of having been a pro, serviced by a team of mechanics and riding the highest tech, fastest kit known to man, he was reduced to trying to teach an unwilling student like me how to fold up a commuter bike. Obviously, as he made me try it for the first time, standing in the lobby of a Best Western hotel, watched on by TV colleagues from across the *zone technique*, I made a repeated and total balls of it, getting everything wrong and the mirror opposite of the correct angle. What was supposed to be over in seconds, took me whole confused minutes, only to achieve a kind of monstrous deformity of tubes, wheels and chains, all dislocated and unrideable. In fact, it would be weeks before I would master the method, a deficiency of technique that left me like a helpless child in the company of a capable parent whose patience was wearing thin. By the time we got to the Alps, I had finally figured it out. But by then I'd almost broken myself by riding the damn thing.

There's never a spare inch of space in our car.

It had all started so well. The morning of stage two of the 2016 Tour dawned wet, grey and blustery. It was the kind of weather that Normandy considers with pride to be a local speciality, even in the height of summer. Later that day Mark Cavendish would relinquish his very brief but very satisfactory hold on the yellow jersey amid squally showers and then proper cloudbursts as the race approached the finish line somewhere in the suburbs of Cherbourg.

ITV's new commentary team arrived in embarrassing style, at least partly. We were chauffeured to the outskirts of town in a white Maserati. I know how bad that sounds, but sadly there is no other way of describing our transport, because that's exactly what it was. For the first two Tours that David and I commentated together on for ITV, we swanned around in what we secretly referred to as 'the wedding car', an endlessly long-bonneted, white thing that growled like a wounded walrus and had no space in the boot for our bikes and barely any for humans. The car enraged people wherever it went, up to and including the puce-faced gendarme who pulled us over on the autoroute as the race left Germany in 2017, hauled David out of the passenger seat and almost pistol-whipped him before realising that he wasn't the driver. It was a right-hand drive.

'I totally knew that,' the police officer had said in French, when David politely pointed out that he wasn't actually in the driving seat. Somewhere in the darkness of the back seat, hidden by three Bromptons, I was convulsed with laughter.

The high-end sponsorship lasted until Maserati realised they were getting nothing from their side of the bargain and withdrew the ridiculous motor car from our clutches. By way of mitigation, I will never forget how we were forced to abandon the wedding car just as we started the long drive north after stage 20 of the 2017 Tour de France.

With hilarious timing, the highly prized sports car chose to lose power somewhere near Grenoble, forcing us to freewheel to a halt near a branch of Avis and dump it unceremoniously in a car park at the airport. We got all our luggage and bikes out, and completed our journey in a tiny little Renault that David hired on his credit card. The mighty were well and truly fallen. And that was the end of my co-commentator's rather flattering association with Maserati. However, up until the ignominious and fatal mechanical, the luxury of having a car and a driver, a great friend of David's from Catalonia called Cristian, held huge advantages for us in our ambition to ride our Bromptons every single day, come hell or high water. In the case of the stage two in 2016, it was the latter.

* * *

Cristian dropped us off about 20 kilometres from the finish line. It was drizzling as David unfolded first his, and then my, bike. He then placed a beret on his head, rather jauntily. It was the only time I have ever seen him do that and I will forever wonder whether the beret itself was an act of hubris, because I never saw it again.

Firstly, it started to rain properly. Then properly became heavily, so heavily in fact that within minutes we were both soaked through to the underpants and indeed beyond. I remember the sound of plimsolls squelching as I turned each painful pedal stroke; my accreditation swinging from side to side like a laminated pendulum, sending off arches of water either side of me. That was roughly when I started to put David Millar into difficulty.

We had reached the series of short, sharp climbs that characterised the rather unlovely final eight kilometres that skirted Cherbourg's utilitarian centre. Conscious that I did not want to disgrace myself on the first ride I had ever done both on a Brompton, or in the company of David, I 'pushed on', to use cycling parlance. Actually, I rode pretty much as hard as I could, to the extent that at points I wanted to sit by the side of the road in the rain and cry. It was a wordless, gruelling ride. I was so certain that I was about to be put in my place by a recently retired professional that at no point did I dare to look back.

Dropping David in Cherbourg.

Had I done so, I probably might have crashed in astonishment on the wet roads. David could not hold my wheel. By the time I got to the finish line, he had dropped completely out of sight. Please don't get me wrong; this is neither a boast nor is it a humble brag. I have no idea how it came about and I must stress very clearly that it has never once been repeated. Not once.

Also, I honestly wasn't fast. I really wasn't. Bemused French spectators, braving the rain, were laughing openly at me; not *with* me, you understand, *at* me. The rascals lampooned my bike or 'le vélo de clown' as they dubbed it. They cackled with Gallic scorn, and made all manner of unkind and derisive whistles and clicks of the tongue. But, and no doubt to his mortification and deep shock, my risible lack of speed was actually faster than David's total horror show of a ride. For one rainy day in Normandy the moment of my greatness flickered, then promptly went out.

* * *

We never once mentioned what had passed between us on the road to Cherbourg. He must have decided that such a shameful reckoning could never be openly discussed and would never be allowed to happen again. The fact of the matter was that, since his final ever race in the autumn of 2014, not only had David not ridden a bike, he'd also not done any form of exercise whatsoever. Given 20 months of total inactivity, he had stopped (temporarily) being good at the only thing he'd ever been brilliant at: being incredibly fit. But still. Neither of us expected the outcome that had just come to pass.

As I say, it couldn't last, and it didn't. As the race wound its way south, we rode our bikes further and further and up ever bigger obstacles. All the while, David started to take himself more seriously. With each passing revolution of the pedals I grew more tired and he grew stronger. Exponentially so. It was as if his body, for so many years accustomed to an insane workload, woke up again and remembered what it was all about. 'Oh, I remember this. It's called exercise. I used to be really good at doing this.' And very, very quickly the athlete reappeared, like a snake shedding its skin, the memory of David Millar the Layabout was dumped by the side of a sodden Normandy road, never to be seen again.

On the first rest day we rode out on our Bromptons to a hilltop village to the south of our tiny townhouse in the middle of Bergerac, stopping only for a coffee in the same courtyard as Adam Yates and his Orica-BikeExchange teammates. Temporarily unsure which identical twin was sitting at the table next to us, sipping a coffee, David greeted him in a manner which left both possibilities open: 'Hello, Yates!' I remember looking at my shoes, then a tree, then at the wall, but not at Adam Yates.

Over the course of a delicate and lovingly prepared lunch of sole and lightly steamed new potatoes, and no doubt emboldened by a bottle of white wine, we hatched a plan as we ate and drank overlooking the plain below. We would spend the afternoon making a mockumentary about our lives and it would feature live action on our Bromptons.

Within hours, we had developed the script, filmed it and post-produced the resultant movie. It told the story of my secret belief that I 'could have been a contender' and David's secret humouring of my delusion. It featured me racing him to a village sign and him letting me win the sprint, with me none the wiser.

Thematically, the whole venture was uncomfortably close to the bone, like all great art is. And believe me, this was great art, filmed entirely on location in Bergerac on our iPhones and edited on my laptop (by me) while David played boules with some locals outside our rented house. The evening degenerated after that and we ended up at a random BBQ miles into the French countryside, at which Richard Virenque was mystifyingly present. I made a speech to everyone and then sang, before trying to order an Uber and collapsing on a lawn. It had been an emotional day.

* * *

Day by day, our Brompton adventures grew in scale and ambition. Towards the middle of week two, we had ended up in the Pyrenees, where we really lifted off. I managed to conquer the Col du Peyresourde, a climb which Chris Boardman and I had abandoned a few years previously, on proper bikes, as the mountain grew dark and stormy and we both suffered from (in Chris's words) a 'double leg puncture'. So the beastly Pyrenean mountain had become something of an albatross around my neck ever since. In 2016 I got to the top on my own (riding with David was becoming a bit less fun every day) and felt so uncommonly pleased with myself I asked a tourist to take a picture of me for posterity. I had not been aware of quite how much I had been sweating until I looked at it later that evening. Then I descended half of the mountain on the other side to find our accommodation and to meet up with David and Cristian, and, of course, the silly white car.

A sweaty mess at the top of the Peyresourde.

The next morning we woke up in a remote hotel deep into the mountains above Luchon, the spa town visited by the Tour on at least a bi-annual basis. The hotel proprietor was a big fan of motor sports and therefore a big fan of the Maserati that had just appeared outside his establishment. As he served us the standard French mountain breakfast of nothing more than a slice of baguette, a packet of butter and some jam, he wanted to know if the car parked out the front was ours.

'Oui, Monsieur,' answered David without looking remotely ashamed. Perhaps Monsieur would like to see it? Perhaps he'd like to sit inside the car at the wheel? Monsieur would. He even posed for photographs of him pretending to drive it. As I said, he *really* liked cars.

Once back in the breakfast room, we started to make our plan for the day. Luchon was only about 10 kilometres away, but that was almost all downhill. This we deemed insufficient 'sport'. We needed to find a climb. Well, we didn't need to, but we were rapidly becoming a bit obsessed. We *wanted* very much to find a climb and we were damn well going to. David, whose memory for the geography of the Alps and the Pyrenees is even worse than mine, despite having raced over them 13 times at least, surprised us both. He asked the patron whether the Porte de Balès was close by.

'Oui, Monsieur.' It was his turn to be helpful. Apparently the hotel, which we had arrived at during the night when it was already dark, was actually at the foot of the climb. All we had to do was turn left out of the front door. The plan was coming together. David then asked him how long it would take to get to Luchon by going over the top of the mountain.

'Une heure et demie,' the hotelier guessed, after a monetary wrinkled brow and a sudden inspection of his wooden boarded ceiling while he made the calculation.

One and a half hours was perfect and would allow us to get to the finish line comfortably in time for a shower, perhaps a bite to eat, and then to commentary (on the day, it would later transpire that Chris Froome effectively won the Tour by attacking on the descent into Luchon). We ate the remainder of our bread and jam in a single bite, took one gulp of his very dark, very difficult coffee, and we headed for the hills.

* * *

It was a bright morning with a frighteningly blue sky, the kind of emptiness above that reminds me just how thin the atmosphere is and how much inky black nothingness lies beyond. But our delicate planet looked perfect that morning, the increasingly barren mountainside empty to all but the click and squeak of our two Bromptons toiling side by side up the unwinding ribbon of road. The climb was not severe, but it was long. Eventually, the conversation dried up. David, showing an exceptional degree of patience that morning, rode at my pace up the climb.

We reached the top together, where the climb opens up on to a plateau and the views in every direction unfold in an infinitely self-replicating pattern of peaks and valleys, the vast landscape quietly basking in the mid-morning sun, mist clinging to the pastures and summery clouds building on the horizon. David, who had eschewed his Cherbourg beret and was now sporting a flat cap for some deep sartorial reason I could not fathom, insisted on us taking a photo at the top to record our ascent.

We were in great spirits. The Tour de France had all but melted away. All that remained in its place was each other, the mountain we had just climbed together and our silly little folding bikes.

Moments later we realised our mistake.

'How long did that take, David?' I asked, suddenly vaguely aware that despite our blissed-out state, we still had a job to do.

'An hour and a half,' he replied. We looked at his watch, then at one another, then at his watch, then at one another again. That was how long the *whole* ride to Luchon was supposed to take, according to our host.

'Oh shit. He thought we were going in a Maserati, didn't he?'

We weren't in a Maserati. We were on folding bikes. 'How far is Luchon?' I asked, with sudden massive anxiety.

'It's about 40 kilometres from here,' said David, trying not to sound totally panicked, 'but half of that is downhill, to be fair.'

The next hour and a half of my life was a passage of time defined by two things: horror and then agony.

The horror came by trying to match David Millar's speed on a folding bike over the course of a 20-kilometre descent. That nearly ended prematurely when I encountered the first vehicle of the morning, a Land Rover coming towards me around a blind corner. I think I closed my eyes as we passed one another. It had seemed the only viable option. I somehow slipped through an almost non-existent space between the front grill of the oncoming car and a cliff face on the inside of the bend. After that very close call, I simply watched David's impeccable form on his bike fly away from me and did the rest of the descent at my own teetering pace, my wrists in agony, pulling hard on the brakes, with the slight smell of heated rubber coming from both little wheels.

The agony came after that, when I was reunited with David at the foot of the climb. How long he had had to wait for me, I shall never know, but there was no time to ask, because he was issuing a very simple-sounding instruction. 'Stay on my wheel,' he said. And then he mounted his bike and off we went along the arrow-straight, pan-flat main road to Luchon. We had to maintain a certain speed if we were going to make it to work on time for the start of the show. And that speed was: Unreasonable.

With a time triallist's precision, David held a constant power, just enough to get the job done, while simultaneously keeping me alive, although only just. My entire body felt like a pot of simmering water with a lid that was lifting off and clattering. I kept my eyes fixed on David's rear wheel as he got himself into the closest approximation to an aero tuck he could manage on a 'clown's bike'.

Only once did we stop between the foot of the mighty Porte de Balès and Luchon. And that was only because a wasp had managed to fly up David's shorts, causing to him to slam on the brakes, dismount and momentarily run up and down the grassy verge slapping himself with both hands in the genitals.

I watched on, too tired to actually laugh, but inwardly absolutely howling. After his brief cameo as a bit-part character in an early *Carry On* film, the former *maillot jaune* of the Tour de France re-mounted his bicycle with small wheels and on we went. We arrived at the finish line to a grim-faced director who was less than impressed and with 10 minutes to spare. We had only made it because of our two-up time trial in which only one of us was actually doing the work on the front. David's burgeoning fitness had saved the day. Had that been Cherbourg David, complete with sodden beret and scowl, we'd have watched the start of the transmission go sailing by.

* * *

We should have learned our lesson, but instead, by the time we got to the Alps, our ambition had ballooned once more. We peaked out on stage 17, a day of folding-bike ignominy. That day we decided it would be wise to ride to work over the category 1 Col de la Forclaz and then straight up the *hors catégorie* Finhaut-Emosson. It was the same day that the weather decided to go mad, pouring heat across the Alps under a scorching sun. It was also on that fated ascent that we really noted, for the first time perhaps, the lack of a bottle cage of any description on a Brompton.

With no way of carrying water other than in our hands, we were reduced to begging from campers at the side of the road, between us deploying a wide a range of European languages to get what we needed to survive. Mostly it worked, despite the widespread bafflement our dishevelled presence on the climbs elicited. 'Go on then,' said a particularly brusque Austrian, having measured out a thimble of mineral water for us each to consume. 'Off you go again on your stupid fucking London city bikes.'

'Thank you!' we smiled back, pathetic in our snivelling gratitude, but stopped again 100 metres further up the climb and had to negotiate for another sip of water with a man from Auxerre, who thought everything was a right hoot.

This design fault (let's face it, Bromptons were not made to be ridden up these huge climbs) has plagued us for the best part of a decade. I remember David in 2022 bringing along a sort of fabric bottle-holder that you could Velcro to the handlebars. It was big enough for one tiny bottle of water, which I had drained entirely by the time I made it to the first of Alpe d'Huez's 21 switchbacks. In 2024 I was begging again on a hot windy ride through the exact centre of France, stopping just outside Bruère-Allichamps to accost a charming elderly couple from Brittany, who not only had plentiful water for me, but a home-made syrupy donut, which they insisted I rode off clutching. But not an edition of the race goes by without a tale of near desiccation. In 2019 David and I had both nearly expired, riding from Albi to Toulouse, and were saved by some Harley-Davidson mechanics by the side of the road. In 2022 somewhere near Brives, I think, only a remote well and ancient washing basin prevented our demise.

Cooling off in a fountain on a ride near Toulouse.

With the cat 1 climb done, and after a short descent, we started to the final climb: over 11 kilometres at an average of nearly 8%. It was quite hard. So hard in fact that I started to feel empty, then dizzy, then sick, then cold, then euphoric, then numb, then like I was drowning. I gazed in distress at David's back as he rode a consistent 30 metres ahead of me. Then, to my astonishment, he started to drop back ever closer. Just as we passed a big open tent where there appeared to be some kind of ad-hoc catering set-up, we both had the same thought at the same time.

'David, I...'

'...need to stop.' He completed the thought that I had begun and which we both suddenly shared. We were blacking out.

We rode off the tarmac and let our bikes fall into the soft, long grass. I let myself drop to the ground, too, while David wobbled drunkenly off to where they appeared to be selling food and drink, already waving his credit card and muttering to himself. Then he tottered back, crest-fallen and almost at the point of tears. 'They don't take cards.'

Fortunately, I had withdrawn 50 Swiss Francs the previous day, which was *just* enough for two cokes and two hot dogs. Honestly? I would have paid 500. It was then my turn to limp off and return with no money, but lots of calories. All the sugar, salt and fat was gone within seconds and we both turned our ketchupy faces into the grass, closed our eyes and drifted off.

How we ever got going again, I cannot recall, but somehow we must have, because I can remember the lanky Tartar Ilnur Zakarin won the stage. And much more pertinently we blagged a lift off the mountain with EF Education in their team bus. That was also the day I sat next to Pierre Rolland. You don't forget days like that.

* * *

Our Brompton adventures have endured for years and still we ride them. In 2017 I rode most of the way up Mont Ventoux, finishing just past Chalet Reynard, where the altered stage finish had been placed that year, high winds making the top of the mountain unsafe. It was the day that Chris Froome was left running up the mountain, bikeless.

David had no desire to join me that day, so instead opted to meet me at Chalet Reynard in the ridiculous Maserati, then drive over the top of Mont Ventoux and down the other side to the distant *zone technique* in Malaucène. By the time he met me on the mountain he had steam coming out of his ears. It seems that nudging an ostentatious high-performance sports car through the thousands of cyclists making their way very, very slowly up the 'Giant of Provence' on race day had tested his occasionally brittle patience to snapping point. By the time I popped open the boot and jauntily dropped in my folded bike (I had mastered the technique by now), he was barely able to talk. So, he didn't.

It might have been for that reason that he dropped me off by the side of the road about 15 kilometres from where I needed to be. It was either that or the fact that former Labour press chief Alastair Campbell had just invited him for tea at his Provençal home just north of Ventoux. Perhaps it was a combination of the two.

But either way, as his white sports car roared off into the lavender fields Campbell-wards, I found myself all alone on the road, trying to turn the pedals into the teeth of the strongest headwind I have ever tackled and already exhausted from having climbed most of Mont Ventoux on my Brompton. Had it not been for the sudden arrival of a French rider, a veteran, as he explained, of the ultra-endurance Paris-Brest-Paris, who took pity on me and sheltered me from the worst of the gale, I think I would still be on that interminable road to Malaucène, cursing the day I ever unfolded a bike or met David Millar.

* * *

Over the years, of course, we have pulled others into our orbit. Pete Kennaugh, once he understood that they needed to be fully unfolded to function as bicycles, also spent a few years enjoying Bromptons in his own dynamic and sometimes overly ambitious way.

Our few days with Marcel Kittel in the car in 2023 will be perhaps best remembered for a Brompton ride back to our hotel from the Puy de Dôme. Marcel had taken some convincing about the wisdom of the adventure. Having never experienced a folding bike before, he conducted a few exploratory and mildly uncontrolled loops of the car park before agreeing to the ride, by which time we were helpless with laughter: the bike looked like a small toy when sat on by the most powerful sprinter that Germany has ever produced.

It didn't take long before Pete Kennaugh, inspired perhaps by the magnificent presence of Kittel as an adversary rather than just boring old me and David, started to attack with a frequency and venom that left me instantly gasping for air. Marcel, it goes without saying, fared much better. He was slowly mastering the Brompton, despite the treacherous gravel paths we were all riding along. I was navigating and kept getting us lost, which at least meant that they both had to wait for me at each junction so that I could tell them which way to go. Then I'd be dropped again as Pete launched off once more.

But Marcel Kittel, the multiple *maillot jaune* and 14-time stage winner of the Tour de France, never once reacted to Pete's crazed and short-lived accelerations, staking his long-term strategy on Pete's predictable tendency to attack himself into submission whenever the road tipped up ahead even slightly. On the final little ramp we had to get over, Pete launched his Hail Mary offensive. Seconds later, and near to the top of the 300-metre climb, he fell off the bike clutching his heart and gasping theatrically for air, and then had to watch on, bent over the handlebars from the side of the road, as first Marcel ground impassively past him and then I followed many minutes later. As I rode past the prone Manxman, all I heard was an increasingly distant-sounding 'I nearly died just then...' as I left him behind.

And so through the years the folding bike has forever been at our sides. These bikes, one way or another, have conveyed us over the cobbles of Roubaix and on to its famous velodrome. They've carried us through the vicious slopes of the Massif Central, up and over just about every major Pyrenean and Alpine climb. They were how I got to work in 2018 on the Mûr-de-Bretagne, the day after my birthday, when England had lost a football World Cup semi-final.

They were my means of transport to the finish line in Brussels the following year, and Copenhagen, when we were allowed on to the race again after the pandemic. I rode my Brompton in 2023, the day before the race got underway, wildly overestimating my strength and taking almost four hours to complete a 60-kilometre loop around Bilbao, finishing on the crazily steep Pike Bidea.

And my folding bike came with me to Florence for the 2024 edition, enabling me to get wonderfully, dreamily lost on the way to Dijon, rolling through vineyards and Burgundy's mellow little villages, getting doused in intermittent showers and then, when I was completely clueless about which way to ride, being shepherded home by a couple of young lads from a local club who took care of a lone lost fool.

Rescued by some local riders in Burgundy.

If it's possible to distil my experience of so many years at the Tour into one single absurd meme, then it is probably the daily hubris of seeing David Millar riding a folding bike. That's probably it. Ever since we set out on our Brompton adventures, there has been a curious alchemy at play: for all that the folding bike diminished David, it enhanced me, so we could meet in the middle.

The poignancy of watching a once specialist time triallist, who despite everything was unarguably one of the very best in the world, reduced to riding the same roads as the pros he left behind but on a tiny little joke bicycle, will never quite leave me. But the thing is, he *loves* it! And I am a willing accomplice. David and my pioneering use of the Brompton at the Tour was the meeting point that we needed to find common ground with one another, as friends, as commentators, as *amateurs* of the Tour de France.

The whole experience does nothing more than make me laugh at my own perennial lack of preparedness for whatever it is that life at the Tour throws at me, which is a lot. And in the end, that must be the reason why the folding bikes so perfectly match our mood: they are, when all is said and done, an extremely silly way to try and ride round France. But then again, riding a bike around France is a pretty silly thing to try and do in the first place, especially when there's a bunch of people chasing you on their bikes.

Ready for the next ridiculous adventure.

19

MONDAY MORNING

For these past 23 years, my summers have been marked by a singu-
lar obsession: the Tour de France. Time has passed and I have
drifted with it. I have been carried through the decades, from Lance
to Landis, through Wiggins, Froome and Thomas via Evans and
Contador, Schleck and Sastre, and beyond. Each step from year to
year has presented only subtle change, so slight sometimes as to be
undetectable. But over time these things mount up and it now comes
as a giddy shock to stand at the end of the road and look back at
how far we've come. How the hell did Tadej Pogačar emerge from the
grisly cocoon of 2003? How was that change possible?

Not everything has changed for the better. I miss the days when
French and Flemish were the languages of the bunch, before the
Anglophone world tightened its globalising tentacles across even that
most arcane and foreign of worlds, the peloton.

I have felt at times the irreversible march of commerce as the
race has reached out for a global market, trying to lose its eccentric
shackles. I've noted how primitive photo ID has been replaced by
QR codes, how barriers have gone up at the start villages to keep the
spectators back, as the free-for-all has been replaced by the mixed
zone, the mad bundles at the finish line done away with in favour of a
press conference on Zoom. I have the seen the slow-to-arrive rebirth,
but then sudden success, of the women's race.

Without wishing to sound like Rutger Hauer in the pouring rain, I *have* seen all that and yet I still feel the thrill, because the layers of meaning that prop up the edifice of the Tour are deeper by far than the crust that sits on top.

Not only that, but by gaining access to this idiosyncratic pursuit called road racing, born in the Belle Époque in a spirit of wild ambition and optimism, I have seen whole worlds unfold in front of me. This sport has taken me both physically and spiritually to places I can assuredly say I did not know existed. And I have taken these roads in the company of a changing host of fellow travellers and friends who I will never forget, and who have maddened and amused me, delighted and educated me, for the last 20 years. I understand, having seen the full extent of riders' careers begin and end, how short life is. And I have lost many colleagues who I have treasured, admired, fought against, laughed with, laughed about and respected. All of them were with me on the ITV team for many years: Glenn Wilkinson, Rob Llewellyn, Steve Blincoe, Steve Docherty, Paul Sherwen. Without them there would have been no journey.

* * *

I am dreading our final descent into Paris. I already fear the moment that I will glimpse the Eiffel Tower by night on the last transfer I make to the capital city, as the race returns to the Champs-Élysées once more. To see its white searchlight arcing through the inky night sky above Paris will mean something greater this summer; greater than I could possibly have imagined when I stepped out into that bright and breezy morning in 2003, trying to second guess what would happen next as I made my way to the first of the 483 finish lines I would step over at the Tour. I could not possibly have guessed that I would still be there after so many years.

I already think about the moment when the winner of the 2025 Tour completes his victory speech and hands back the microphone. He will turn around through 360 degrees with a single hand raised aloft, saluting the crowd, signing his name into the thin air of history for a fleeting moment which dissolves no sooner than it is created. I know how ephemeral the Tour is. The podium is cleared, the crowds disperse. The trucks, one by one, pull away. The sun has long since set.

The dew won't fall on the cobblestones for hours yet, if it falls at all. Most likely just a gossamer layer of the lightest moisture will materialise overnight, inaudibly, invisibly, on the streets around the Place de la Concorde, on the mighty roof of the Madeleine, on the ranks of orderly Vélib' bikes and the broken ones haphazardly dropped near the parked cars. I can see the lone revellers, the stragglers making it back to hotels in pairs or perhaps alone. I can almost hear the streetlights' glow. A taxi passes by. A wet rumble on the cobbles.

Paris will eventually fall fast asleep and the story will close down, at last accepting its defeat as the night gets ever deeper. Final sleep and loose dreams of distant mountains will replace the bright noise of what has gone before, until everything has been erased on this last Sunday nighttime of July.

When Monday morning blows in from the northwest, bringing its brightening breeze and the first faintest whisper of autumn, all trace of the Tour will have been ushered out, swept along with the changing months, with the air crossing from the Channel, across the rolling plains of Normandy, and on towards the capital and beyond.

The everyday people of the city will not care as they shrug, glance hurriedly skywards, check their pockets for the housekeys and then dive underground, shouldering their way into the Metro, and waiting for the train to appear and for life to take the course that it always has. But somewhere in that city, that morning, I will wake up and, all around me, the race will have gone entirely.

It was greater than the sum of its parts, wilder than my imagination, richer than I could have guessed and will stay with me forever. The whole adventure may well have been one giant accident, but accidents happen. This one was glorious.

David and I with our little trophies for 20 years of 'service' to the Tour.

AFTERWORD

But it's New Year's Eve, 2025. The morning sky outside is white-blue. Gusts of steam rise past my window from time to time, escaping from the boiler flue and catching on a chill breeze.

Last night I dreamt my final dream of the year. It was the usual psychedelic concoction of plot lines which simply stopped, walls that ran with water or gave way to the lightest touch, details that seemed disproportionately important, and people whose faces were both deeply familiar and quite unknown. Waking to the sound of the central heating ticking, most of the night's dreamworld instantly evaporated. But like when an old television set is switched off, a single bright spot of memory remained for long enough for me to concentrate on it. I knew with total clarity that I had been dreaming about the Tour de France.

We were in Boulogne, I think. Or at least somewhere that reminded me of Boulogne. It seemed to me that we had set up our studio on a little park, surrounded by a parapet and at the top of a little rise. It felt like the road that Mathieu van der Poel had come charging up to claim victory back in July, although in my dream nothing was quite as it seemed and everything was impossible to pin down.

The race was not yet underway. Instead, and in languid slow motion, technical staff were making the final adjustments to camera equipment, lights and microphones; lifting them up and tapping them to see if they were live. Everyone was there, moving with a kind of balletic torpor: Francesco and the crew from RAI raising and lowering cigarettes to their lips, the Germans very slowly eating morose forkfuls of pasta, all the army of men and women from France Télévisions, going through the motions with bowed heads, the Norwegians, the Danes sitting in camp chairs, and us.

Gary was standing alone and looking out over the finish, memorising lines. It was unusually dark, almost night-time. There were perhaps 20 minutes before we all went live. Then suddenly everyone stopped where they were and raised a champagne flute to the grey skies above. The moment lasted only a few seconds, but was awful and beautiful. That was when I realised that this was the absolute end of the Tour de France and that it was about to cease to exist entirely. I woke up feeling profoundly sad.

It's only now, writing these words, that I can shake off that sadness and see the dream for what it was: a pompous, self-congratulatory, overblown melodrama. So bad is the storyline and crass the characterisation that I have had to consider quite hard whether to include its retelling in this addendum to the book. But I reckon that if you've got as far as reading these words in a 'cycling' book, you've already waded through my ramblings about Malaysian soup, Italian pastries and Pete Kennaugh's inability to understand hay bales, so I think I'm safe enough.

Saying goodbye to the Tour de France this summer was an intense experience. For a small story about a small programme on a small channel showing a small sport in a parochial country, ITV's withdrawal from the race kept making headlines. It was the source of press and radio coverage all the way from the previous November, when the announcement was made, through to the very end of the 2025 Tour de France, when we finally went off the air. The loss of free-to-air Tour coverage was even debated in the House of Commons, for heaven's sake, meaning that the names 'Imlach' and 'Boulting' have now been entered into *Hansard* for the first, and almost certainly last, time in history. I'm sure there must have been a better use of 15 minutes of parliamentary time given EVERYTHING ELSE going on in the world, but obsessions are strange things and this one is stranger than most.

It was a curious thing to lose one's job slowly over three weeks, in French, and to do so very publicly: to be asked about it repeatedly; to have to answer the question about how it might feel when I finally signed off. I didn't mind the question, and indeed was very touched by the depth and warmth of the support that was afforded us all, but I eventually found the process wearing. And towards the end I wanted it all to stop.

Nevertheless, when the ITV crew gathered at one final start line in Lille, we approached our last task with great enthusiasm, determined to go off air having given our very best version of ourselves for the final Tour. Matt and Daniel shot and scripted finely crafted features that celebrated the past of the race, analysed its present and unflinchingly sought to ask the questions which will shape its future. In Paris, Tadej Pogačar, having won his fourth Tour, turned to Matt and told him with real sincerity that he'd miss him. Chris Boardman (back *again!*), Jacopo Guarnieri, Alex Dowsett and Pete all offered their wit, insight and humour in their contrasting ways. David and I did our level best in the commentary box, facilitated by a team of producers who backed our instincts for storytelling, allowing me to indulge my interest in a wide variety of tangential issues, from the unavoidably colossal *Les Misérables* to the Normandy landings, Alfred Jarry's unpaid hire purchase bill for his bike and the history of the mirage fighter jet. Sometimes I even spoke about the bike race on air.

The first block of racing was one of the longest in Tour de France history. Ten entire stages passed before the first rest day; stages which brought us all the way across the north of the nation and down in gigantic leaps through the Massif Central to Toulouse, after which we collectively paused and drew breath.

We had passed once again through the La Suisse Normande, the hilly part of Normandy, which Guillaume Martin calls home and where Jacques Anquetil lived in a castle. There I had got incredibly lost on a bike ride through fields, until, an hour later than planned, I pitched up in a sunlit garden where Jacopo and Alex had ordered a bottle of Sancerre on ice. I had marvelled at Rouen's church towers, ascended the arrow-straight climb of the Mûr-de-Bretagne for a fourth and perhaps final time, called in on Châteauroux once more, evoking memories of Mark Cavendish's maiden win, 17 years previously. And here we were on the first rest day, waking up in an odd little hotel in a scruffy part of Toulouse, getting ready to spend the day taking stock over steak-frites and Corbières. It was only later, as I sat with David and Alex in a launderette, watching socks gyrate, that the realisation struck me: the race was already half gone. I would never again experience that opening week.

In all honesty, the intense scrutiny of the first stages of the race is impossible to sustain. By the time the double-digit stages come along, the focus perforce gets fuzzier. That is an experience shared by both viewers and commentators alike. Who knows? Maybe even the riders, too. And in the case of 2025, our cursory dip into the Pyrenees was enough to kill the Tour de France off as a competitive spectacle. Pogačar ended Jonas Vingegaard's challenge on the Hautacam and Peyragudes, and Remco Evenepoel climbed off the very next day. The much-anticipated, three-way tussle blew apart and what remained of the intrigue centred around Pogačar's extraordinary nascent existential crisis, as he admitted to finding the procession through the Alps rather dispiriting.

And we started to think about the finish line, too. Ours arrived at night. We approached Paris from the west, passing through the city at midnight. From the back seat of our car, I leaned forward to glimpse the Eiffel Tower. The little Romania flag that Pete had unaccountably bought on a whim from a trucker's stop in the Alps, and hung from the rear-view mirror, now swung from side to side as our car rumbled over the cobbles of the Place de la Concorde. Hundreds of barriers were stashed in waiting on the pavements. By morning, kilometres of the city, including the climb to Montmartre, would be cordoned off. Heavily armed French riot police would be waving people away from the Rue du Faubourg Saint-Honoré, where the President would be eating a croissant and unfolding a crisp copy of *Le Monde* to read of the latest horrors.

The race came and went, with Wout Van Aert crossing the line in first place and the victorious Pogačar behind him in the wet gloom of an unseasonable late July evening. David and I remained where we were to commentate over the endless podium ceremony, pausing only for the anthems and for Pogačar's fourth winner's speech. After that we reappeared briefly in vision, the camera cutting to us in the commentary booth that had been our home for the previous three weeks in the back of a truck now parked up between the Petit and the Grand Palais.

'For the best part of ten years,' I remember telling the viewers (or words to this effect), 'David and I have been sitting in two shonky, torn, second-hand office chairs, which collapse when you're least expecting it and roll away from the desk when we're parked up on the slope of a summit finish. But for both of us, they've been the best chairs in the world.'

The director cut back to Gary, standing on the set, with Paris now pitch black behind him. 'You should have brought your own chair,' he said. 'That's what I've been doing for years.' Out of vision and off mic, David and I roared with laughter. It was the most perfect Imlach reply. I cracked open a can of beer and stepped out of the truck, intensely relieved that it was over.

Later that evening, laden with bags and crossing the Champs-Élysées with Kath, who had come to Paris as she usually did, we spotted a pancake stall that was still open. Its light stood out against the dark foliage of the horse chestnut trees behind. A family were standing at the counter: a few kids, a tall mother and a shorter dad, ordering the pancakes and handing over the money. I recognised his silhouette instantly.

Mark Cavendish waiting for pancakes.

Here was the greatest sprinter in the history of the Tour, a year on from his final win, ordering pancakes for his kids, unnoticed by anyone. Mark Cavendish had simply returned quietly to the real world.

'How are you feeling, mate?' he asked. 'Shit,' I told him, suddenly overwhelmed. Then I apologised for the language I'd used in front of his family. He waved my apology away. 'Don't worry. What fucking language do you think they get to hear every day at home?' Kath and I pushed on into the night to go and meet up with the rest of the ITV team. An hour later, I got a message from him:

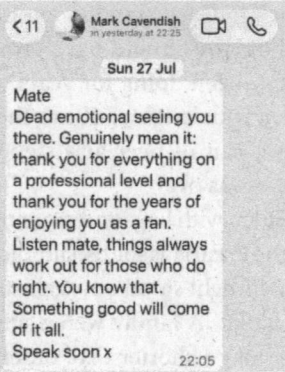

A message I won't delete.

And now, six months on? I am planning for so much in the coming years. The notion that I would somehow renounce my devotion to the accidental tourism which has driven my curiosity for years was always far-fetched. This pursuit of riders, races, people and places sits far too deep in my DNA to be extractable any longer. I am doomed to wander the globe like the Ghost of Tours Past, haunting finish lines far and wide. I shall rattle my chains in the faces of riders across the world!

I will return to the Tour, of course, but it will be different. And in the meantime I am busily making plans. Unshackled by the constraints of telly, I am going to visit races I've never heard of before, new races that haven't even existed until now, races in parts of the world I have never seen. There is a universe of experience out there, spinning in the orbit of this most extraordinary human endeavour that somehow calls itself a sport, even though it is so much more than that.

I feel like I've only just begun.

ACKNOWLEDGEMENTS

The list of my co-tourists over the last quarter-century is so endlessly long that I have no idea where I should begin with it. Perhaps I owe the biggest debt to the trio of good people at the top of the production company, latterly known as Vsquared, which crafted the ITV Tour de France output (and before that, Channel 4); Brian and James Venner and Carolyn Viccari.

I will never forget working with Gary Imlach, Matt Rendell, Daniel Friebe, Chris Boardman et al. They have all been great influences on me. More recently, I have had the support and loyalty of some excellent colleagues in Italy; so my thanks and respect in particular to Massimiliano Adamo, Jess Sheehan, Roberto Nitti, Lisa Ponsford,

Davide Terraneo, Andrea Basso and Martina Centemo. My work in the UK at both the men's and women's Tours of Britain were for a long time the fiefdom of the excellent Rohan Browning, one of the most loyal and hard-working people in the business.

Along the way, I have worked with many hundreds of dedicated technical staff, producers, camera operators, sound supervisors and editors; the seldom-credited staff who take the rough edges of our output and smooth them off until they are polished and fit for consumption. To all of these excellent colleagues from Norway to Wuxi, Abu Dhabi to Weimar, many of whom I never had the time to get to know, my thanks. To my co-commentators Pete Kennaugh and David Millar; I will miss the hours we have spent at the Tour de France. And to Matt Stephens and others, I hope to spend many more in your company at other races.

I could not have written this book without the support once again of everyone at Bloomsbury Sport. From Charlotte Croft and Sarah Skipper on the editorial team to Neil Stevens who designed the cover, Katherine Macpherson in publicity, Xanthe Rendall on the marketing team and Rachel Murphy in production; you've all been tremendous, for the third time in my career!

The patience of my family is immense. My partner Kath had to bear a heavy load of solo parenting when our kids were still kids, and I was on the road. My debt is immense, probably too big to pay back, if I'm honest. And to Suzi and Edie, who are my everything when I am away.

But the biggest debt of gratitude I owe is to road racing itself; a grand notion that shouldn't work but somehow does. It has changed my life.